IMAGES
of America

MARTIN COUNTY

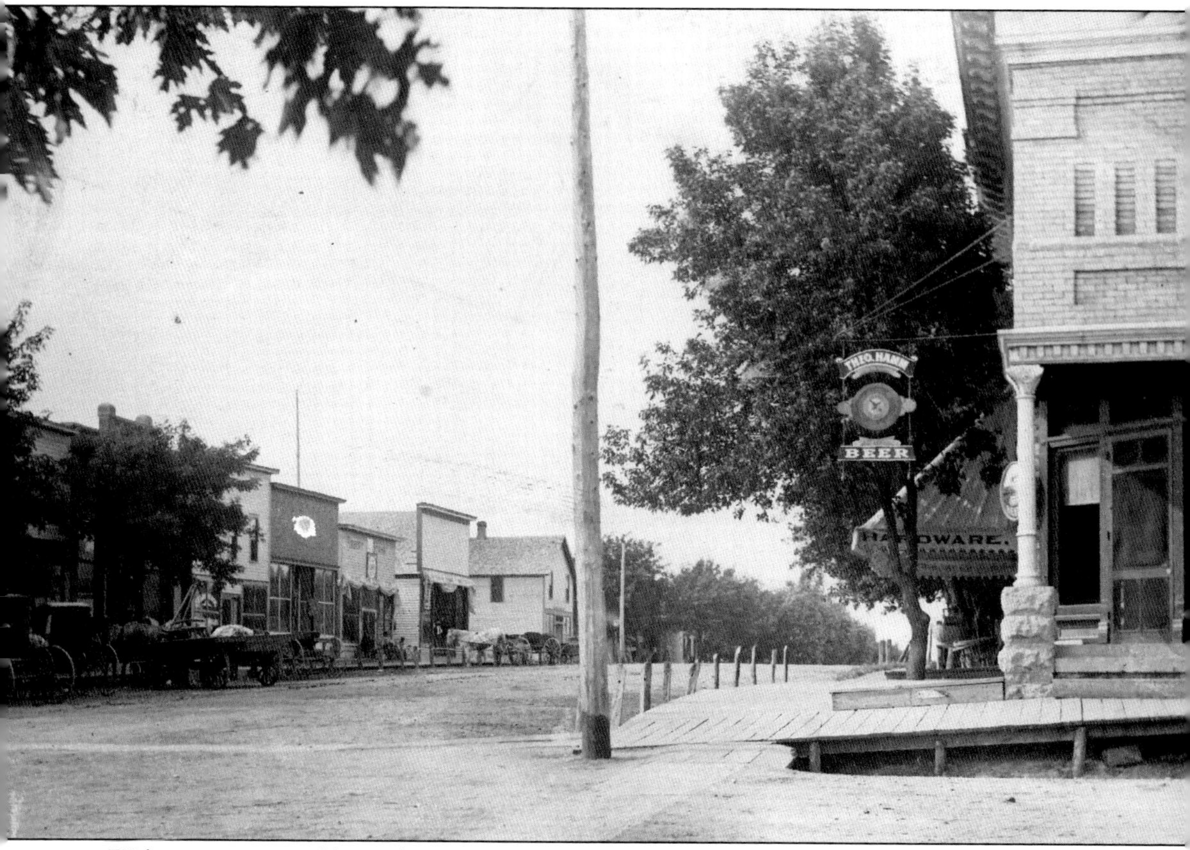

Welcome is pictured here about 1899. (Author's collection.)

On the cover: This is the hillside farm of John Jorgenson in section 16 of Waverly Township. The home is still occupied by a descendant of the Jorgensons. The home has changed somewhat, and at the request of Anna Jorgenson, it was picked up and rotated since she did not like it facing the road. The festivity taking place is unknown. (Author's collection.)

IMAGES
of America

MARTIN COUNTY

Chris Hanning

ARCADIA
PUBLISHING

ISBN 978-0-7385-7721-0

Published by Arcadia Publishing
Charleston SC, Chicago IL, Portsmouth NH, San Francisco CA

Printed in the United States of America

Library of Congress Control Number: 2009931863

For all general information contact Arcadia Publishing at:
Telephone 843-853-2070
Fax 843-853-0044
E-mail sales@arcadiapublishing.com
For customer service and orders:
Toll-Free 1-888-313-2665

Visit us on the Internet at www.arcadiapublishing.com

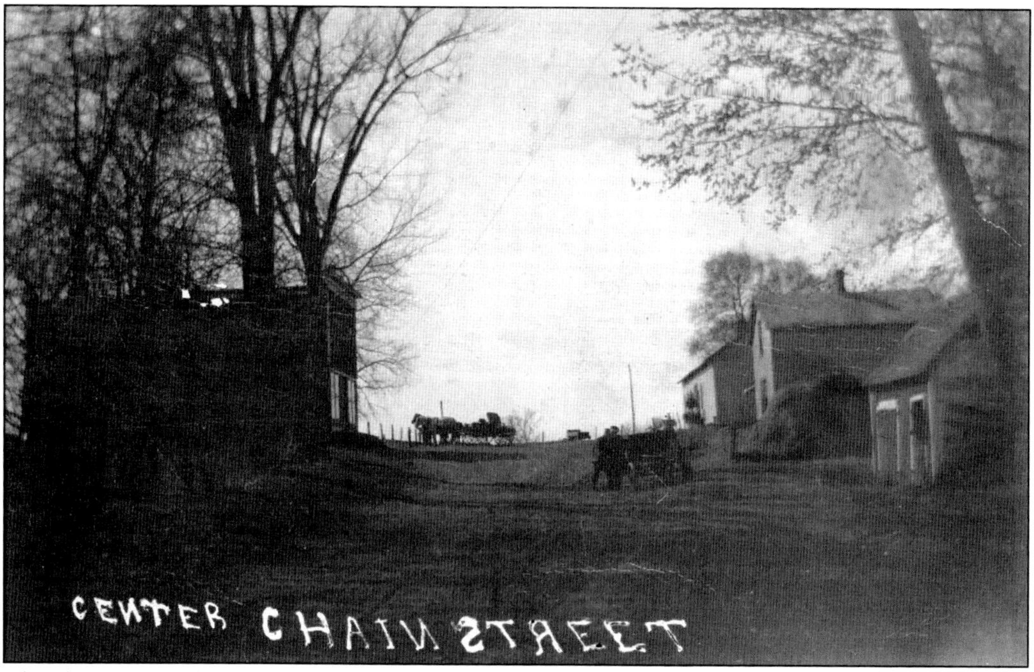

The "lost town" of Center Chain actually had a Main Street. This photograph dates from about 1909. The Center Chain Store is on the left. (Author's collection.)

Contents

ACKNOWLEDGMENTS

Martin County has been very lucky to have many local historians who published pamphlets and books since William Budd's *Martin County before 1880* in 1897. In addition to those many resources, I also gleaned information from old telephone books, directories, plat books, and newspaper clippings. This is a photographic history of the county, and the bulk of the images are postcards made between the early 1900s and the 1930s. Some come from the Granada Historical Museum archives. Unless otherwise noted, the images are from the author's collection.

I hope you enjoy this book. It is an abbreviated version of *Greetings from Martin County*, which I published in 2006. Many thanks to the people who made that endeavor a success. I am grateful to Helen Simon and Muriel Malliet. They are two former curators of the Martin County Historical Society and were a joy to work with. Of course, thanks to my wife, Linda, who puts up with me, and my grandmother Dora Eisenbarger. Even though she has been gone for many years, her love of history is still in me. I also want to apologize for any errors, as it is most certainly inadvertent. Please contact me if any are found so I can make certain to record any corrections. There was so much I wanted to include as it was very difficult to condense the entire county to fit into this project. I certainly would not disagree with anyone that a certain photograph or subject should have been included. Please visit the Granada Historical Museum's Web site for a link to a bibliography and consider printing it out and putting it with the book. Please note, when I identified a business, I tried to label it how it appeared when the postcard or photograph was made.

INTRODUCTION

The first pioneer families of this county came here most likely by covered wagon and ox team; single men pioneers came on horseback. The point is, these pioneers wanted to get here one way or the other. In one case, they literally walked here from the East Coast. According to family lore, the Davison family pioneers of Center Creek Township were said to have done this. Plus they even walked back and then returned in a covered wagon. On that trip, Mrs. Davison carried on her lap the entire way a soup tureen that is now a treasured family heirloom.

If these pioneers had not endured that long, slow trip and suffered through many hardships, Martin County would not exist as it does today and be one of the best places to live. Their first hardship was to survive just getting here. This was not always easy. Along the way, they had to gather their own food. Granted the hunting grounds provided much more food than it would today, but they still had to do it almost everyday since they had no practical means to preserve anything. Once they got here, their first order of business was to procure shelter, which in the beginning was quite often made of sod or simple dugouts. The roofs of these sod homes did make a good pasture for small livestock.

Once they arrived, they worried about the Native Americans, with whom, quite often, the white man was not on friendly terms. There was also the isolation from one's fellow man, which surely caused issues for some folks. Then again, that isolation was a good thing for a select few settlers, as crime did not evade this great prairie land in the beginning. The very first unsolved murder happened in Martin County when Charles White's body was discovered in Fox Lake Township in 1864. Another tragedy almost happened again, when a settler shot at a man named Richardson for filing a claim the settler wanted to save for a friend. A true Martin County resident prevented a mob from dispensing their justice by refusing to let them hang the accused from the lone tree on his property in Center Creek Township.

The many blizzards of this time were to be reckoned with, especially the ones of 1866, 1870, 1872, and 1873. In all these storms, there was loss of life due to people freezing to death. Reuben Wagar of Silver Lake Township even wrote a poem called "The Blizzard of '73" and recorded the deaths of two settlers. The biblical stories rang true in Martin County when the grasshopper plague of the mid-1870s descended on this area and sent some of the English farming pioneers packing. It is almost unimaginable what these women, children, and men went through for a better life; their struggles never seemed to end. They had to tolerate droughts, hail, and if that was not enough—the occasional prairie fire. Martin County in 1870 was a land of log cabins, ragged men, dirty children, and overworked women, as a local pioneer woman put it.

Many of the Englishmen who were able to remain were "on the whole, a colony of gentlemen." They stayed and established several businesses, but not all were prosperous. The Bank of Fairmont and a young British man who brewed "genuine English ale" were pretty much finished by 1880. However, many were successful businessmen. The Victoria, which was a $10,000 gristmill, was one of the victories. A photograph of this mill is on page 31.

The St. Martin's Episcopal Church was also established by the Englishmen, who have worshipped at the same place since 1876. This "neat Gothic Church" was a considered to be in the suburbs of Fairmont in 1880. Martin County has a colorful history, and it seems like every town has some sort of claim to fame, albeit small.

Ceylon is the birthplace of the 42nd vice president of the United States, Walter Mondale. It is also home to the youngest mayor ever elected in Minnesota, John Gibeau, who began his term in 1998 at the age of 21. East Chain is close to where Reuben Wagar wrote his poem "The Blizzard of '73" and the freezing deaths of Andrew Anderson and Isaac Foster. The first blacksmiths shop was also built in East Chain in 1864. This shop was made of sod, which at least made it fireproof. Astronaut Dale Gardner spent part of his life growing up in Sherburn. During two of his trips into space, Gardner orbited the earth more than 200 times. During World War II, Fairmont nervously watched over a prisoner of war camp that housed many Germans. Most of these prisoners worked for the local canning company, and a few of them found the United States to their liking and became citizens. Back when the area was still being developed, there was a minor civil war in what is now Granada. In 1888, the students and teachers literally did not know where the schoolhouse would be the next day. The northerners and southerners each wanted the schoolhouse located on their side of Center Creek, and the school was clandestinely moved several times. Northrop was known as "Flag Town USA," as every home donned a flag. It was also home to this county's first liquor store. Welcome had the first radio station in the county. KFVN was started in 1925, and the next year, the *Voice of Martin County* had its trial run. Of course there is Ormsby, the "Biggest Little Town in Two Counties," and the two towns of Triumph and Monterey became one in 1959.

Martin County is home to many historic preservation sites. The old post office, the Chubb house, the Martin County Courthouse, the George Wohlheter mansion, and part of the main street of Sherburn are all on the National Register of Historic Places. Fairmont is home to two high-quality cultural institutions: the Red Rock Center for the Arts and the Fairmont Opera House, which are also on the National Register of Historic Places. Several of the smaller cities have museums dedicated to their history, and in Fairmont is the newly dedicated (2009) Hobo Camp Nature Trail. Martin County is truly a historic destination.

One

Ceylon and Dunnell

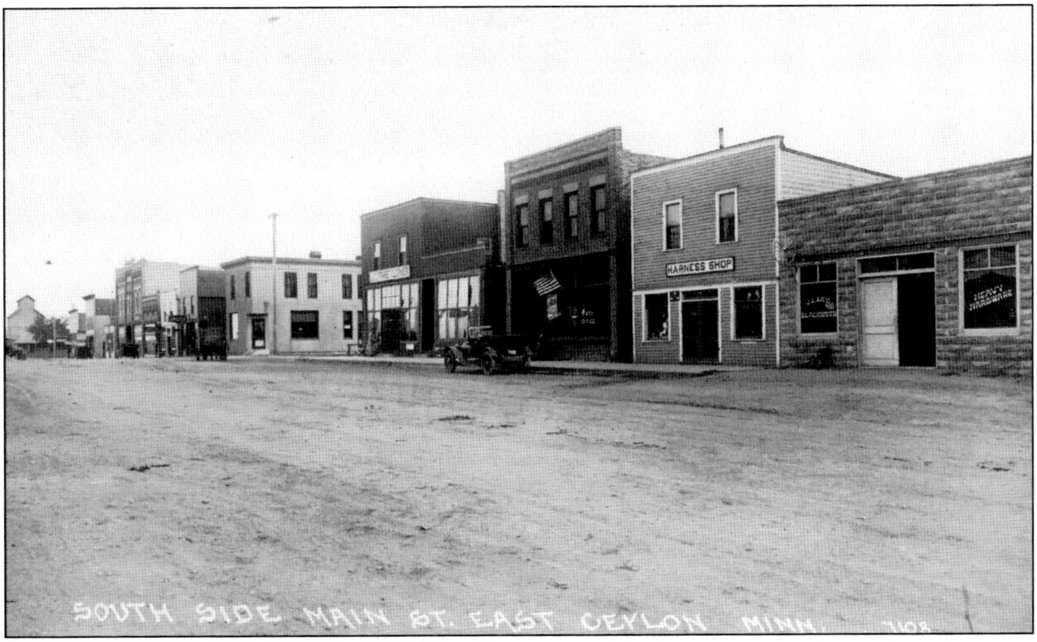

Ceylon was first named Tenhassen by the Chicago and North Western Railway when the town was formed in 1898. The U.S. Postal Service rejected the name, and according to local lore, the name Ceylon came from the brand name on a box of tea. Above is the south side of Ceylon's Main Street in 1914. The first building on the right is J. E. Ray's Blacksmith Shop. Ray had the first blacksmith shop in town and built a new building in 1913, which is shown here.

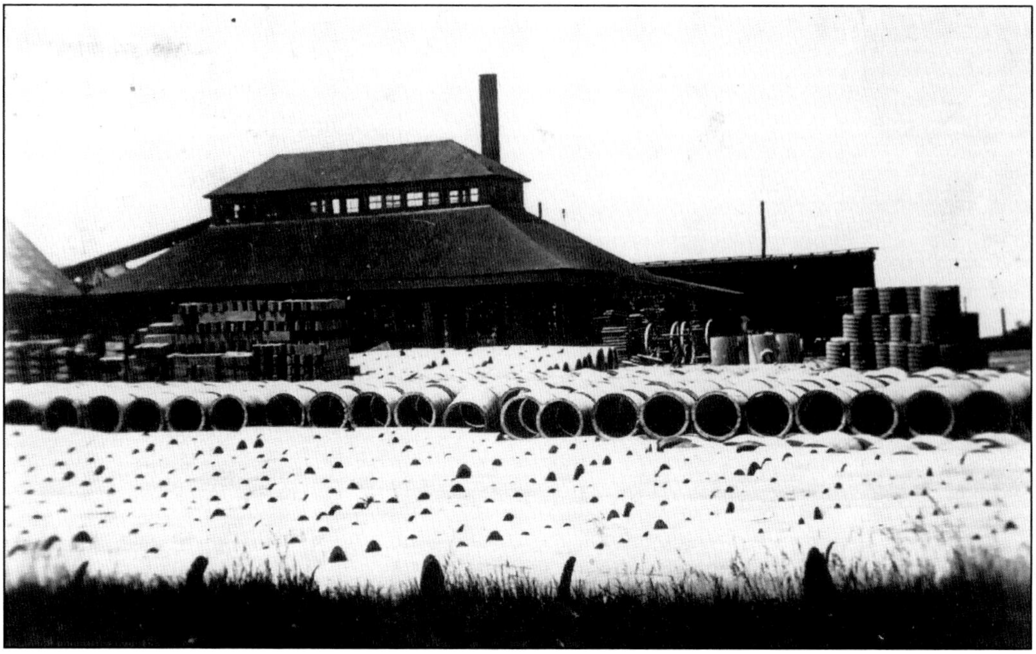

The Ceylon Tile Factory was a large, successful enterprise located north of the elevators. Mr. Belknap of Gold Field, Iowa, built it about 1906 and sold it to W. H. Kelling and David Keith not long after. Many local homes and businesses were built with cement block made by this factory. When general manager Keith passed away in 1924, the factory closed. This photograph was taken about 1913.

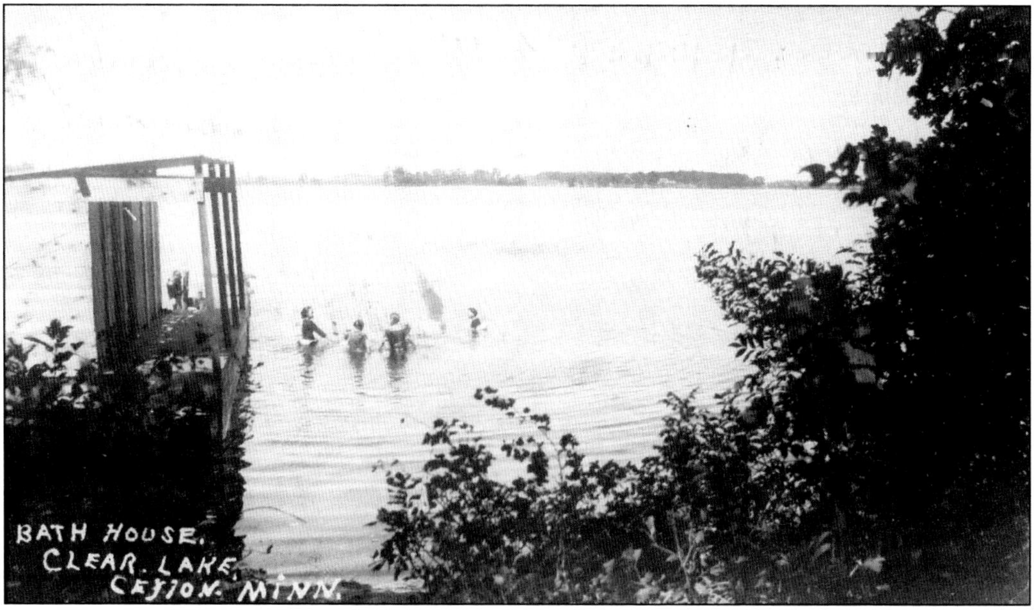

The Ceylon Tile Factory built a bathhouse on the north shore of Clear Lake for its employees. On hot summer days when the employees were finished working, they went out there for a swim, or as it was called then, a bath. It is doubtful that this was used exclusively by the factory employees. This pre-1917 photograph may be of the bathhouse the factory built.

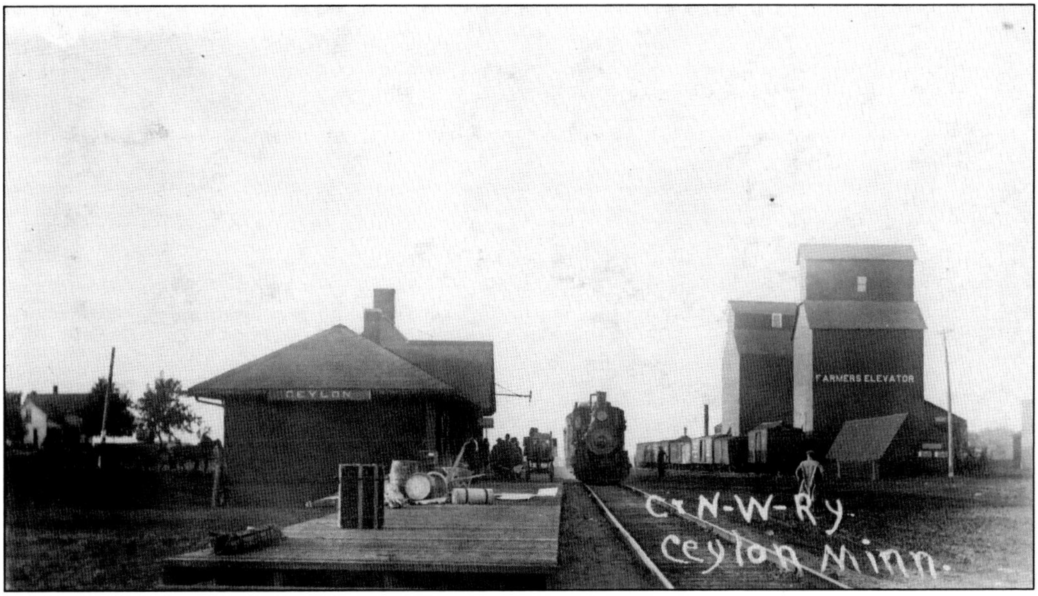

The Chicago and North Western Railway depot was built about 1900. The first depot was a train car that the railroad dropped off. On September 30, 1899, the first train pulled into Ceylon (Tenhassen at the time) when E. K. Davis was the depot agent. The trains stopped coming in 1969, and the tracks were removed in 1970. Some of the railroad ties made their way to Fairmont and were used to build a retaining wall at the residence of Dr. John and Ella Hanson at 828 Albion Avenue.

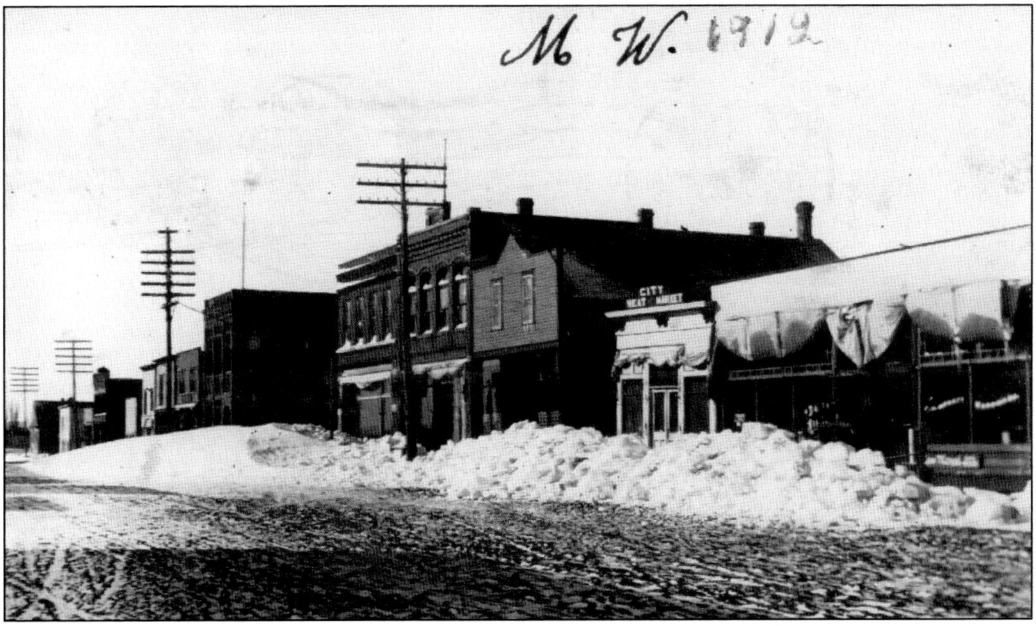

This is the north side of Main Street in the winter of 1911–1912. Shown is the City Meat Market, which was burglarized in May 1922. The thieves got away with a whopping $2. That same evening, the Anderson Hardware and Furniture Store and the Rautenkraur Barber Shop and Billiard Hall were also broken into. The sixth building from the right is the State Bank of Ceylon. It was built in 1901.

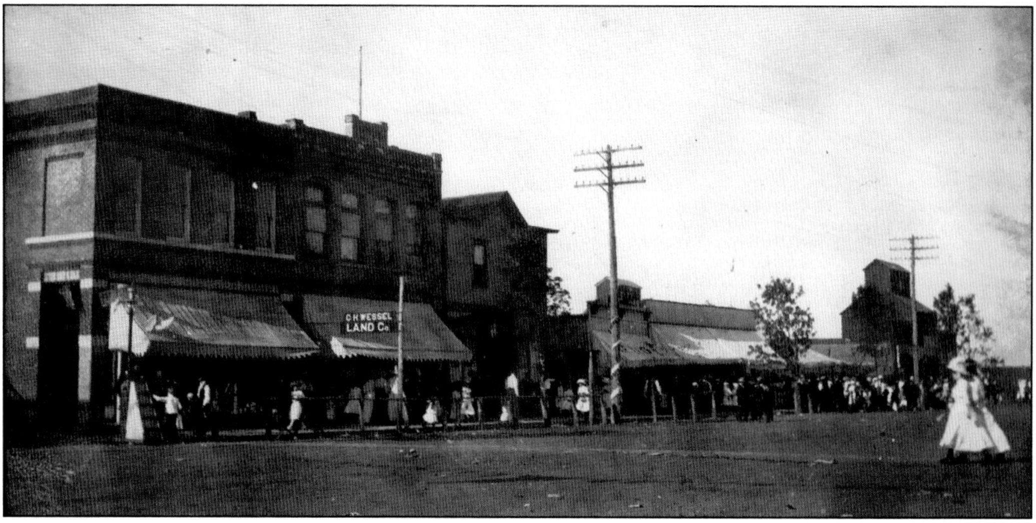

This postcard was sent in September 1910. The notation on the back says, "Flosie will be married Oct. 1st in Swell Style." From the left, the first building once housed the Prust Market. It was razed in 2006. The second structure at the time this photograph was taken was the C. H. Wessel Land Company building. Later it became Bailey's drugstore and most recently Peterson's Coffee Shop. The fourth building (behind the telephone pole) is the City Meat Market.

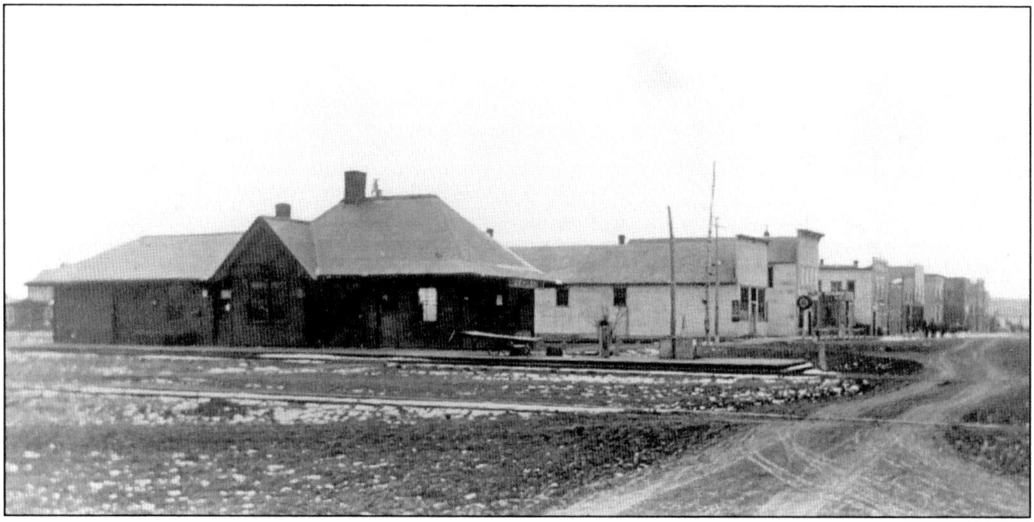

This postcard photograph was taken about 1905 and shows the south side of Main Street in Ceylon. The depot, Henry Siem's Saloon, and the hotel are the first three buildings from the left. Siems came to America from Germany in 1883.

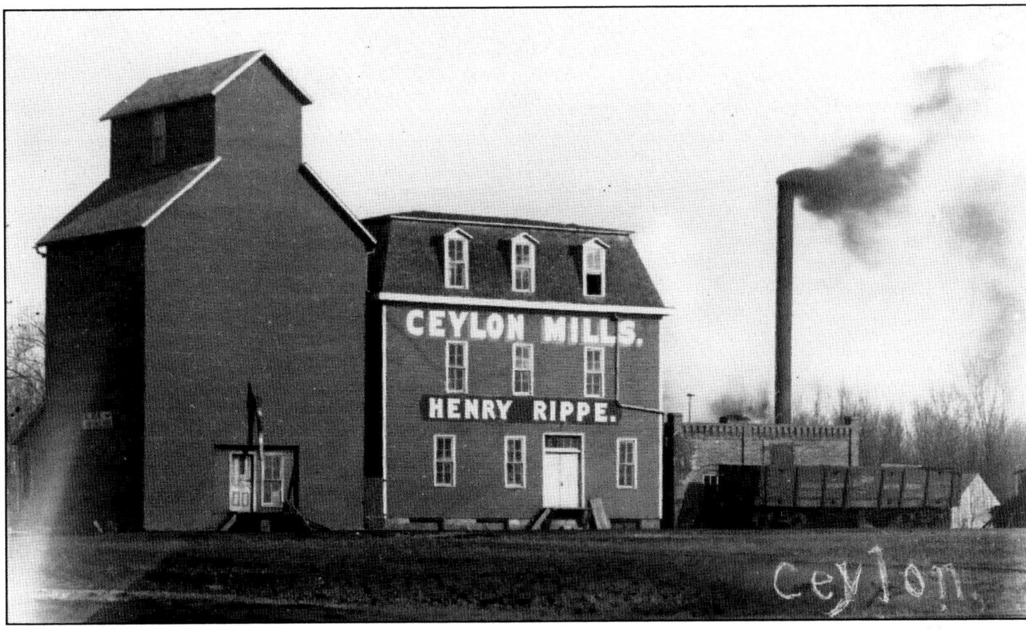

The Ceylon Mills was a branch business of Rippe Grain and Milling Company, owned by Henry Rippe of Fairmont. Rippe started the business in 1891 at Fairmont and built the Ceylon Mills about 1902. It is pictured here about 1906. The business was short lived because of the poor rail connections. Travel was slow and proved to be too costly, and within a few years, it closed and was torn down.

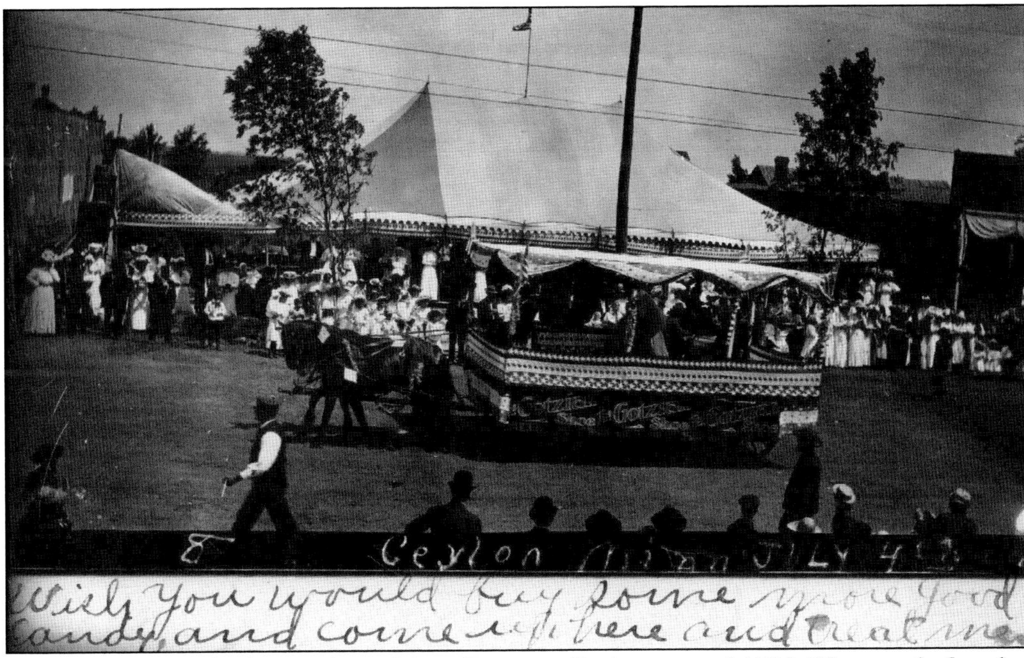

This is a Fourth of July parade on Main Street in Ceylon around 1906. The parade float has advertising for the Gotzian Shoe. The name of the business that sold it is too faint to read but is probably the Frase Clothing Store. Most businesses had floats decorated with a large amount of patriotic bunting and some kind of advertisement touting their business.

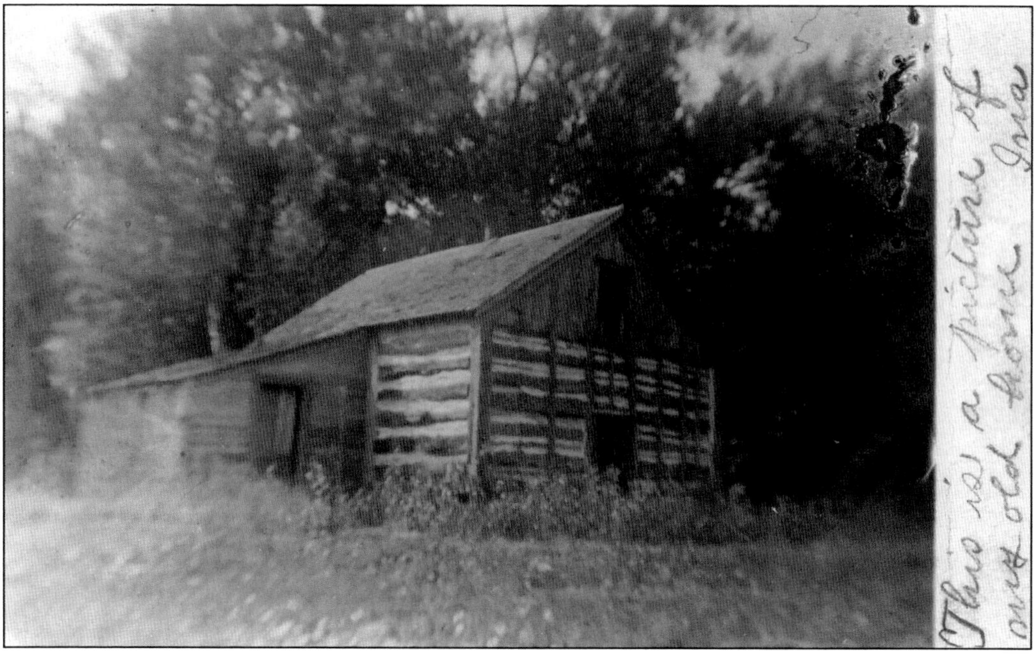

At the time this photograph was taken, between 1902 and 1907, this was the oldest house near Ceylon. It was built in 1864 and was the home of Andrew S. Personius. In 1880, Personius owned land in the northeast quarter of section 30 in Tenhassen Township. This may be where the home was located, which is roughly a mile or so east of Ceylon.

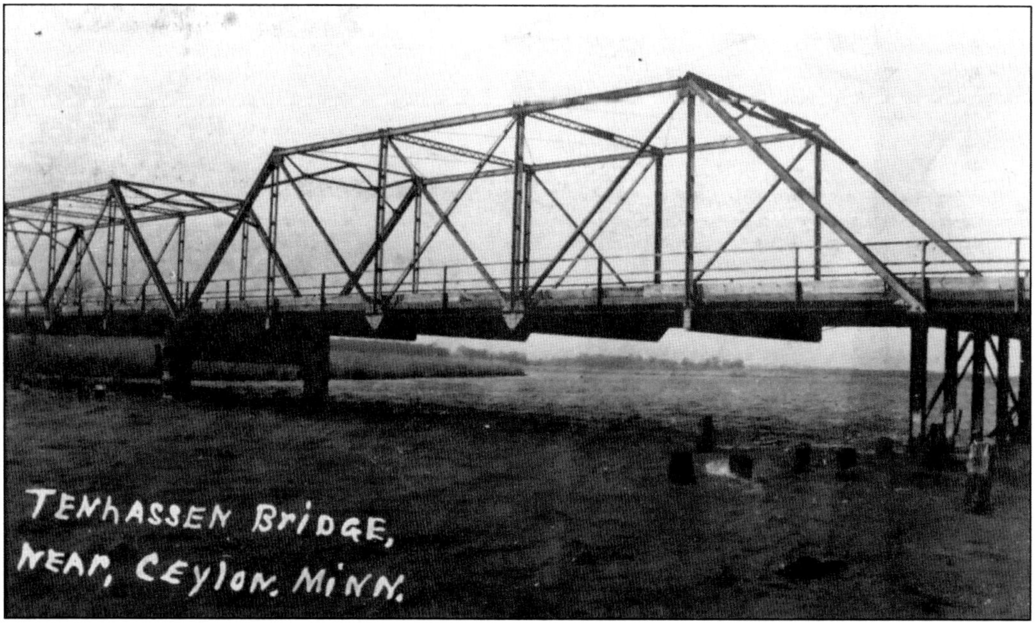

This is a photograph of the Tenhassen Bridge over Tuttle Lake. It was built in 1908. The first bridge across the inlet of Lake Okamanpeedan was built in February 1858, and Calvin Tuttle and Sons furnished the timber. It was 160 feet long, and when the time came to raise it, some folks from Center Creek Township helped. They stayed until the job was done, which took about two weeks. This postcard dates from between 1912 and 1914.

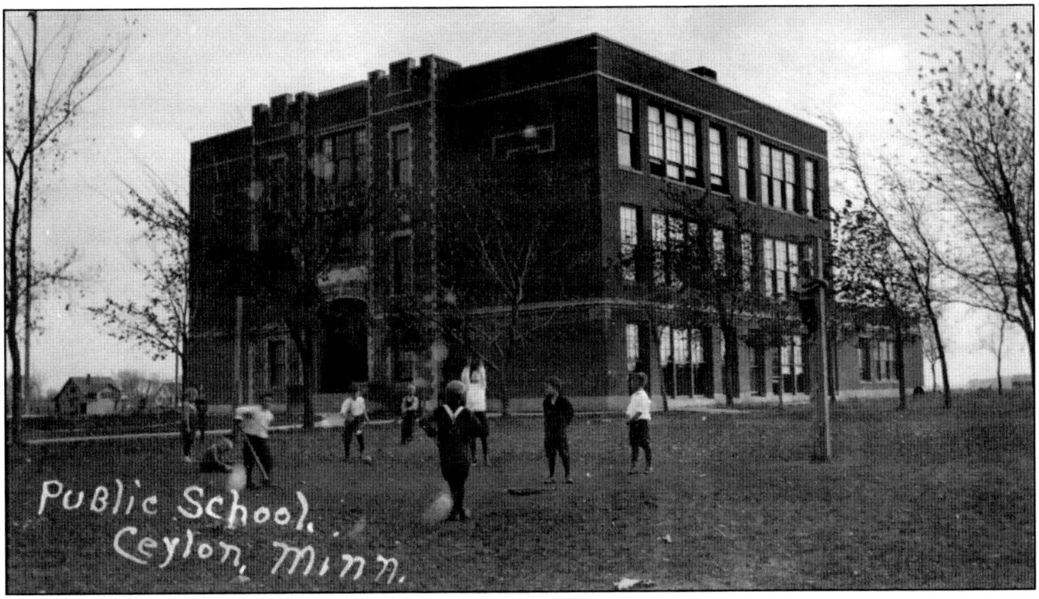

The Ceylon School District No. 29 started about 1868 on Clear Lake until 1901, when a two-story schoolhouse was built in Ceylon. The school above was dedicated on March 4, 1920, and this part of the school closed in 1991. The class of 1992 brought the high school era to a close.

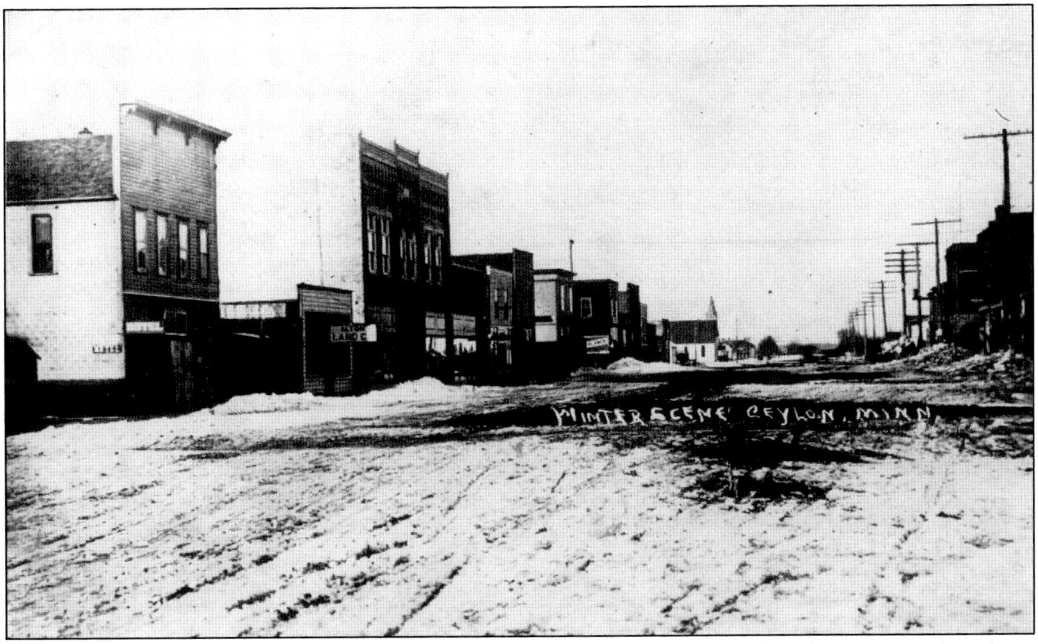

This is the south side of Ceylon's Main Street about 1912. Ceylon's hotel was moved in from Sherburn and was a basic structure. Straw bedding from the rooms upstairs would sift down onto the dining tables below. The first building on the left replaced that hotel. Down the street was the J. C. Frase Clothier store. Yeggs burgled this store twice in 1923, stealing $1,500 in clothing and then 89 suits the second time. The *Ceylon Herald* thought "a rope and a telephone post would be proper punishment for such thieves."

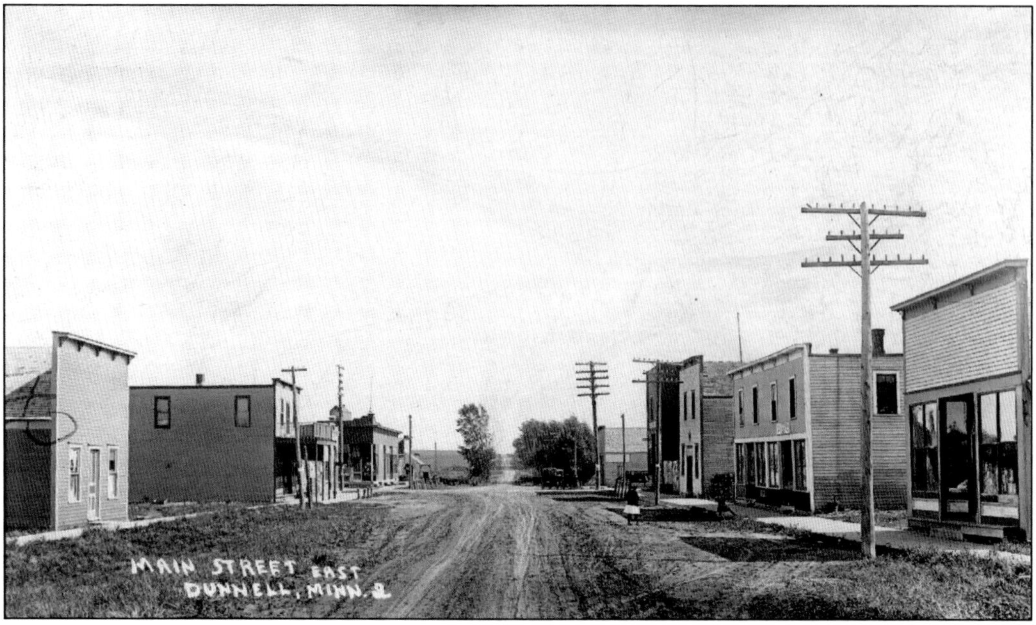

When four local landowners donated land and lots were sold at auction in February 1900, Dunnell was born. It promptly grew and incorporated the next year. Dunnell was a sleepy little town when this photograph of Main Street looking east was taken about 1915. The first building on the left is currently the U-Turn Bar and Museum. The second building on the right in 1915 was A. G. Peterson's business. When it was first built, it was J. N. Smith's Hotel. It was located where the municipal building is now.

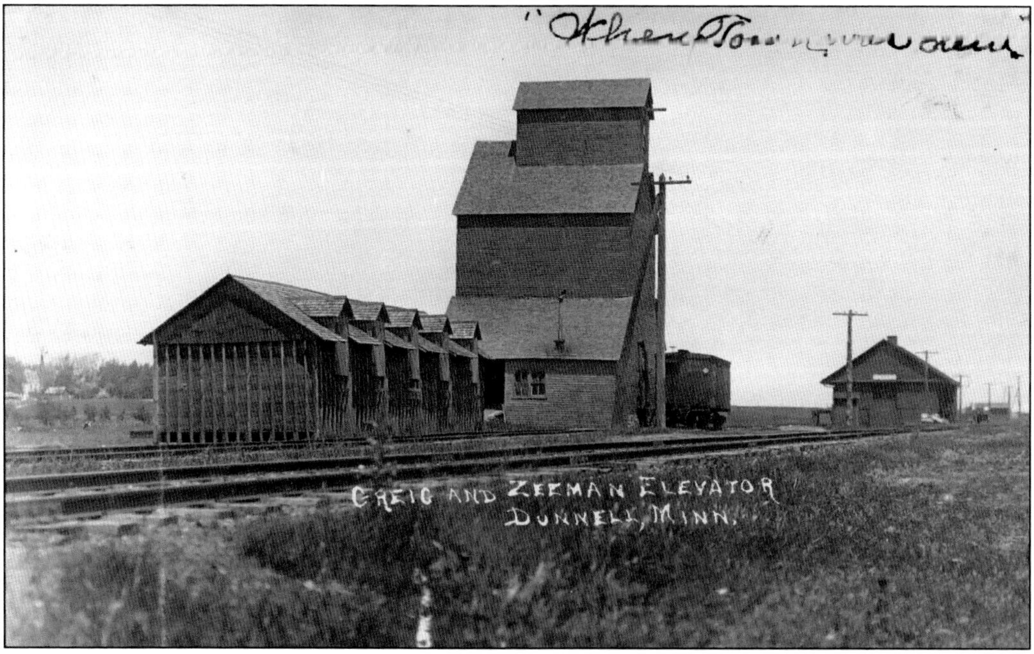

The Greig and Zeeman elevator was built about 1900. The depot was also built that year. The Great Western Elevator Company was the other elevator in town; George Weir was the manager of one, and E. A. Cooper ran the other. This photograph was taken about 1908.

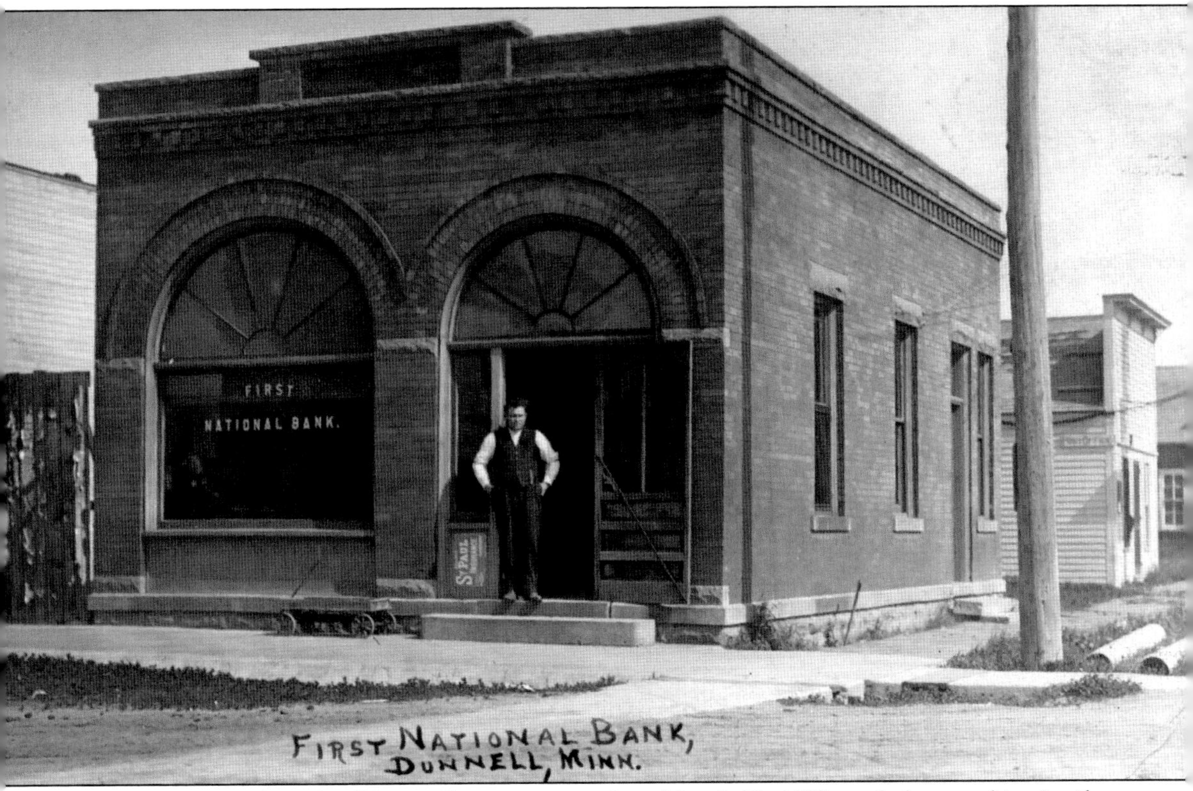

The First National Bank of Dunnell was organized on March 12, 1903, and chartered in April with a June opening. Cashier George Gruwell is the man in front of the building. He was the first cashier and a stockholder for many years. This bank was burglarized on Friday, September 9, 1921. The yeggmen (burglars) poured nitroglycerin in the crack around the door of the safe. The building suffered greatly after the safe was blown up, and many items flew out onto Main Street. Surprisingly, nobody heard the explosion, but hotel proprietor Albert Ronnei was awakened by the glass hitting the sidewalk. The burglars cut the telephone lines into town, and Dunnell became isolated. Ronnei was discovered by the burglars and told at gunpoint to stay quiet. The burglars did not get too much loot since they miscalculated the force of the explosion and left much of it behind. A new building was constructed at this site and is still in use. It is now the Dunnell Branch of the Farmers State Bank of Trimont. The old Dunnell Post Office can be seen behind the bank.

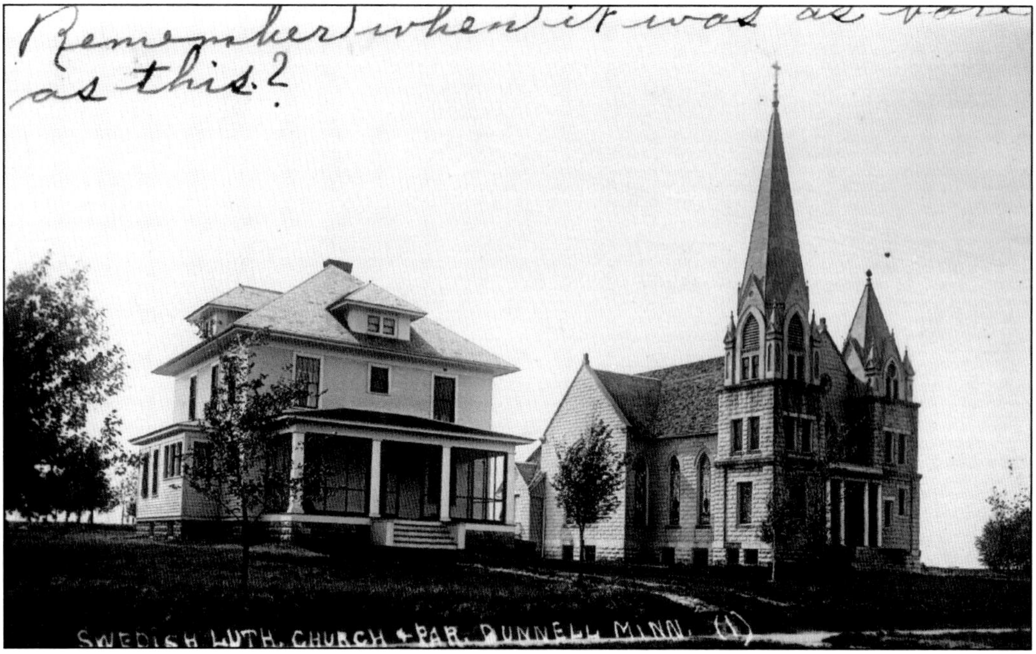

The first meeting of what became the Blooming Prairie Congregation was on August 26, 1871. The first church building was constructed in 1886 and located a half mile north of Dunnell. On May 25, 1903, it was decided to build a new church in Dunnell. The cornerstone was laid on September 3, 1904, and dedicated on May 30–31, 1905. It is now called the Immanuel Lutheran Church. The parsonage was built in 1914.

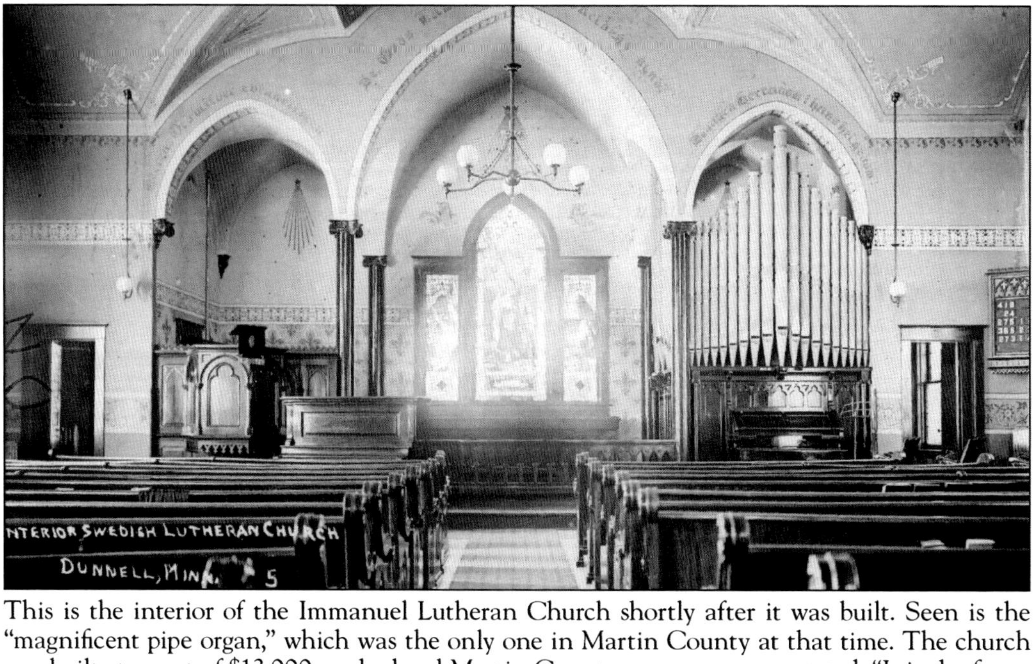

This is the interior of the Immanuel Lutheran Church shortly after it was built. Seen is the "magnificent pipe organ," which was the only one in Martin County at that time. The church was built at a cost of $13,000, and a local Martin County newspaperman stated, "It is the finest church in the county at this time and the largest block building." The cement block for this church may have come from the Ceylon Tile Factory.

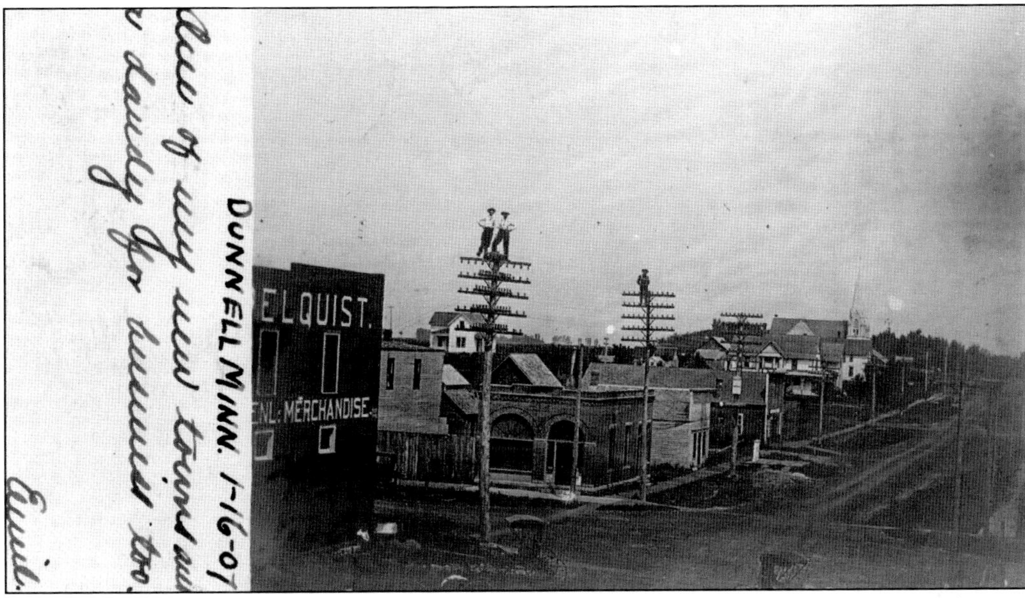

This photograph was taken in 1906 right after the telephone poles were erected. Note the men standing on top of these poles. The Dunnell Farmers Cooperative Telephone Company was formed in 1904, and shares were sold that year for $10 each. The Dunnell Telephone Company was the first in the United States to provide one-party service to all its subscribers. Carl Rupe accomplished this in 1964, and after he passed away, the local workers set up Rupe's private line to Heaven. A telephone and service pole was setup by his grave marker.

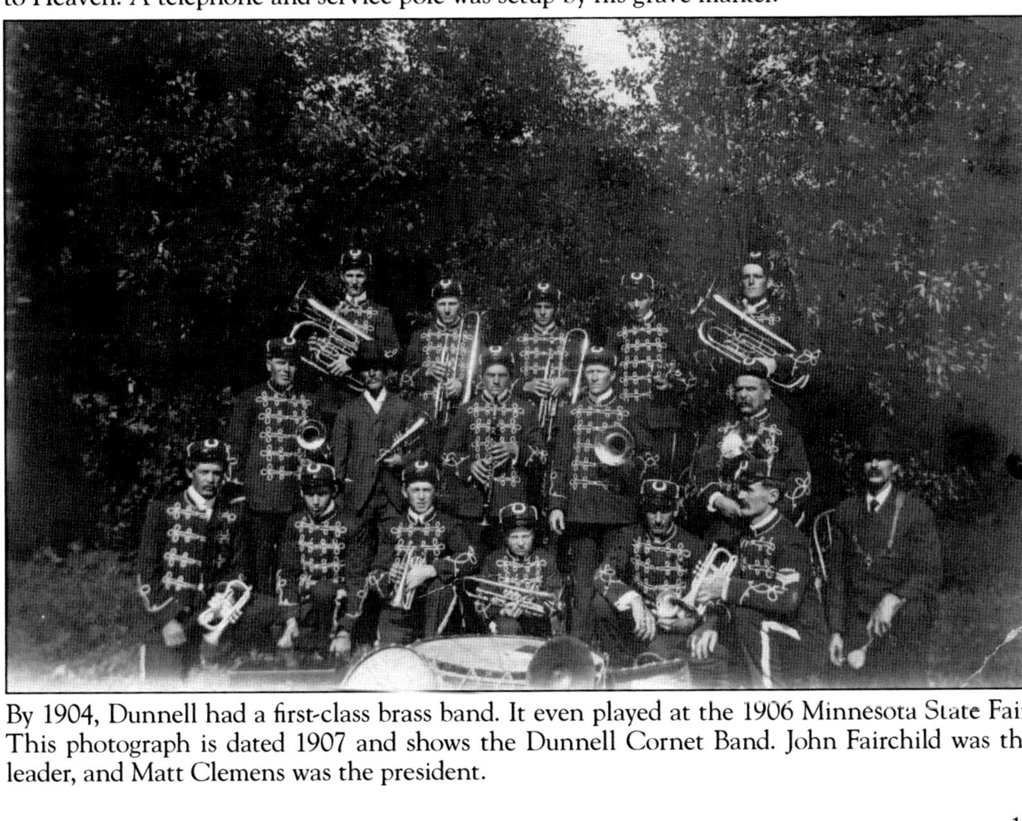

By 1904, Dunnell had a first-class brass band. It even played at the 1906 Minnesota State Fair. This photograph is dated 1907 and shows the Dunnell Cornet Band. John Fairchild was the leader, and Matt Clemens was the president.

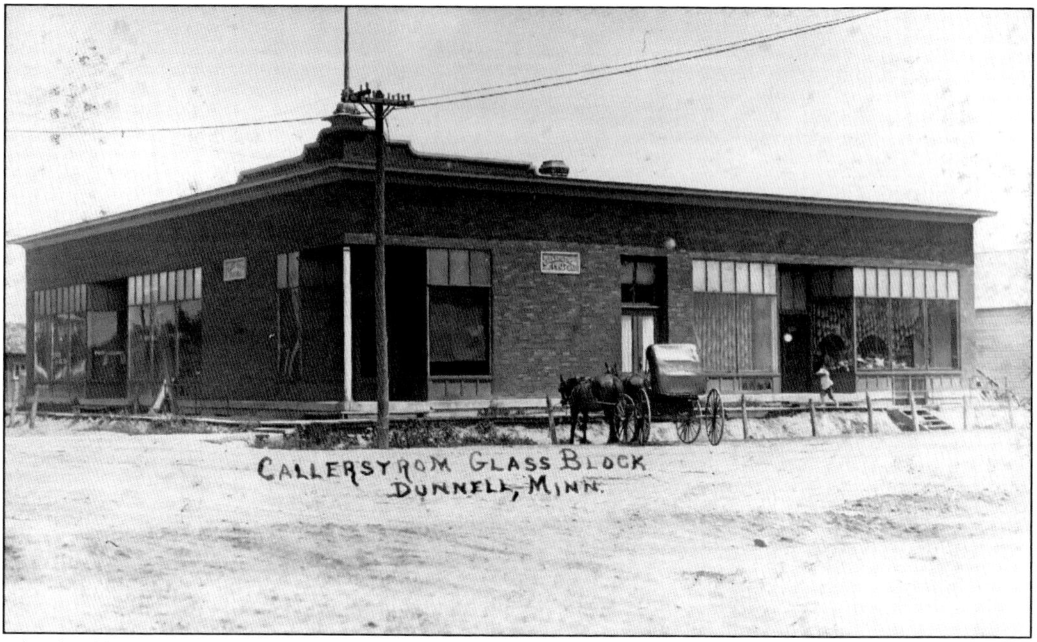

This building was called the Callerstrom Glass Block, which was constructed in 1907 by Dunnell's first resident physician, Dr. Godfred Callerstrom. Later businesses in this building included the Sandquist Barber Shop and Ostergren and Linder General Store. This postcard was taken about 1908 and was also sold in this building.

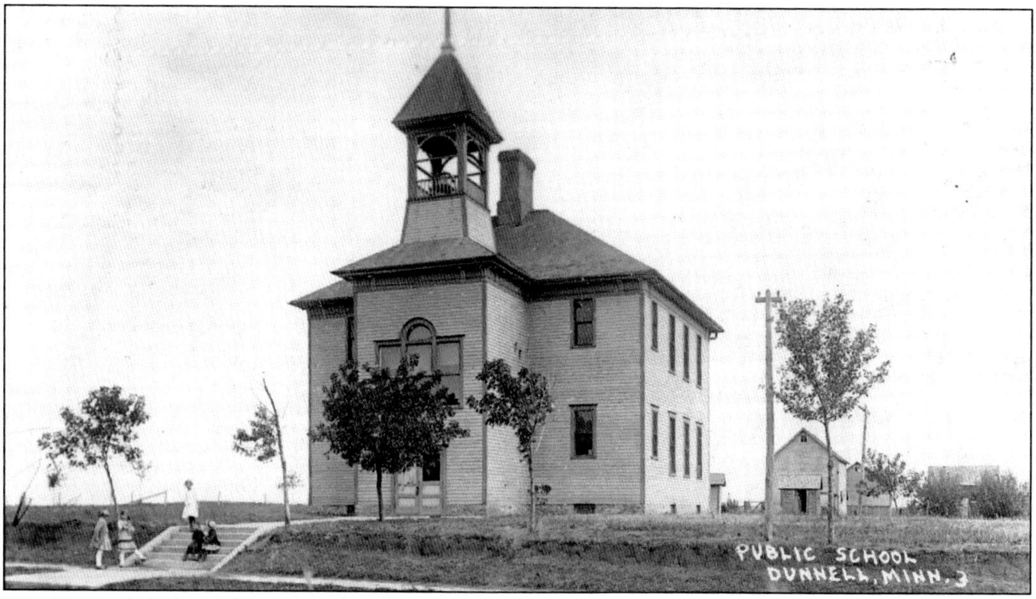

The Dunnell School first started as district No. 60 in 1876. The following year, a schoolhouse was built on Eric Olson's land outside Dunnell. High winds destroyed it in 1882, but it was rebuilt. In 1902, the school was moved into Dunnell, but in 1903, it was decided a new one should be built. Dunnell's third schoolhouse, shown above, was finished in 1904. The fourth building was built in 1929. The Dunnell School consolidated with Sherburn and closed in 1969.

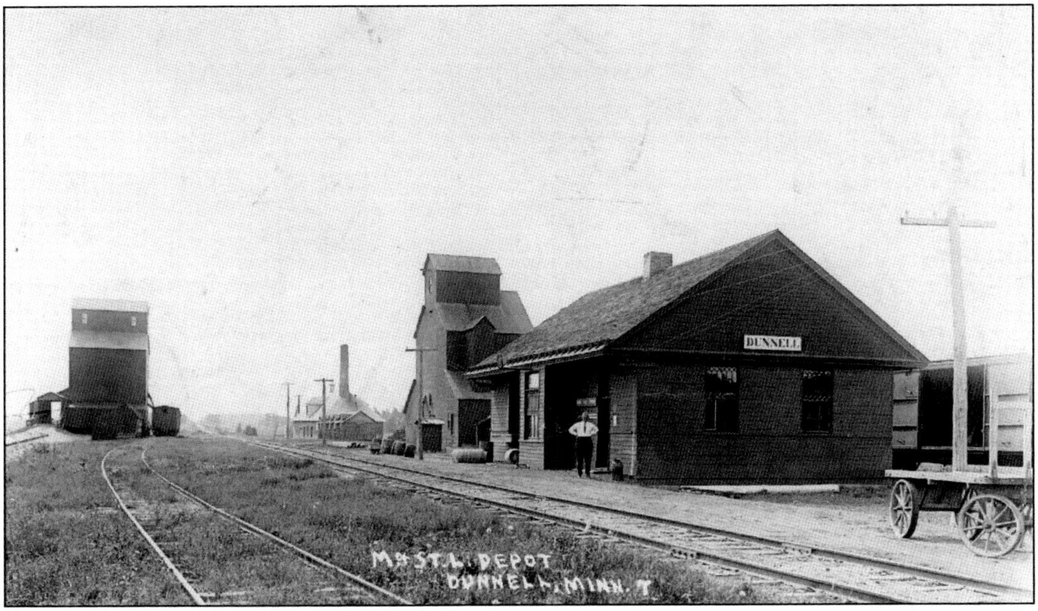

J. J. Gourley was the first agent of the Dunnell Minneapolis and St. Louis depot that was built in 1900. The first train chugged into town and stopped here on June 1, 1900. The tall chimney in the back is the Dunnell Creamery. The first creamery building was constructed in 1901 and destroyed by fire in July 1913. The one in this photograph opened for business in January 1914. This postcard dates from about 1915.

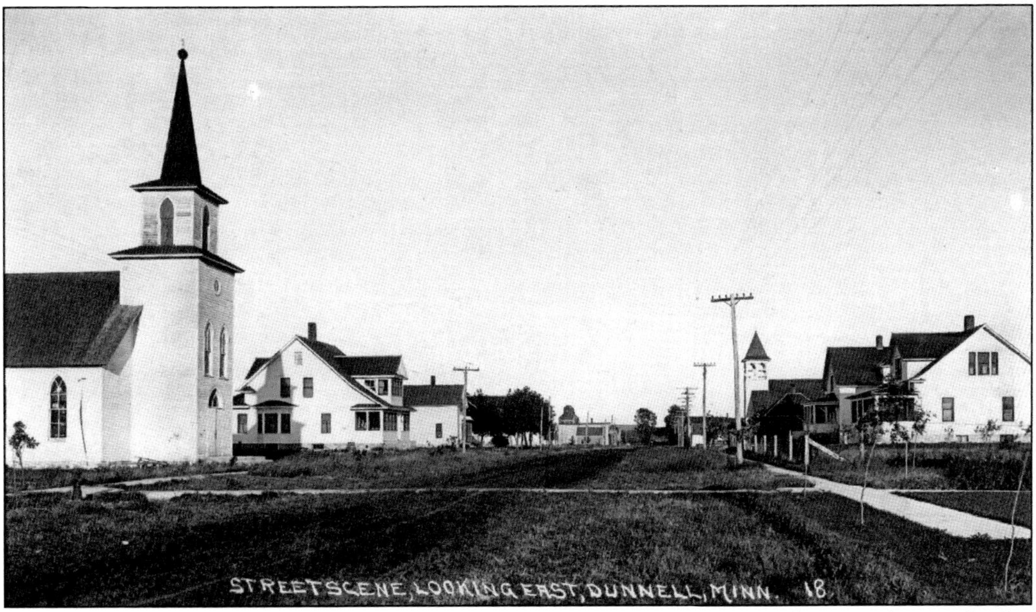

Here is Wenberg (Main) Street in Dunnell sometime between 1914 and 1918. The Methodist church on the left was originally the Immanuel Lutheran Church and moved into town in 1904. The Methodists sold it in the 1930s. St. John's Lutheran Church was built in 1914, and the steeple can be seen on the right. After 103 years, it was closed in 2003. This postcard is one of the first to show the new cement sidewalks in town.

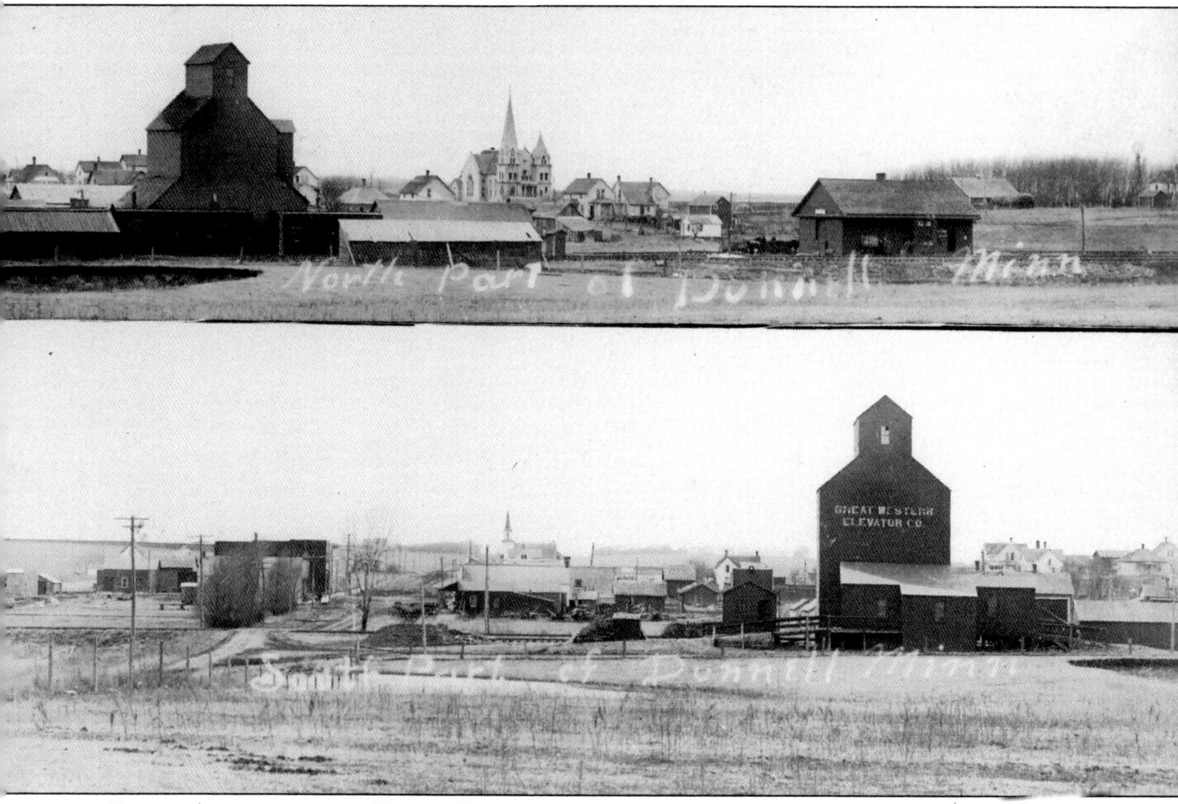

Here is the entire town of Dunnell on one postcard. Moving the top section and putting it to the right of the bottom one makes a panoramic view. This was taken about 1909.

Two

EAST CHAIN

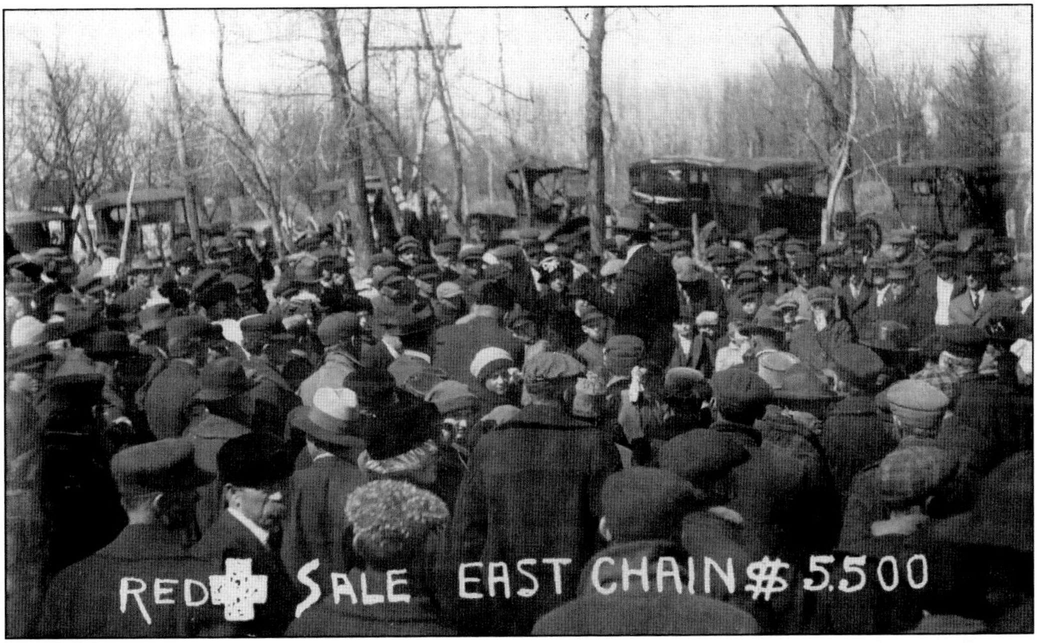

This postcard shows the 1918 Red Cross auction at East Chain in which the actual proceeds were $5,455. The area people would donate a fowl, livestock, or something of value to be auctioned. The successful bidder would then donate it back, and this would happen several times, bringing in large amounts of money for the Red Cross. A calf was sold in this manner at Truman, which raised $3,955; another at Welcome brought $4,250. The East Chain Red Cross branch was organized in 1917 at the Woodman Hall.

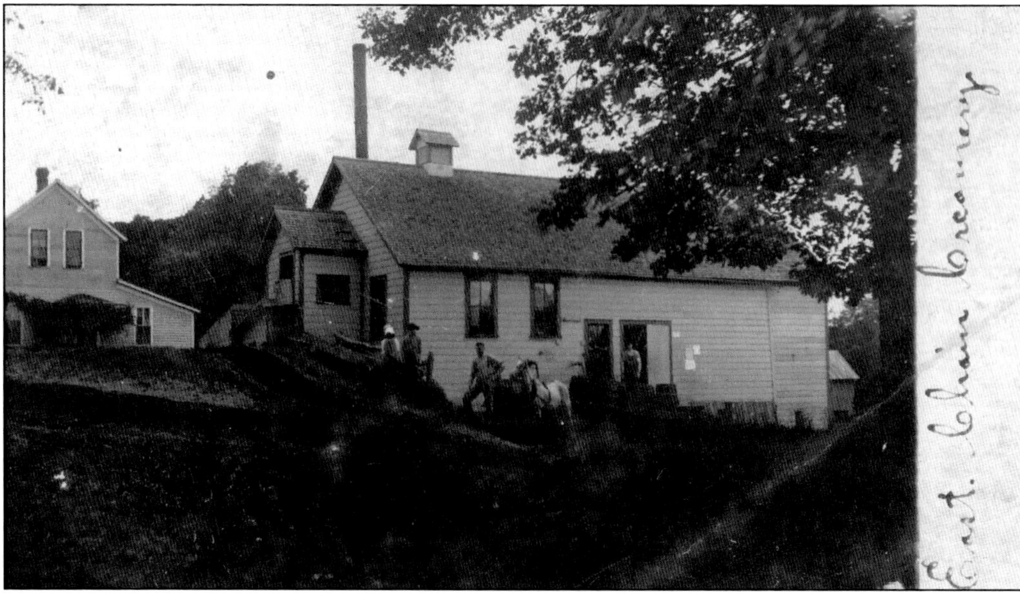

In the summer of 1895, it was decided to take a census of cows in the area. If pledges could be made for 500 cows to serve a new creamery, one was to be organized. Much to the delight of the organizers (George Elwess, Martin Gaworski, James Hand, R. B. Leet, E. S. Miller, G. H. Nicholas, O. G. Rowley, and J. E. Ruble), 600 cows were pledged, and the East Chain Lake Creamery was organized. The creamery building was constructed shortly thereafter. Under the management of C. R. Boynton, the creamery flourished. This building was located on the far west side of East Chain and is shown here about 1908.

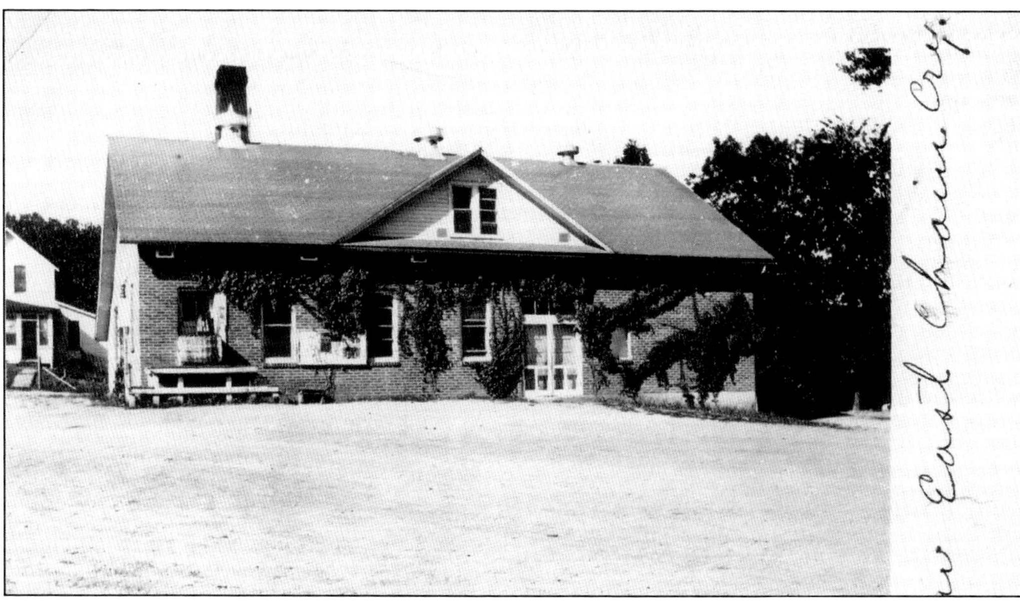

The East Chain Creamery did so well that in 1921, this 30-by-60-foot brick and tile structure was built. It cost $8,100 to construct, and Wagner and Stollman of Elmore were the successful bidders. The creamery closed in January 1961 and was then torn down. Martin County was left with only four creameries at Fairmont, Northrop (merged with Fairmont in 1964 and closed in the 1970s), Dunnell, and Welcome (closed in 1975).

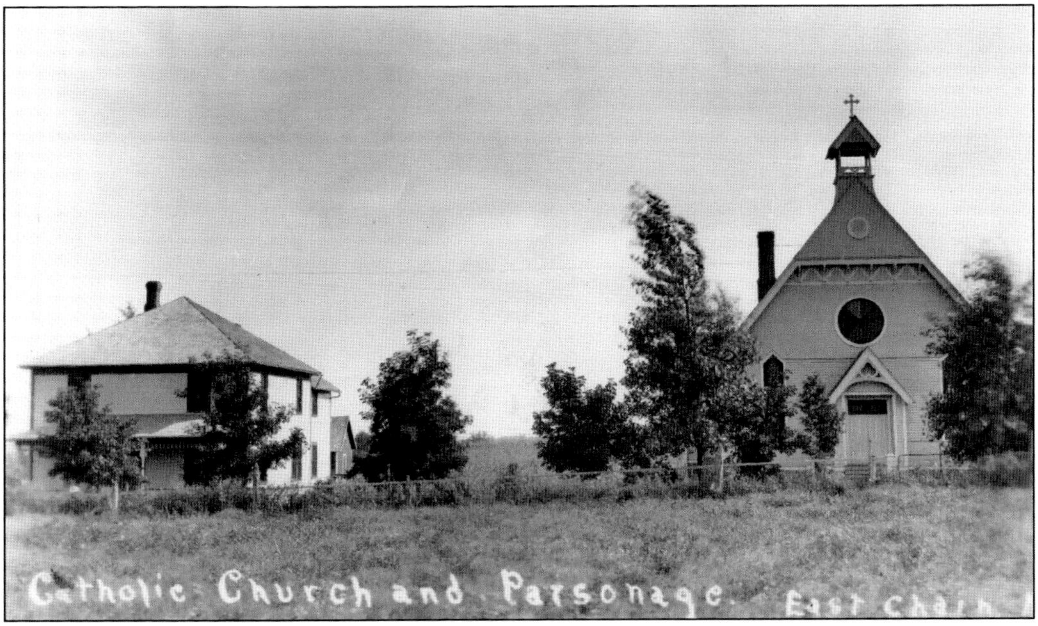

The East Chain Catholic parish was started in 1892 but was not officially organized until June 23, 1897. It is not certain when the church was built, but it was probably around 1893. It was destroyed by fire on December 27, 1924. The parsonage was built in 1908 under the auspices of Fr. Jerome Daszkowski.

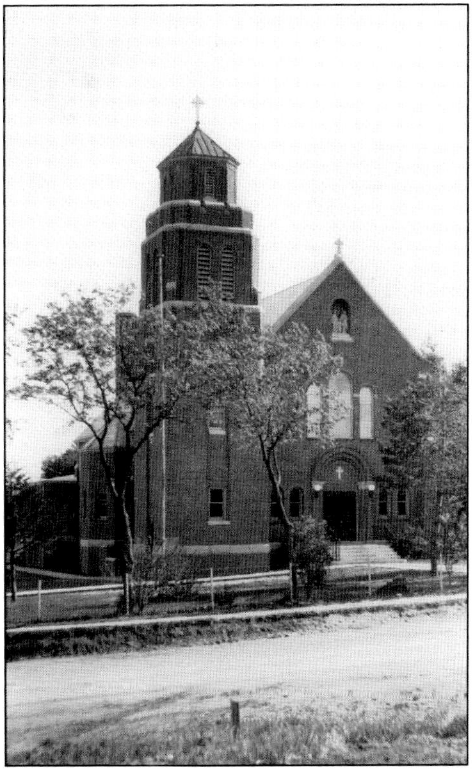

The cornerstone for the new East Chain Holy Family Catholic Church was laid on September 27, 1925. The tornado of 1936 that roared through Martin County did considerable damage to the new brick church, but it survived. The photograph shows the building shortly after it was finished in 1926.

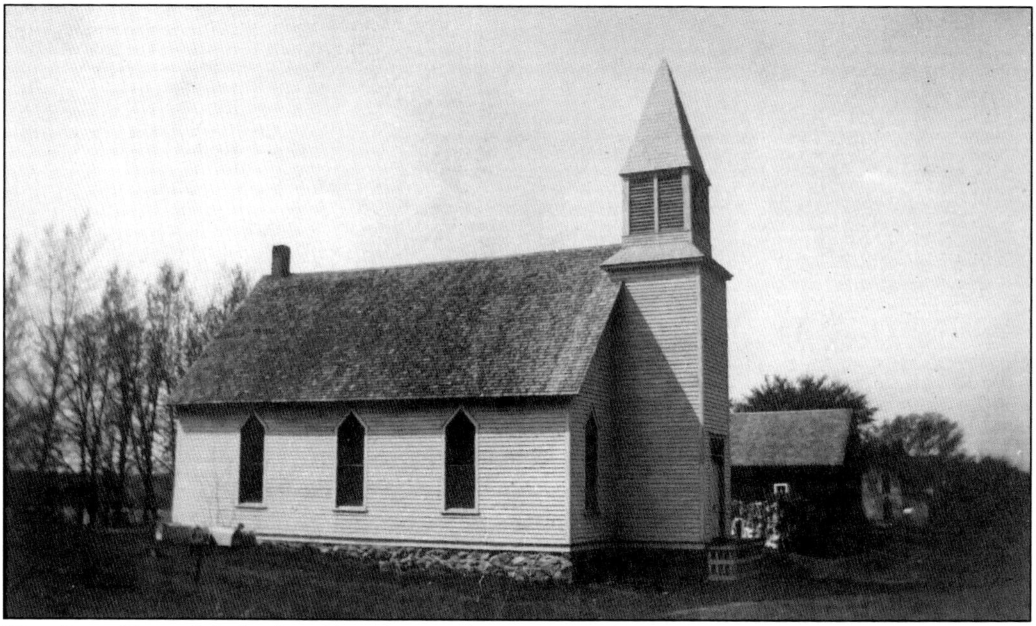

The East Chain Methodist Church was first organized in December 1873 as the Wesleyan Methodists by the Reverend S. C. Davis. The congregation worshipped in a schoolhouse for many years but had so few members that the state conference would not recognize it, so ministers of different denominations served it. It became large enough by 1895 to build a church, which was dedicated on November 1, 1895, and is shown here about 1910.

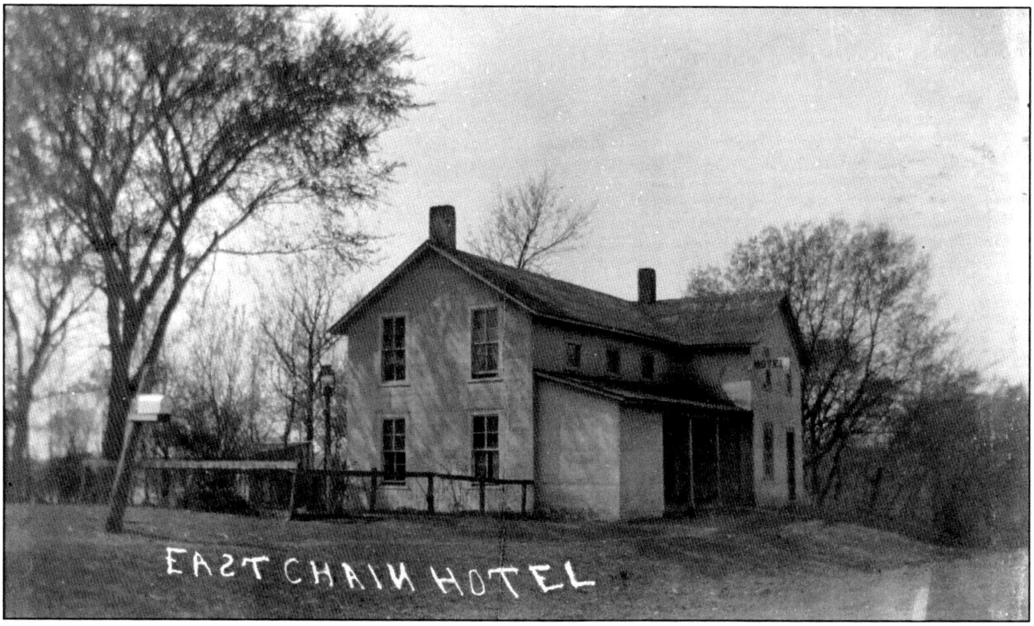

William Hoffman built the East Chain Hotel in 1871. However, it is not known how long it was a hotel. Walter and Cleo Gardner purchased it in 1939. They intended to construct a new house but discovered the building was made with oak studs and black walnut sills. They instead decided to remodel, thus saving the historic building. This is more than likely the oldest business structure still standing in Martin County. It currently is a residence.

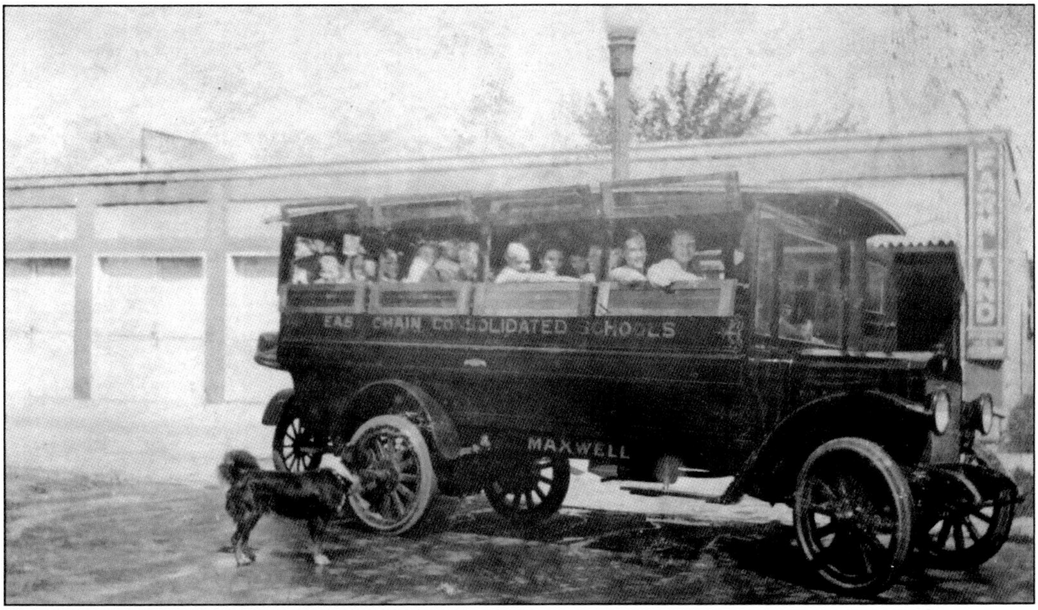

This is the Maxwell school bus that the East Chain Consolidated School purchased in the spring of 1918. A Ford bus was also purchased at the same time. The Maxwell Motor Company was one of the three largest manufacturers and by 1914 had sold 60,000 cars.

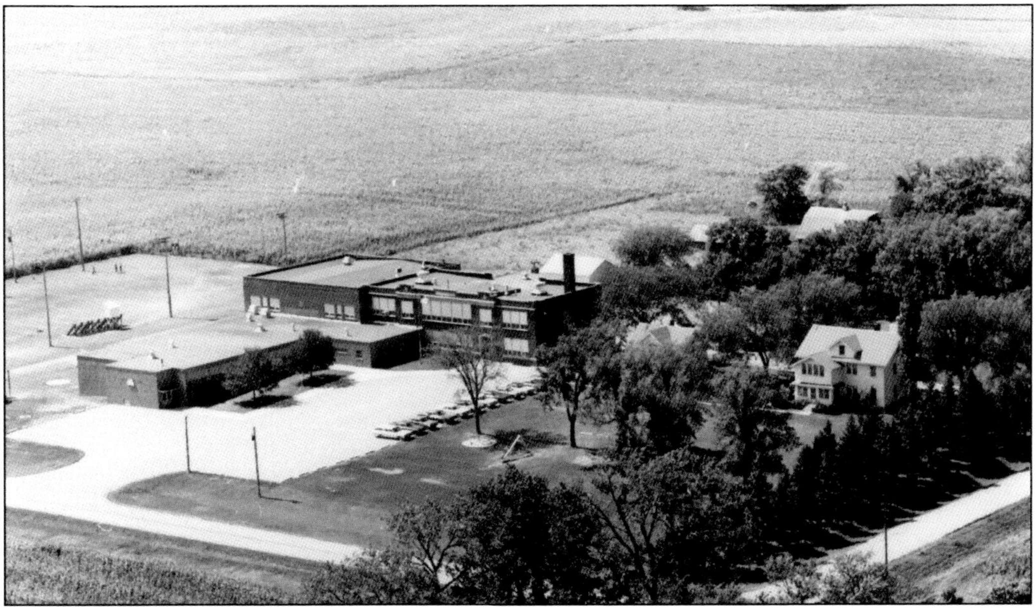

The East Chain Consolidated School was organized in 1916 when many rural school districts came together to form it. The new school was built and has been added on to many times since. In 1939, a gymnasium was added, and in 1955, the elementary section was built. A new gymnasium was built in 1975. Two houses were also constructed on the grounds in 1916. One was for the janitor, and the other was for the superintendent. The old school building and the house most visible were razed in 2002.

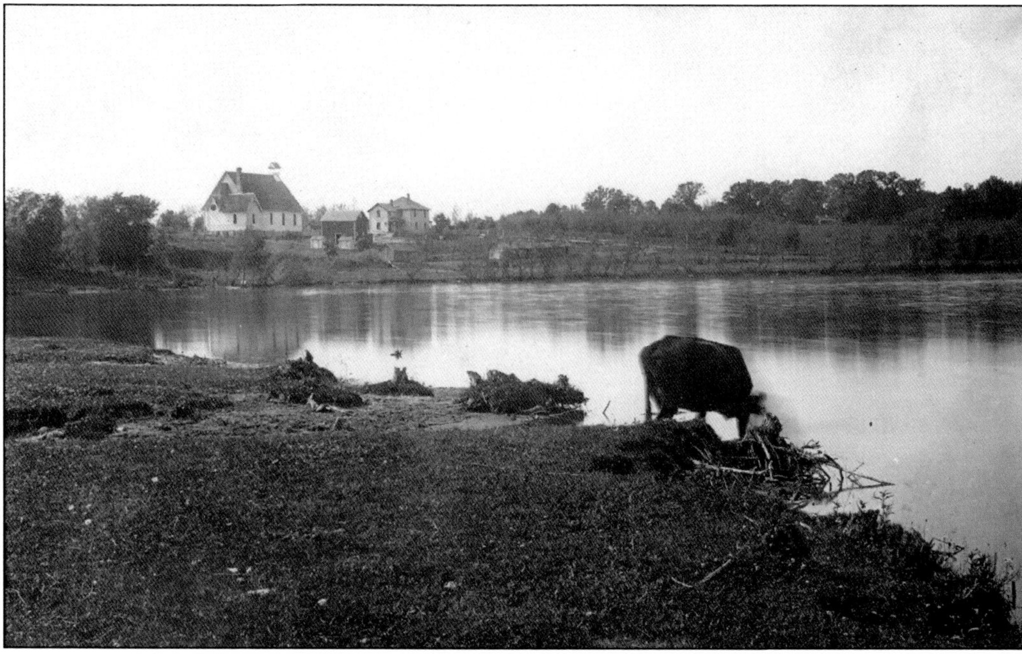

This is a view of East Chain Lake around 1910. The first Catholic church and parsonage can be seen in the background. The first settlers arrived to the East Chain area as early as 1857. When Darius Rowley arrived here in October 1859, the community of East Chain was started. When the post office opened on June 26, 1862, it was known as East Chain Lakes. The last mail delivered from there happened on May 14, 1906.

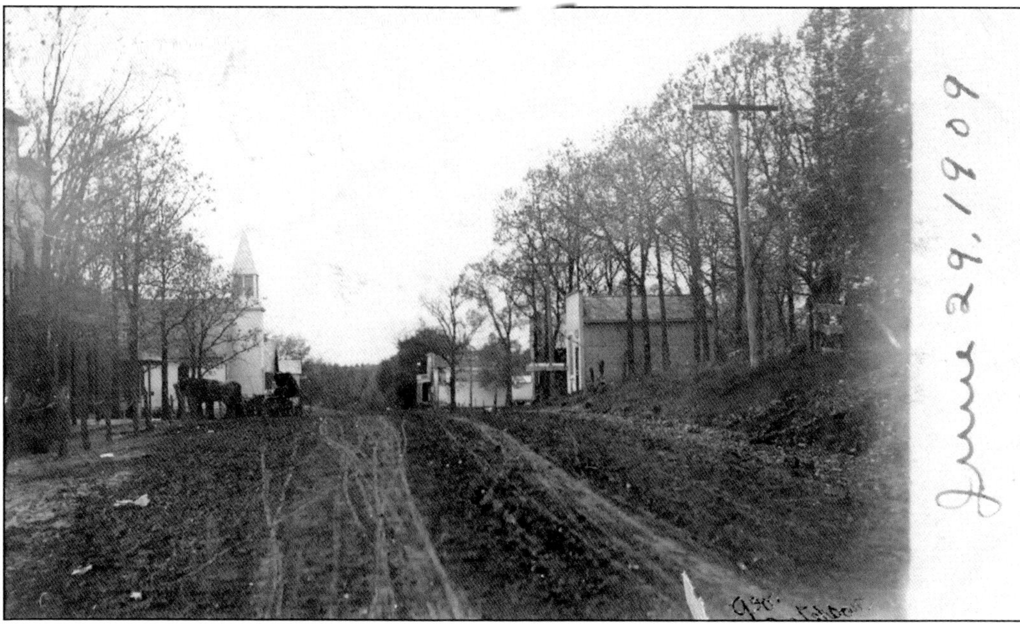

This photograph is dated June 29, 1909, and shows East Chain's main street looking west. The businesses located on the left side were the Vermilya Store, the Miller house, the Methodist church, the livery stable, and the hotel. On the right side were Garret Doyle's real estate office, a blacksmith shop, a butcher shop, and the Doyle Store.

Three

FAIRMONT AND INTERLAKEN

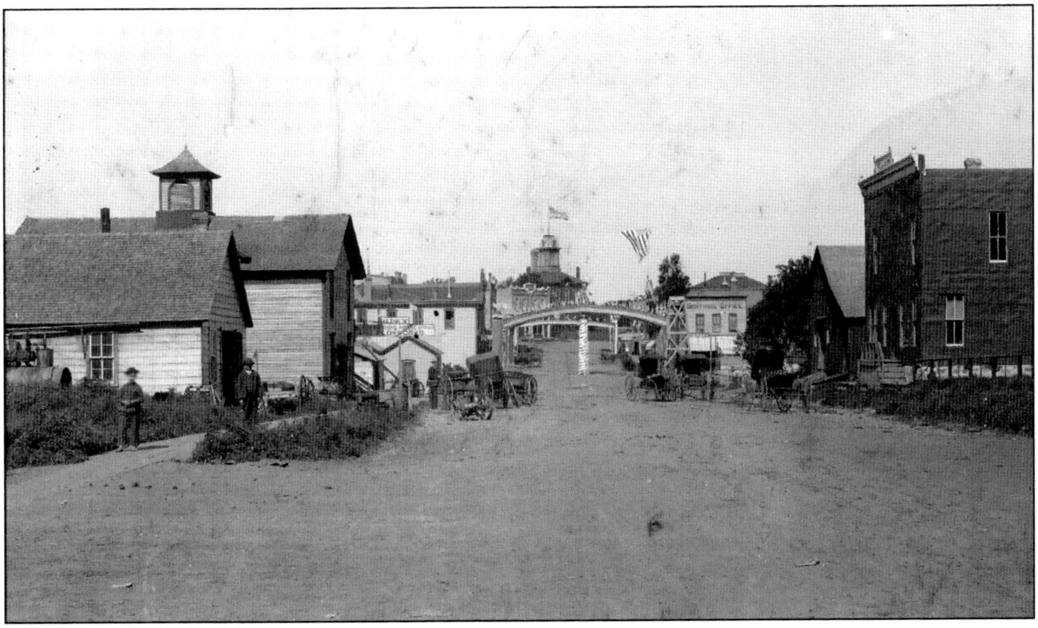

E. Banks Hall and William H. Budd came to what is now Fairmont in July 1856. The new town of Fair Mount was platted in October 1857 and declared the county seat on December 16, 1857. In 1874, Fairmont became home to the 125th newspaper started in Minnesota. On July 1, 1878, the first train rolled into town. Some sort of celebration was taking place when this photograph was taken in 1893 or 1894. The building on the left with the large cupola is Martin Thiede's blacksmith shop.

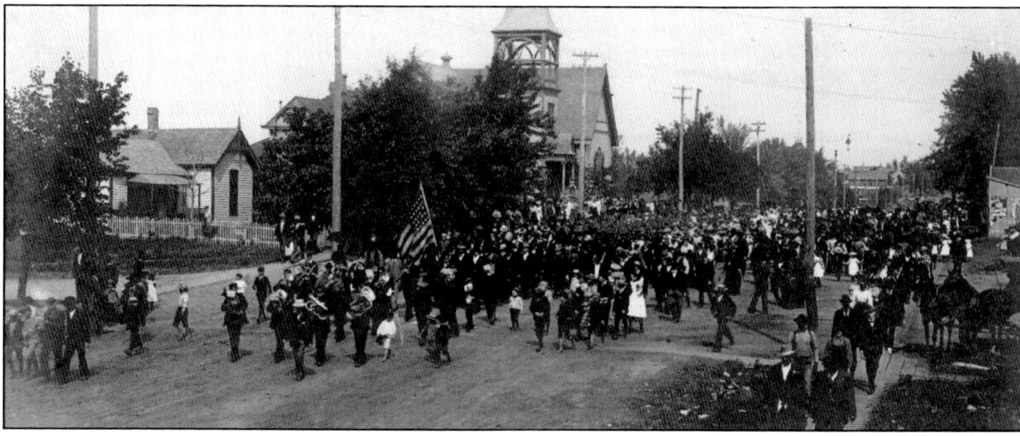

This photograph was taken on September 23, 1898, after Company D of the 12th Minnesota Volunteer Infantry arrived at the Milwaukee depot. They got off on the north side of the train and were met by "the whole countryside." The band leads a procession with great fanfare down North Avenue.

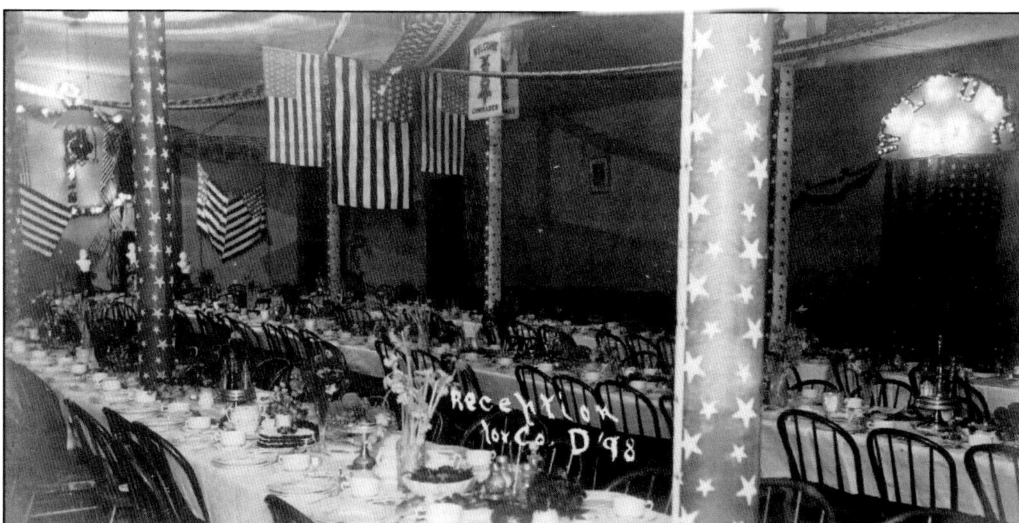

This is "the great banquet" held in honor of Company D at Daniels Hall. Plates were laid for 200, and the menu included consomme et tasse, English celery, pickles, roast turkey, mallard duck, boiled ham, cabbage salad, potato salad, maple ice cream, and coffee. This is also the first time "electric effects" were used in Fairmont, which were in patriotic colors and seen at the top right-hand corner. This photograph was taken on October 7, 1898. Daniels Hall was in the second story of the large brick building that burned in 1914 on North Avenue.

The Victoria gristmill is on the far left. Of the English settlers who stayed in the 1870s, this was one of their successes. The photograph was taken on March 29, 1881, after one of the worst blizzards to hit the Midwest. At the time, this was North Avenue, probably looking north, at the corner of Downtown Plaza and Second Street where Bank Midwest is located. The third building from the right was a billiard hall.

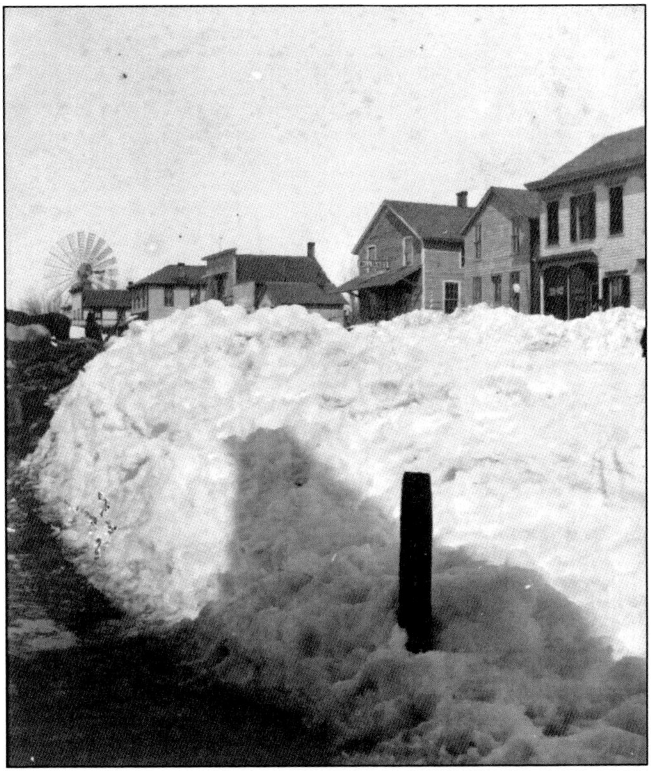

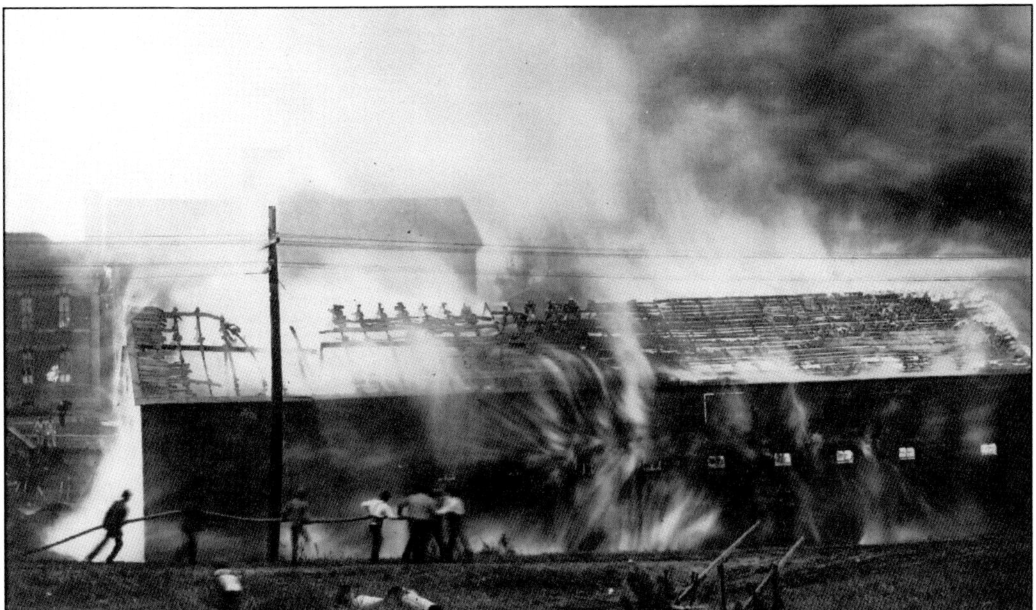

This fire destroyed the Wallace Livery Barn on September 28, 1908. Fifteen horses, fourteen buggies, six cutters, nearly 50 tons of hay, and much more were incinerated. Two horses, one goat, and one buggy were saved. Wallace's daughter ran into the burning building and rescued the singed goat. It is amazing she was not killed. Apparently the building collapsed within 10 minutes of the discovery of the fire, which makes this photograph even more incredible.

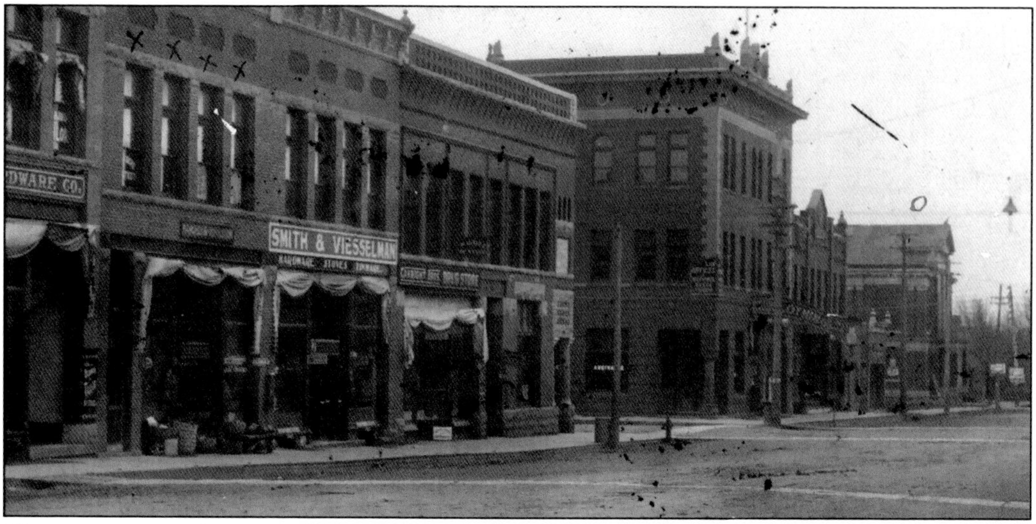

This is a very early view of North Avenue looking south between 1901 and 1903. The first building is a hardware store, and by 1904, it became a furniture store. The storefronts from left to right are the A. P. Smith Hardware Company (partially shown), Fancher and Donaldson General Merchandise store (this was just A. R. Fancher's by 1904), A. H. Smith and William Viesselman Hardware Store, Canright Brothers Drug Store, First National Bank, Hicks and Goetz Clothing Store (tallest building), J. H. Gorman Machinery, August Krumholz Flour and Feed, and the opera house.

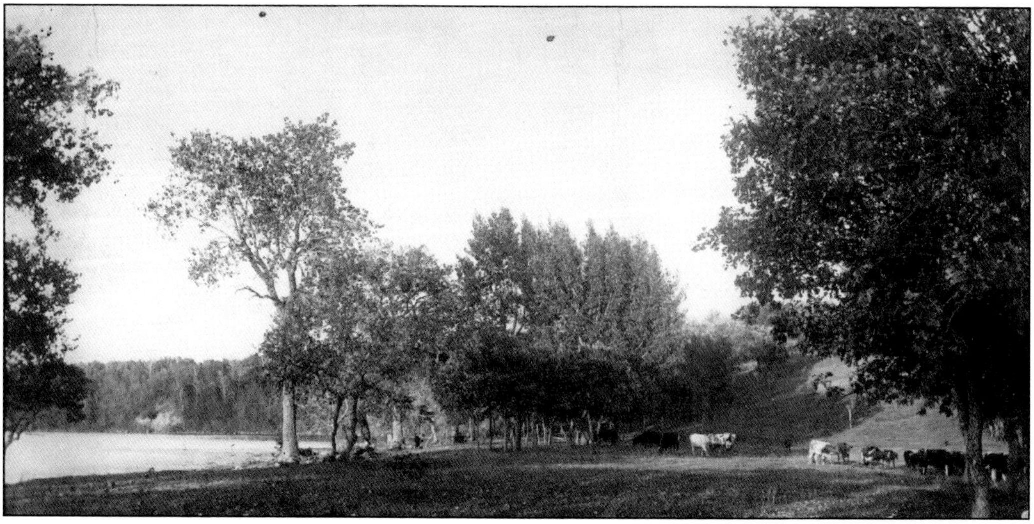

This is Interlaken Park before it was developed. The photograph was taken when F. A. B. Paterson owned it and used it as his summer home. Even at that time, it was known as Interlaken.

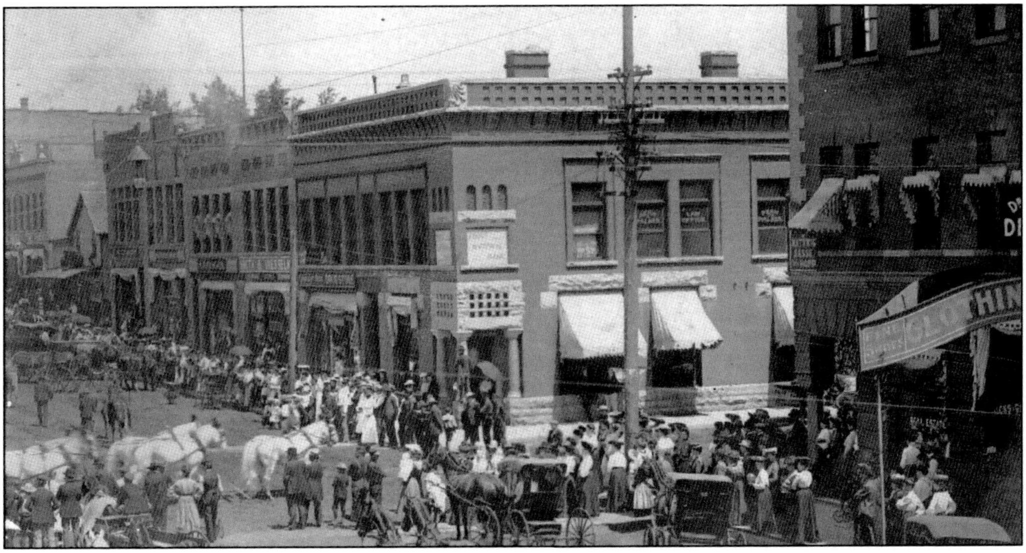

This postcard was mailed on September 9, 1907, and probably shows the Fairmont Chautauqua celebration on July 1, 1907. This parade was led by the Fairmont Juvenile Band. The first building on the right is the Hicks and Goetz Clothing Store. It also housed the Sinclair Real Estate Office and the law offices of Mathwig, Sasse and Hopp. Across the street is the First National Bank of Fairmont with many attorneys having offices on the second floor. In the same building to the left is Canright Brothers Drug Store, with Dr. W. G. Tull, the dentist, overhead. The next shops are Smith and Viesselman Hardware Store, A. R. Fancher General Merchandise, Needham and Symonds Furniture, the City Grocery, T. R. Alston Grocery and Crockery Store, and liquors and cigars dealer the Phoenix.

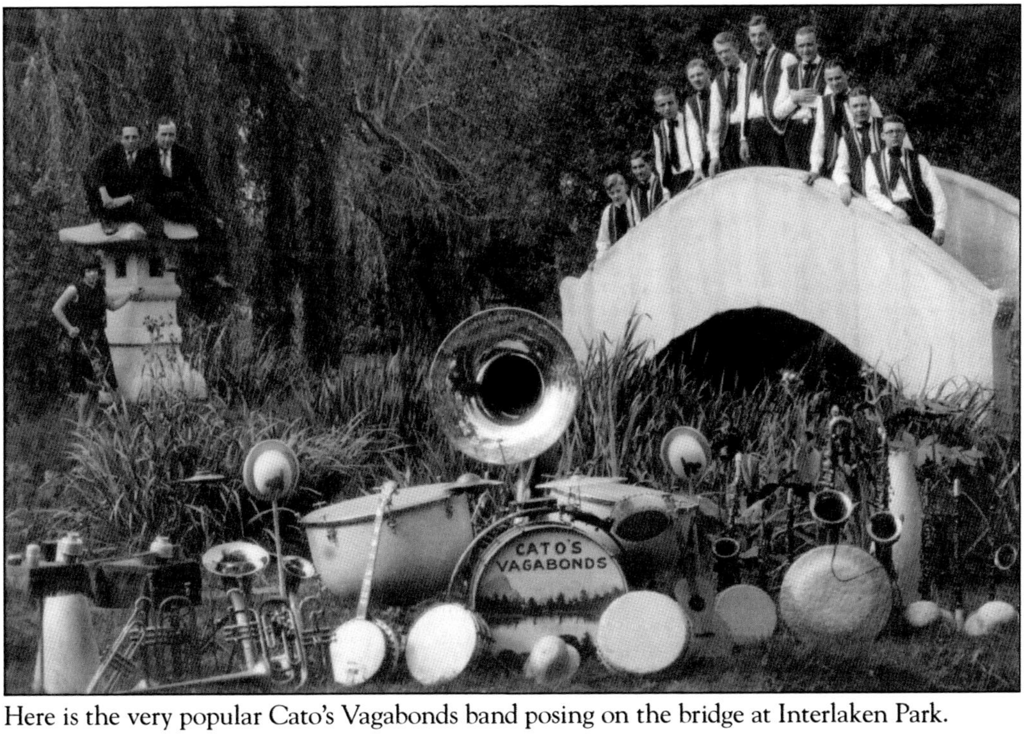

Here is the very popular Cato's Vagabonds band posing on the bridge at Interlaken Park.

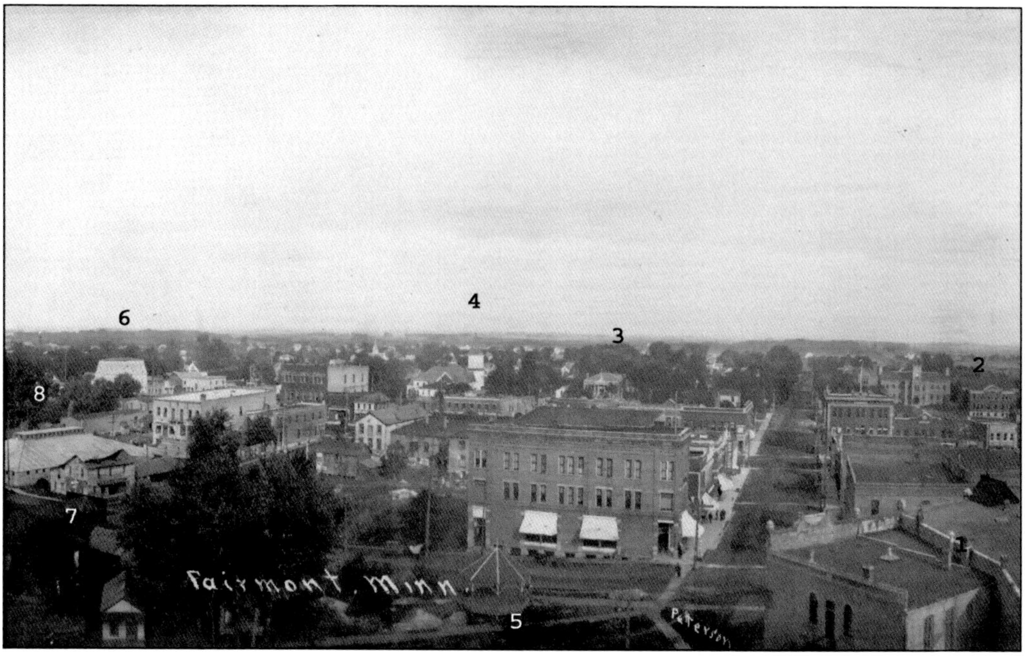

This is what is commonly called a bird's-eye view. It was taken by Paul Peterson in 1907, and quite a few landmarks are visible. The roof of Houghtaling and Coult Hardware Store and Martin County National Bank (1) can be seen along with the three school buildings (2), the Carnegie library (3), old Methodist church (4), the gazebo in the flatiron block (5), Rippe Mill (6), and what appears to be a large burned-out house (7) by Allison's Horse Parlors (8).

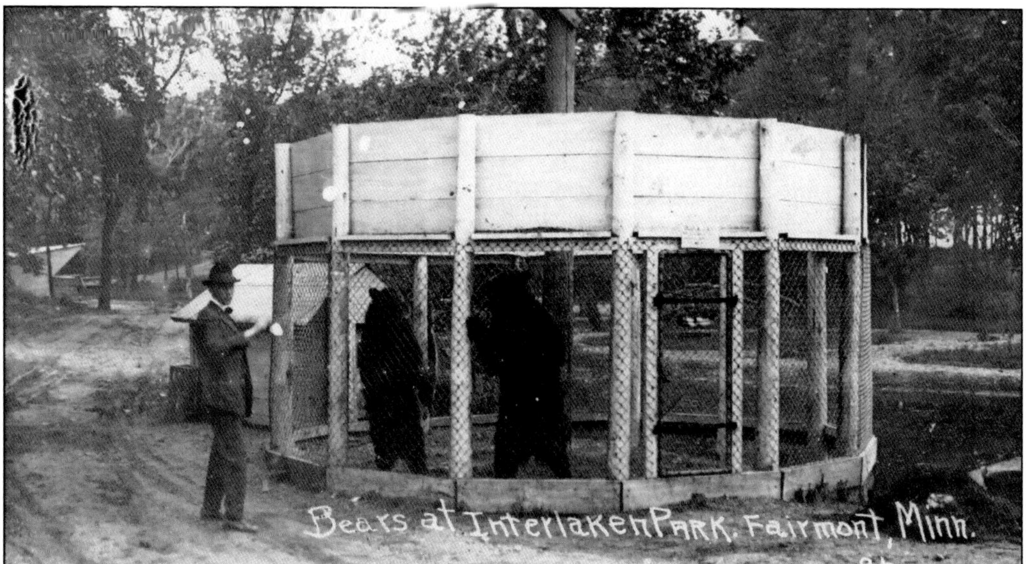

The zoo at Interlaken started in 1916. It was originally called Lenny Burton's Zoo, located where Jake's Pizza is now. It was later moved to George Lake and then Interlaken. The zoo once boasted six bears, three deer, monkeys, owls, squirrels, a parrot, ostriches, seals, and many more animals. Burton almost lost his life at his zoo when he went into the bear cage and the door shut behind him. Thinking quickly, he threw sawdust into the bear's eyes, allowing time to escape.

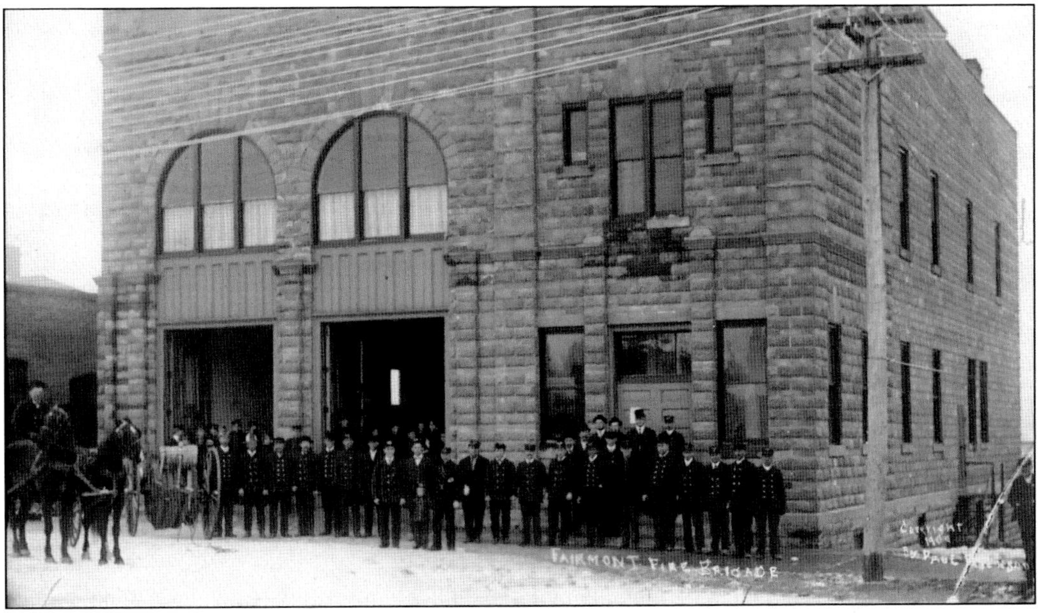

This was taken in 1909 by Fairmont photographer Peterson. The Fairmont Fire Brigade was organized on December 26, 1882, and the Village of Fairmont duly presented them with three ladders, twelve leather buckets, and two axes. C. Roids presented the fire company with an old spring wagon, which was transformed into a hook and ladder truck. This building housed both the city and fire halls. The original 1907 bids to construct the building were over $20,000 and were rejected by the council. According to Albert Niss, it was finished in 1908 at a cost of $12,000.

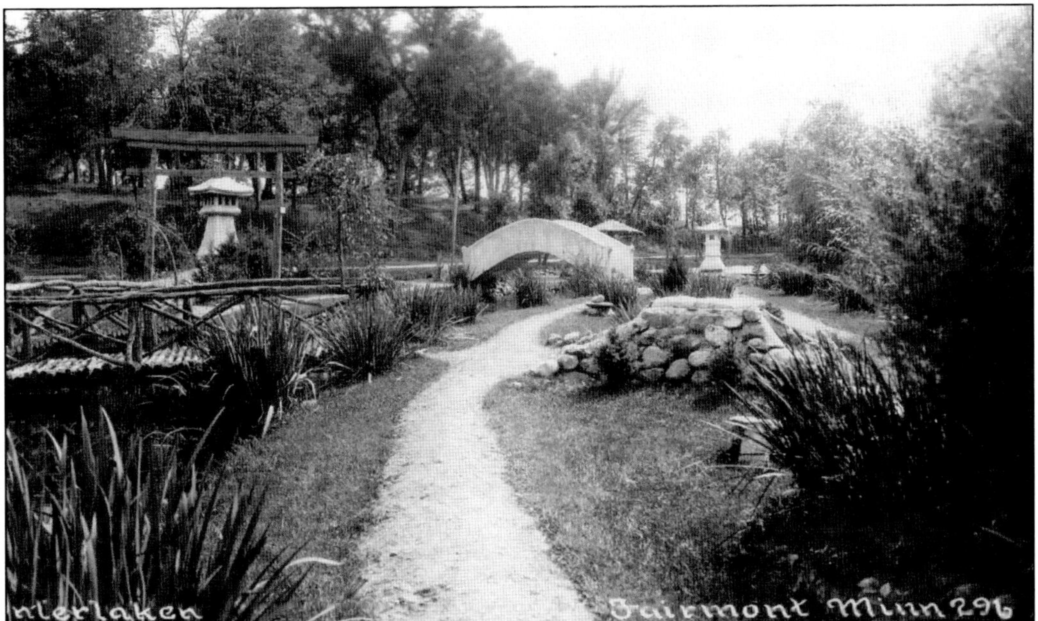

The Japanese gardens were Frank Wade's favorite part of Interlaken. He started these gardens in 1917 and expanded them for awhile, but they fell into neglect in the late 1930s.

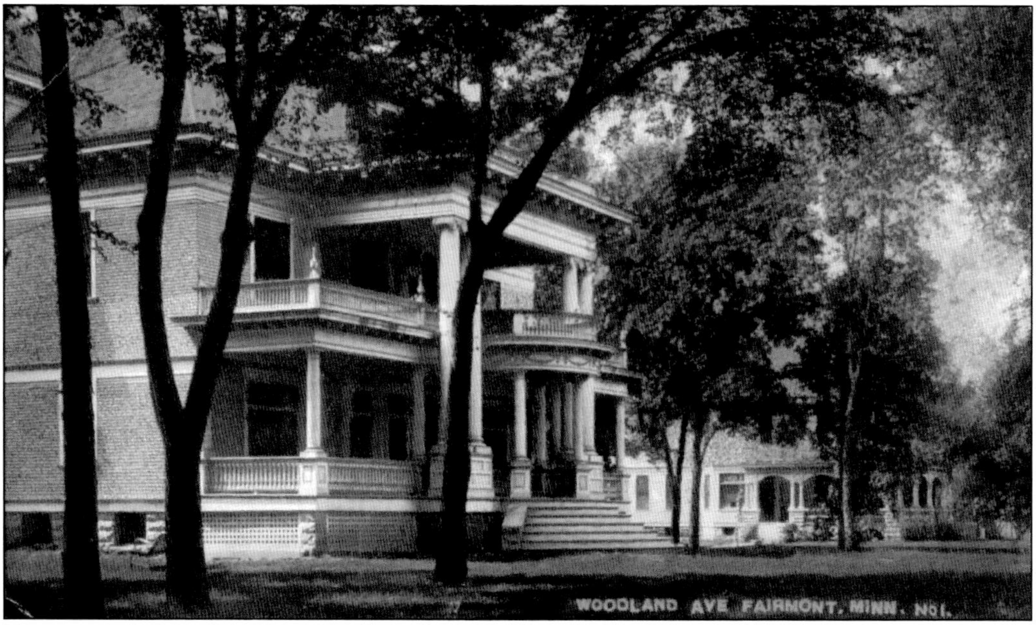

Here are the homes of Henry Rippe at 121 Woodland Avenue (left) and W. L. Lamb at 203 Woodland Avenue about 1913. The Rippe mansion had an extreme makeover in 1935. Roy Palmer purchased the home and intended to make the two-and-a-half-story home into one and a half stories. The second story was removed and, along with the garage, it was used to build another nearby residence. It took three carpenters a full day to dismantle the main staircase in 1935. The mansion was built in 1900 and is presently a fine residence.

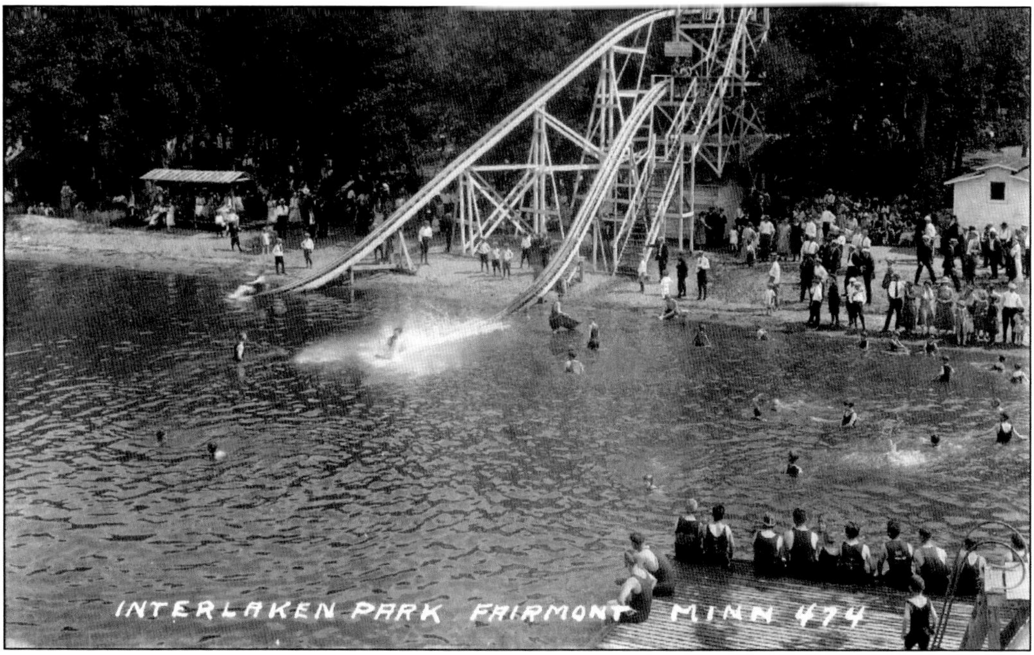

This postcard shows Interlaken's two immensely popular water toboggan slides that were built in 1915 and 1916.

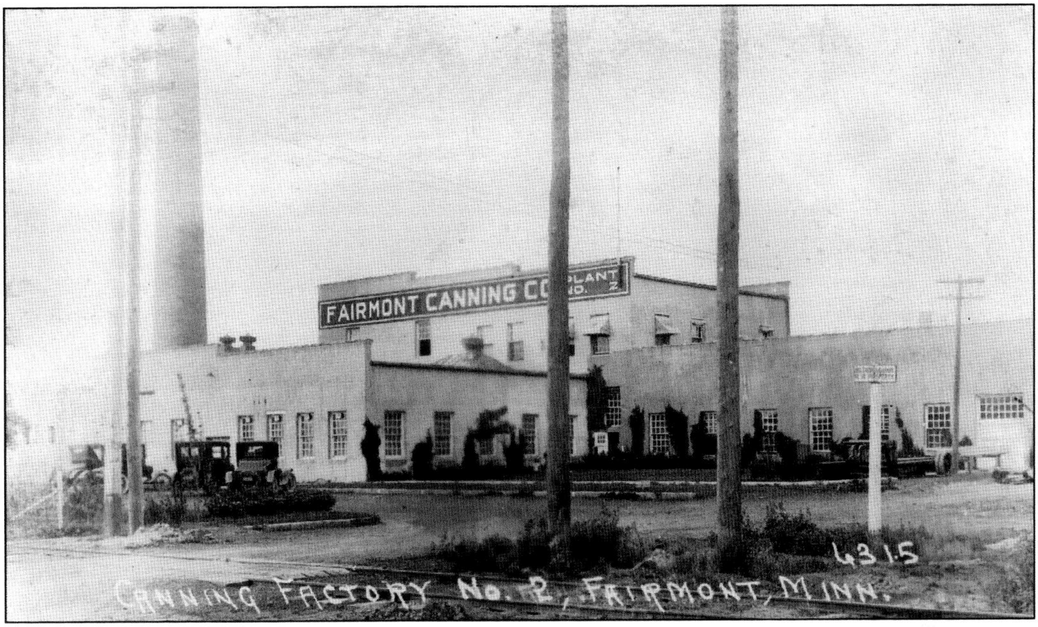

This is the Fairmont Canning Company sometime in the 1920s. This building was originally the Fairmont Tile Plant, which had its beginnings in 1912. The canning company was vying for this property in 1919 but lost out due to a technicality. In 1919, the defunct tile plant was sold to the short-lived Sumner Engine Factory enterprise. In 1922, it was proposed to be sold to the Power Farming Manufacturing Company. It is unknown if that transaction went through, but it was sold to the Fairmont Canning Company in the 1920s.

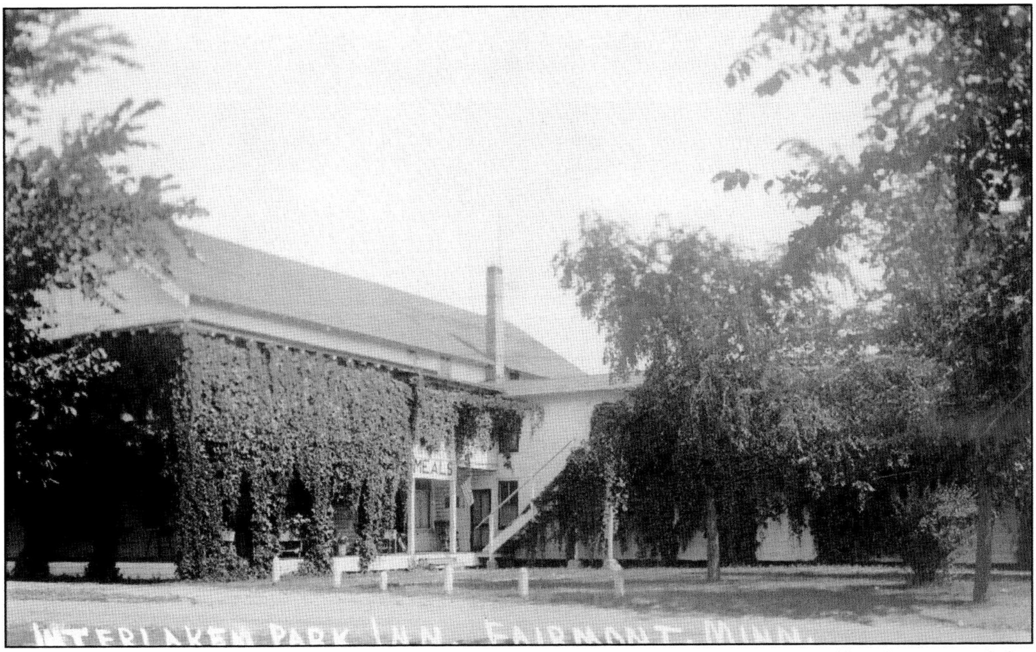

The Inn at Interlaken was built in 1916. It was located along the bank of Hall Lake west of the present Chain of Lakes Yacht Club. It was a large but simple building, and each room had a porch overlooking Hall Lake.

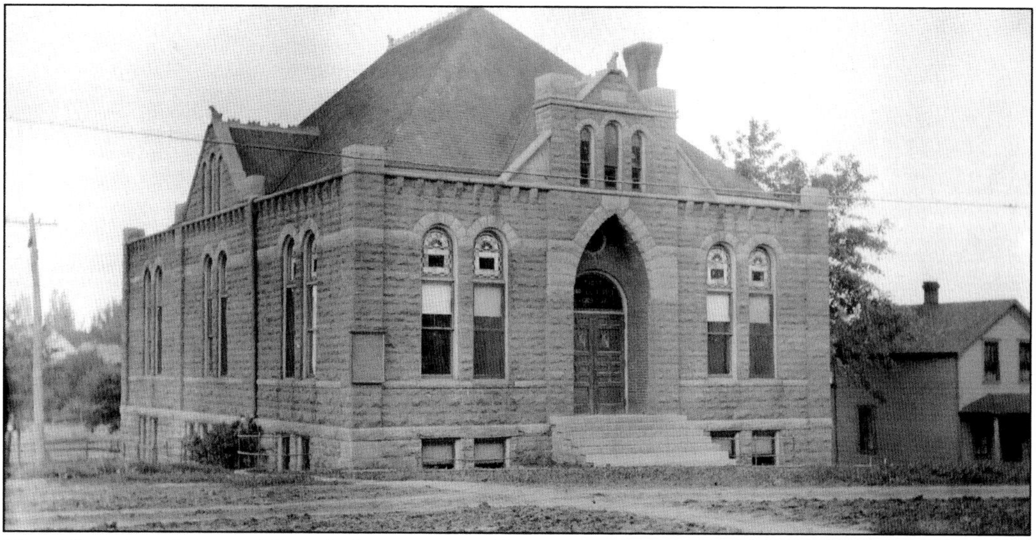

The Christian Science Church first came to Fairmont in 1889, and "a number of chronic and acute diseases were cured," according to an old newspaper. The First Church of Christ, Scientist was incorporated on September 28, 1891. The lot for a new church building was purchased in 1897 for $600. On May 19, 1898, work commenced, and the first services were on communion Sunday in June 1899. This structure was vacant for the last few years and had partially collapsed. With the help of the Martin County Preservation Society, it has been restored and is known as the Red Rock Center for the Arts. This postcard dates from about 1908. Notice the fancy work on the peak of the roof and the lack of stained-glass windows.

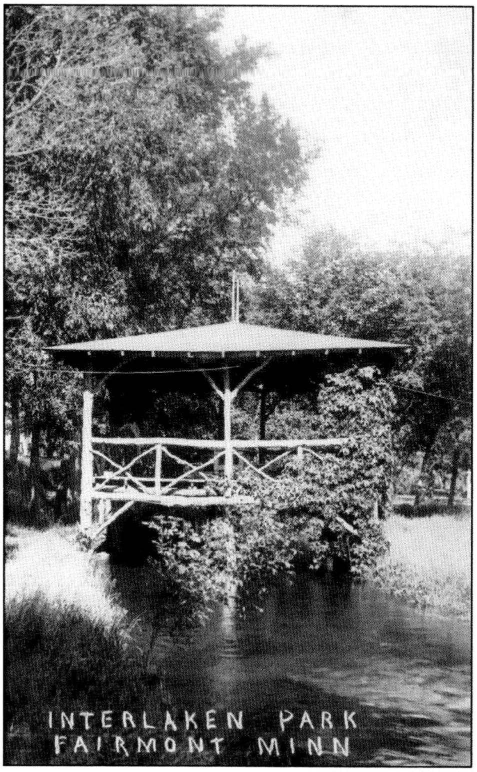

"The Great Commoner," William Jennings Bryan, spoke from this bandstand at Interlaken on July 12, 1918, for two and a half hours. His speech attracted some 3,000 listeners.

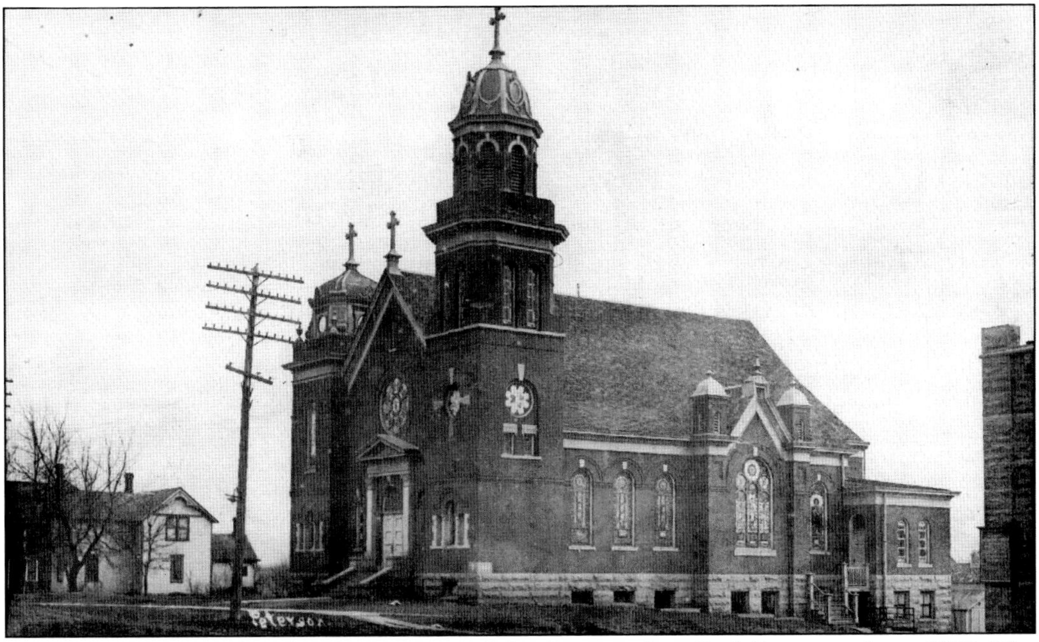

This postcard was taken by Fairmont's prolific photographer Paul Peterson about 1907. The Fairmont Catholic Church first started in 1873 when a mass was held in a farmhouse four miles west of town. In 1882, the first church was built where the library now stands. The church in this postcard was built about 1902 and torn down in March 1956, when even the large, round stained-glass window was smashed by the wrecking ball. The Martin County Historical Society is now located at this site in the former Catholic school.

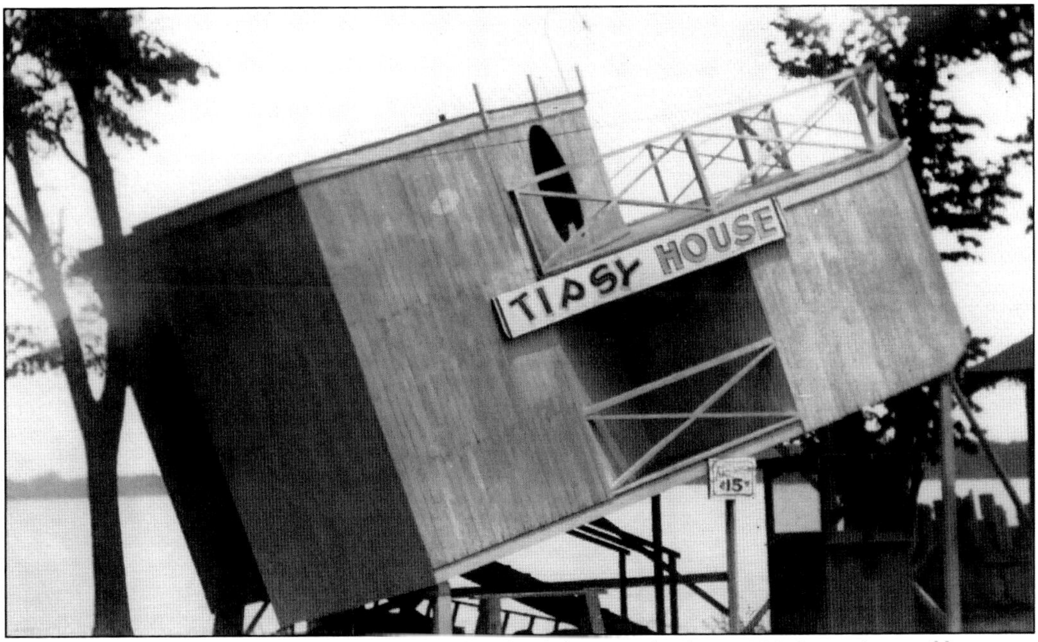

The Tipsy House, modeled after a Coney Island exhibit, was built in 1928. It was located between the dance pavilion and Hall Lake. Many young people enjoyed paying the 15¢ to be entertained in the house. This photograph was made by the Photo Shop at Interlaken Park.

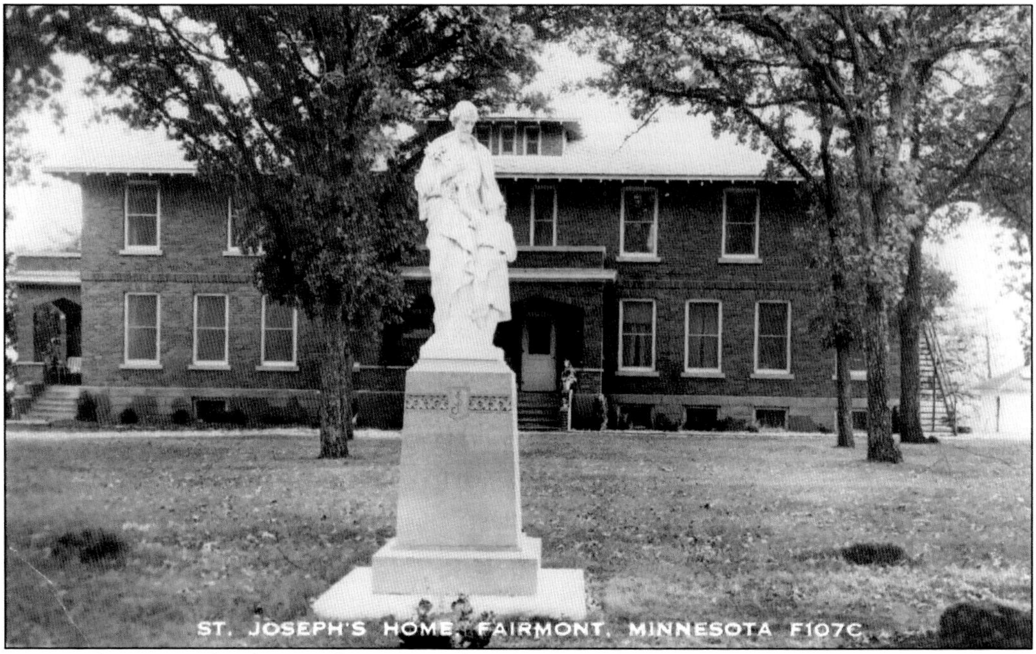

St. Joseph's Home for the Aged was owned and operated by the Sisters of Our Lady Mother of Mercy. It was purchased from Martin County in 1948 for $21,000. This originally was the county poorhouse, built in 1915 for $16,700. The county first acquired the land in 1883 from Somerville and Betsy Hill and Somerville's brother Washington at a cost of $1,400. St. Joseph's Home lasted until 1970. In 1973, it became the Chain of Lakes Halfway House, which closed in 2004. Pat and Jacklyn Beemer purchased the property in 2004 and intend to raze the structure.

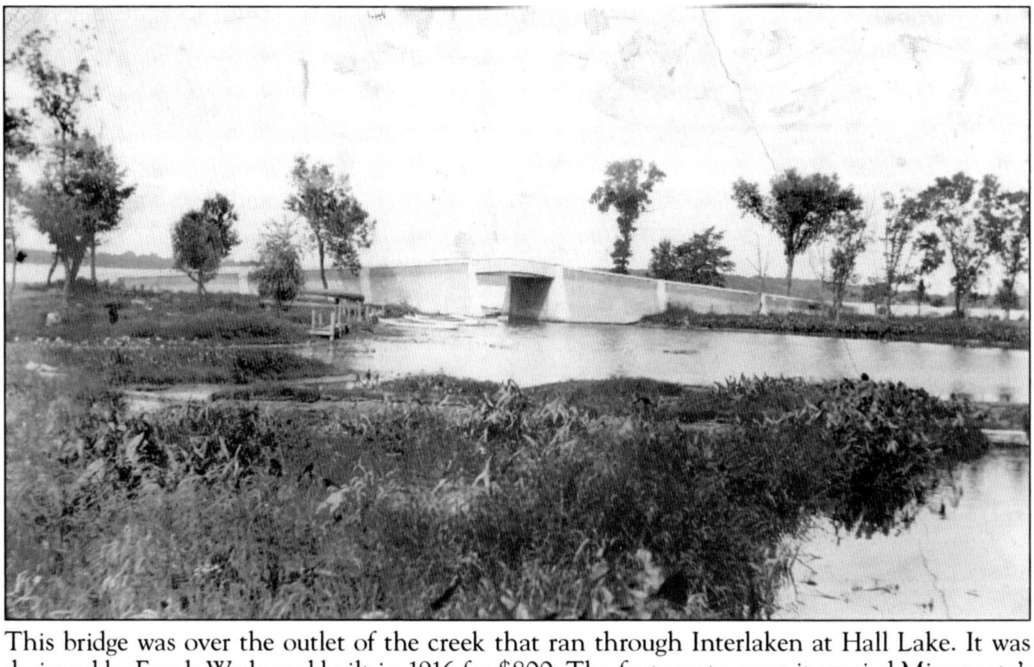

This bridge was over the outlet of the creek that ran through Interlaken at Hall Lake. It was designed by Frank Wade and built in 1916 for $800. The first car to cross it carried Minnesota's Gov. Joseph Burnquist.

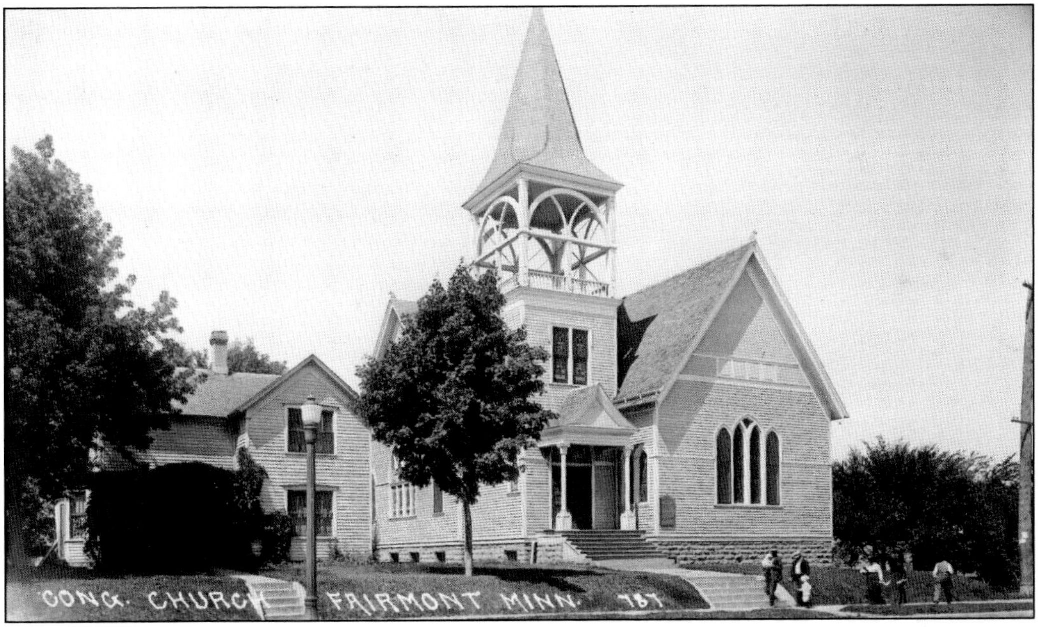

The Congregational Church of Fairmont was first organized on May 23, 1868, and the first church was built in 1876. This is a photograph of the second church, which was built in 1896 and 1897 and dedicated on October 10, 1897. A fine brick edifice replaced this one in 1929. Even though it was organized over 140 years ago, the first Congregational church in Martin County was at Center Chain.

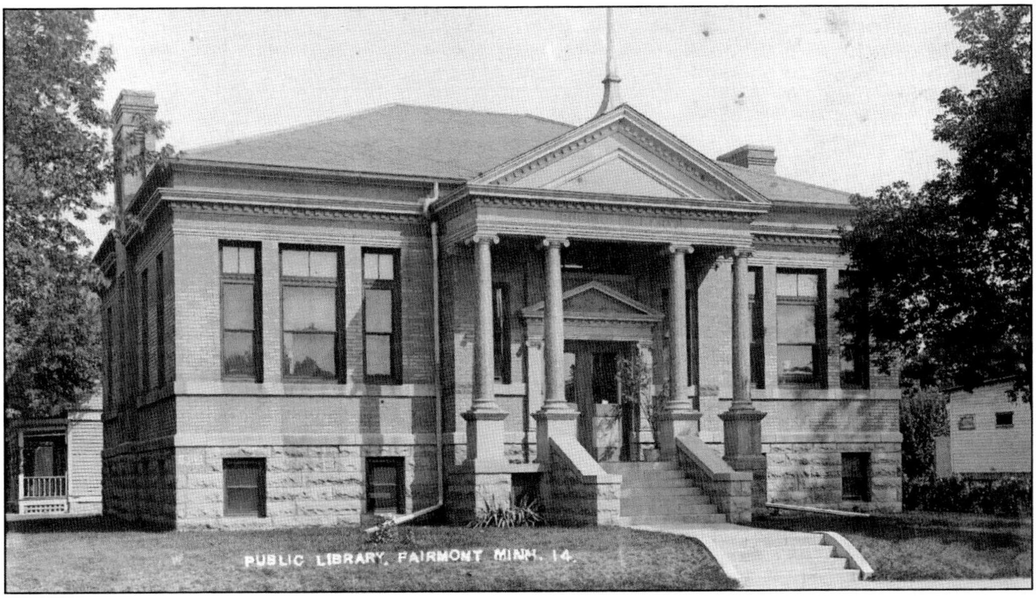

The Martin County Library started in 1880 and was located in the area of the northwest corner of Downtown Plaza and Second Street. By 1900, it was located at 105 East First Street. In 1903, a $10,000 gift from Andrew Carnegie and $800 from "public spirited citizens" enabled Martin County to build a library. On April 26, 1904, the Martin County Library opened its doors. The above library was razed and replaced with a $440,000 structure in 1969. This photograph is from around 1911.

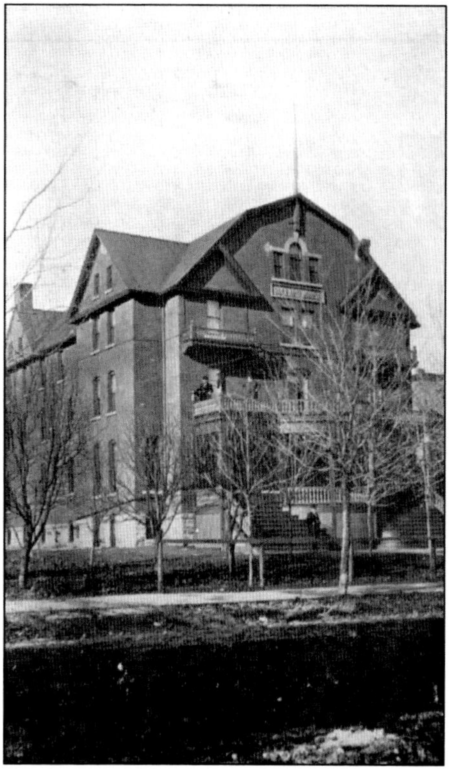

This postcard has a hand-written date of 1907 and shows the Bullard Hotel, also commonly known as the Bullard House. The substantial brick structure was built in 1894 by Charles H. Bullard. On many old postcards showing Lake Sisseton and the courthouse, one can see the rooftop of this building. It was later called the Edgewater Hotel, when from 1912 to 1950, E. A. Luedke operated it. In 1960, this structure was torn down and replaced with a new $160,000, 24-unit motel. That structure has since been razed and is now a parking lot for Profinium Financial (formerly Martin County National Bank).

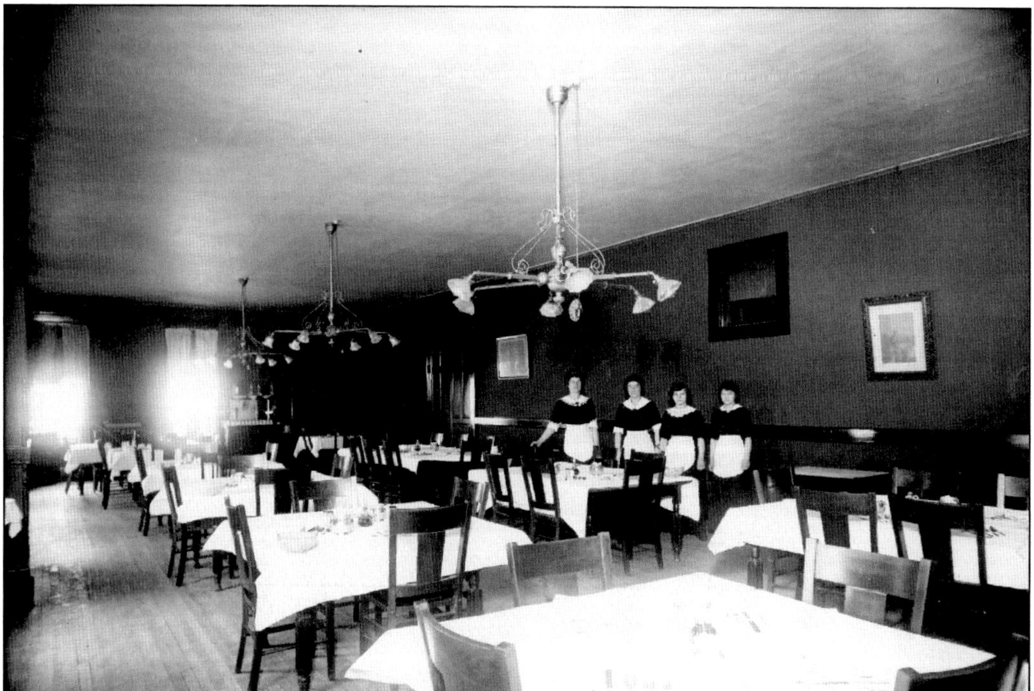

This is the dining room of the Edgewater Hotel about 1914. Bertha Cowing is one of the waitresses. (Courtesy of the Granada Historical Museum.)

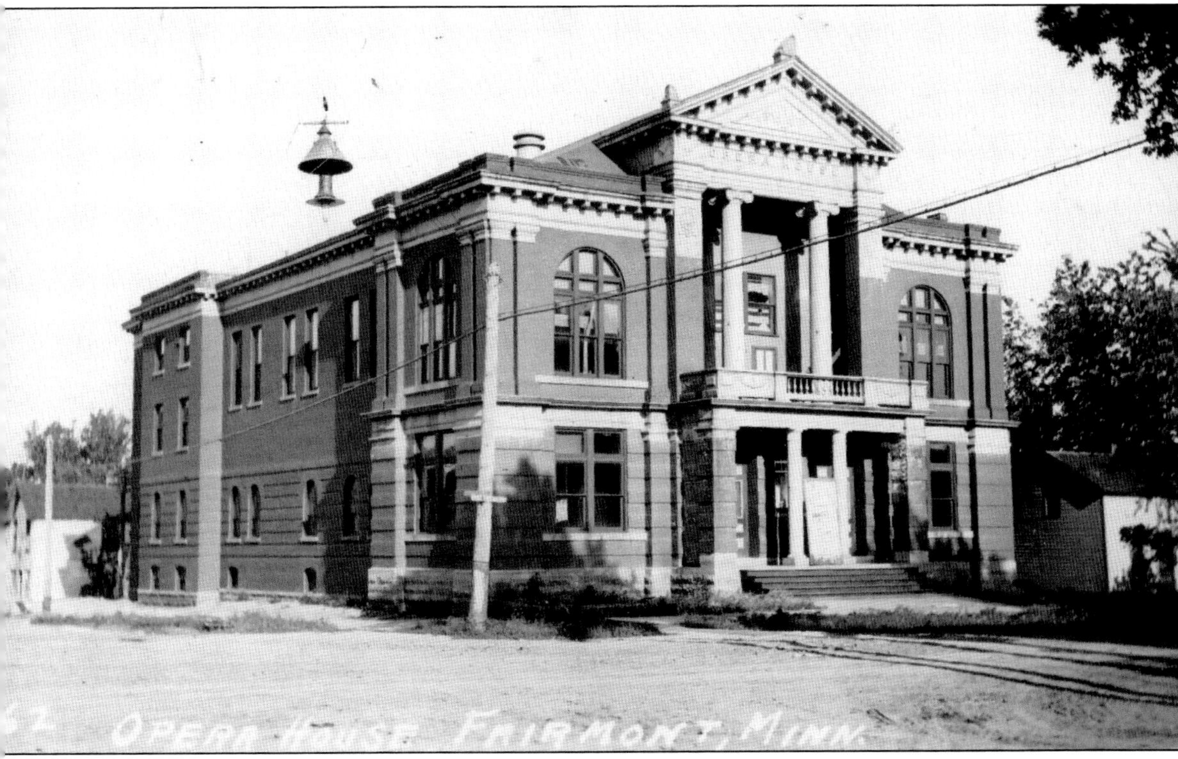

The idea of an actual opera house building and association goes back to 1899 when H. W. Sinclair was reportedly having an architect draw up plans for one. An opera house did exist before this time, but it was housed in the Ward and Cadwell complex. Many towns had opera houses, and they were usually on the second floor of a well-established business. With much excitement, the idea came up again in January 1901, and by March of that year, the Fairmont Opera House Company was organized and stocks were sold. Construction was started that year, and the grand opening was on February 11, 1902. It cost $21,000 to build and had a 700-seat capacity. It was well lighted by red, white, and blue lamps with Thomas Edison's direct current. It became the Haynic Theater in 1912 and the Nicholas Theater in 1927. By 1980, it had closed and its future did not look good. However, Dr. Robert and Mary Arneson and many others came along to save the building.

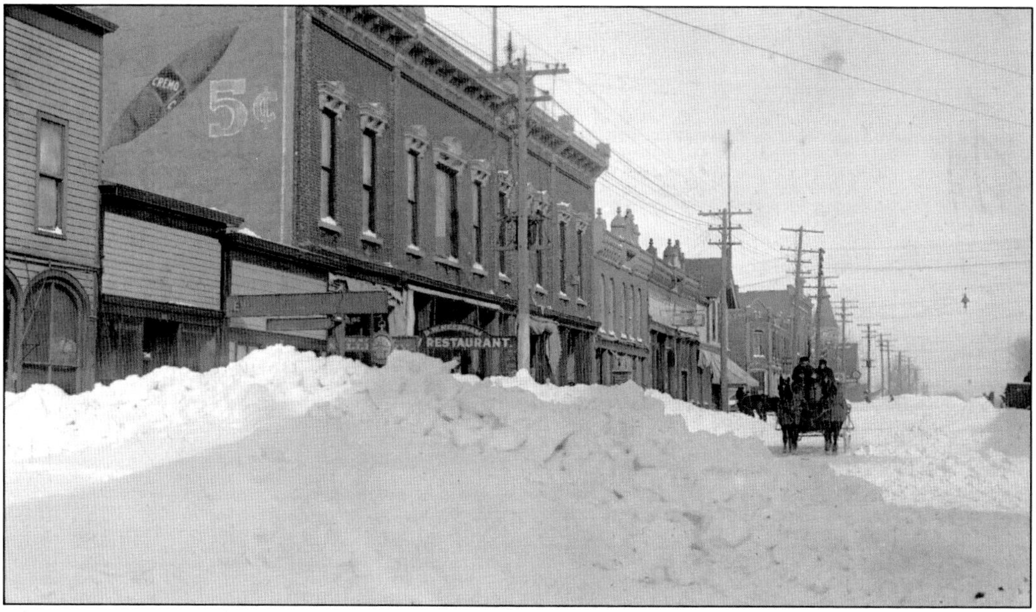

This is Downtown Plaza in February 1909 after a big blizzard. The Syndicate Block (large brick building) was destroyed by fire on December 31, 1914. The businesses from the left to right are E. J. Edwards Drug Store (partially visible), A. G. Crooker Jewelry Store, and in the same tiny building are the Edwin Sisters Hat Shop and Lucas Millinery Store. This little building was partially crushed by the adjoining brick wall that fell during the fire. The following four are in the Syndicate Block: D. W. Needham City Restaurant, S. V. Bomboy Department Store, H. E. Barto Drug Store, and the Ward and Company Meat Market.

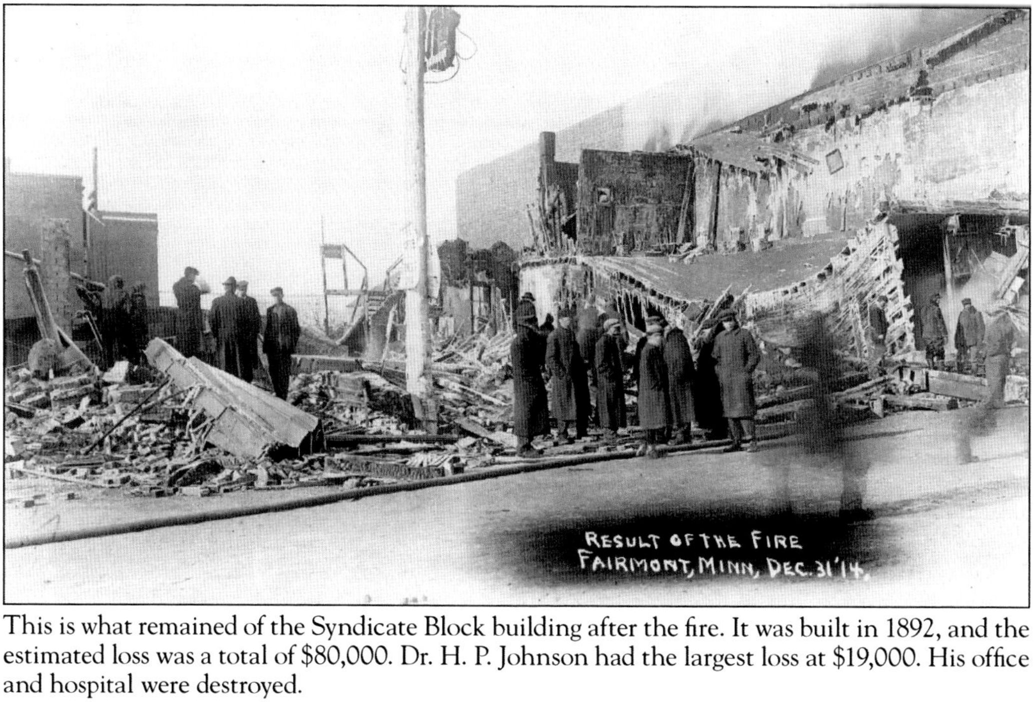

This is what remained of the Syndicate Block building after the fire. It was built in 1892, and the estimated loss was a total of $80,000. Dr. H. P. Johnson had the largest loss at $19,000. His office and hospital were destroyed.

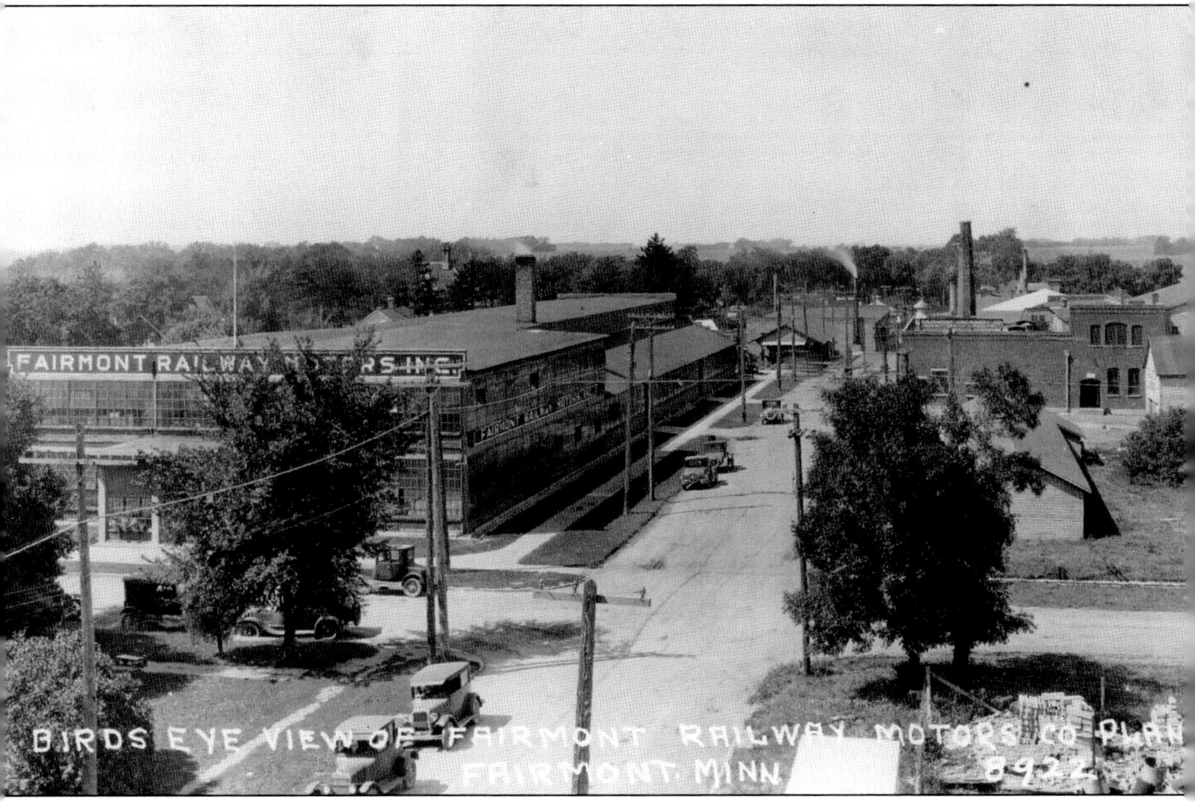

Victor St. John had his foundry at this site in 1904, and by 1906, it became known as the Fairmont Machine Company. In 1907, Horace Woolery and St. John began to manufacture one-cylinder engines for farm use. This was the very beginning of what became "the Motors." In 1909, the Fairmont Machine Company was incorporated and began to produce the "Mighty Fairmont Engine." St. John was the first treasurer of the incorporated company, but he also branched off and had a garage elsewhere in town. The company was prospering, and in 1914, a new office was built. In 1915, the name was changed to Fairmont Gas Engine and Railway Motor Car Company, and in 1923, it was again changed to Fairmont Railway Motors. The impressive milestone of being in business for a century was reached in 2009, plus it became Harsco Rail. This is a bird's-eye view of the Motors that shows how the main office looked when it was first built. The building is still there but has been extensively remodeled. This postcard photograph was taken about 1924 and shows the Fairmont Creamery on the right where the tall chimney is.

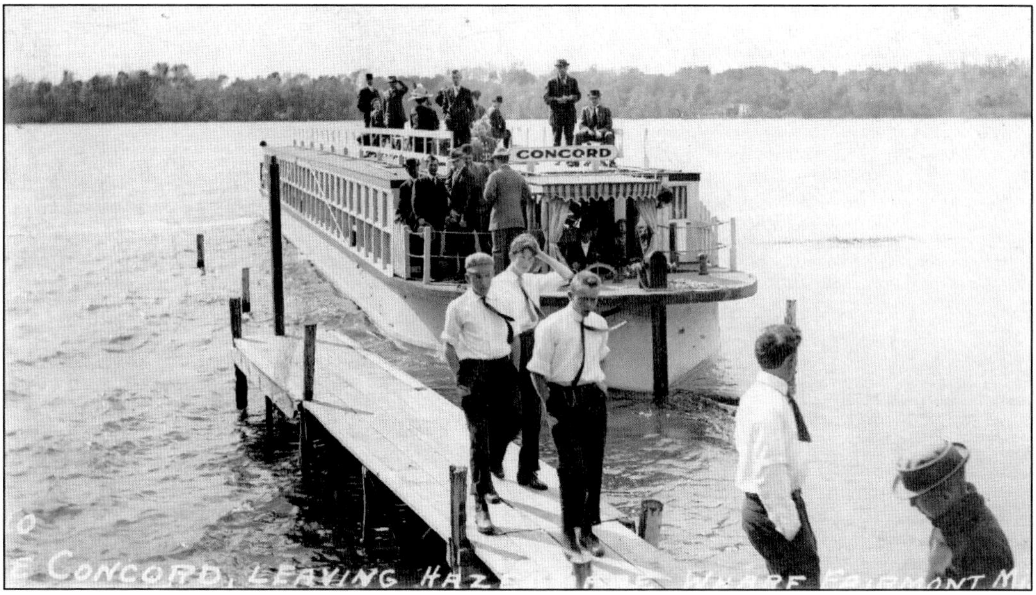

The *Concord* excursion boat measured 112 feet long and was the largest boat to sail the Fairmont lakes. It made stops at Hazelmere, Webster Street Pier, and Interlaken. The *Concord* was built on the ice of Lake Sisseton during the winter of 1908–1909 under the direction of Frank Wade. A 25¢ round-trip was said to have "cost's like hell, but wuth it." The engine was a 32-horsepower Fairmont gas engine. The boat was sold in 1922, and the wood was used to build a cottage at Hazelmere.

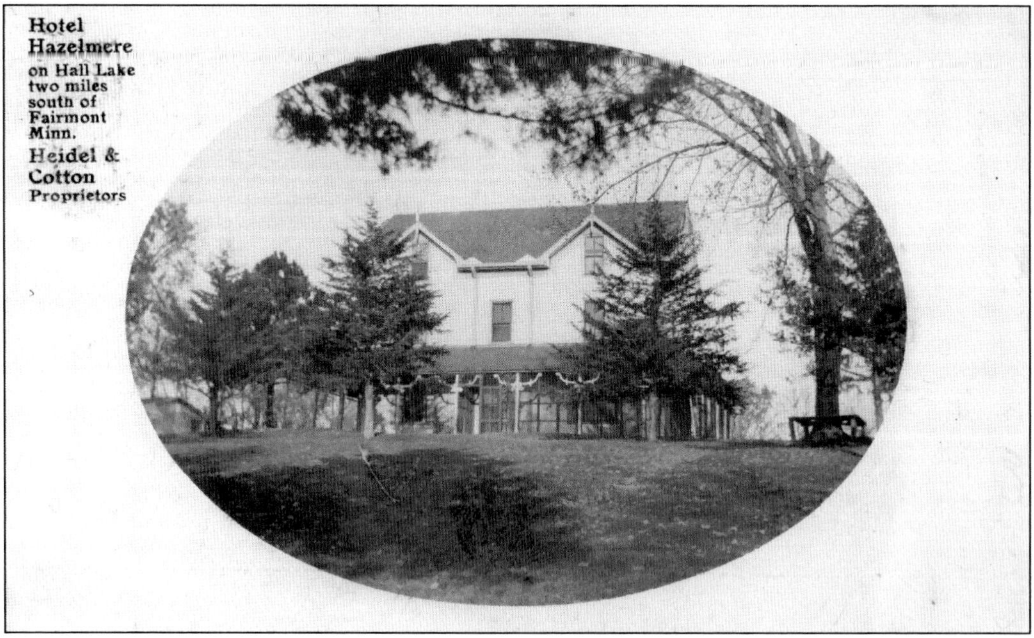

This is Hotel Hazelmere in 1906 after Frank Heidel and Fred R. Cotton leased it. Joseph Ramsdale built this $7,000 house in 1875 and christened it Hazelmere. It was sold to J. T. Swearingen and E. J. Edwards in 1901 for $9,000 with 75 acres of land bordering Hall Lake. Its address was listed simply as Hazelmere. This hotel was razed in the 1940s to make room for new homes.

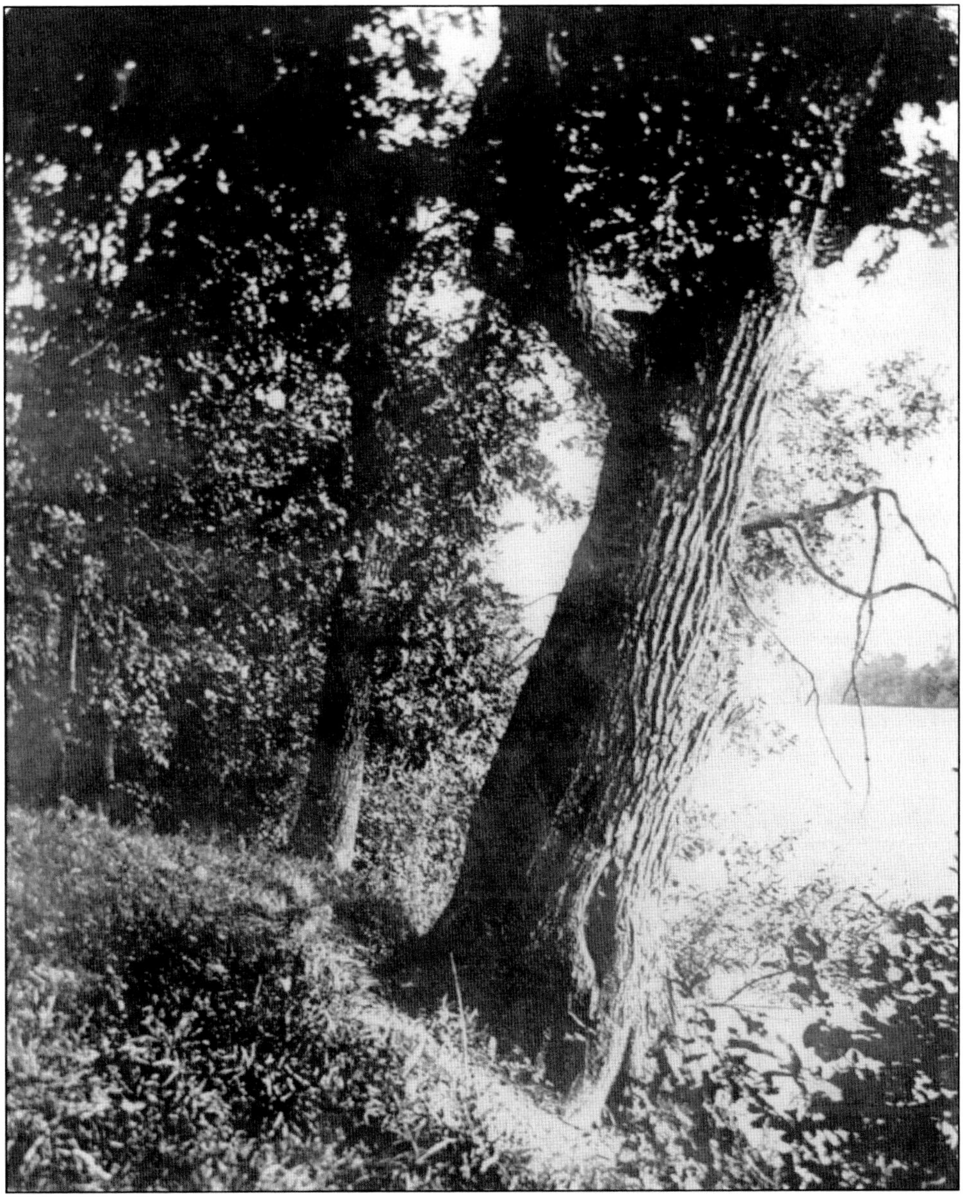

This is a photograph of the famous "singing oak" or "haunted oak" taken by Isaac Flo. The tree was located in the northwest portion of Sylvania Park on the bank of Lake Sisseton. According to legend, a white child was captured and brought back to the Native American village, and they named her Wowihaha. Chibiabas, a very gifted singer and storyteller of the tribe, became quite fond of the child. It was not long before a fatal epidemic appeared in the village that enraged the Native Americans. It was deemed that the great spirit was displeased with the presence of the white child and that she should be sacrificed. Chibiabas was against this and was also condemned. They were both tied to a limb on this tree and burned alive. It is said that at dusk it is sometimes possible to hear his singing and the child's moans at this spot. The tree was destroyed by fire in June 1908 by burning from its center out. The cause is unknown, but it is believed lightning is to blame, and to add suspense, it is even speculated that the fire could have smoldered since the cremation of the Sisseton singer.

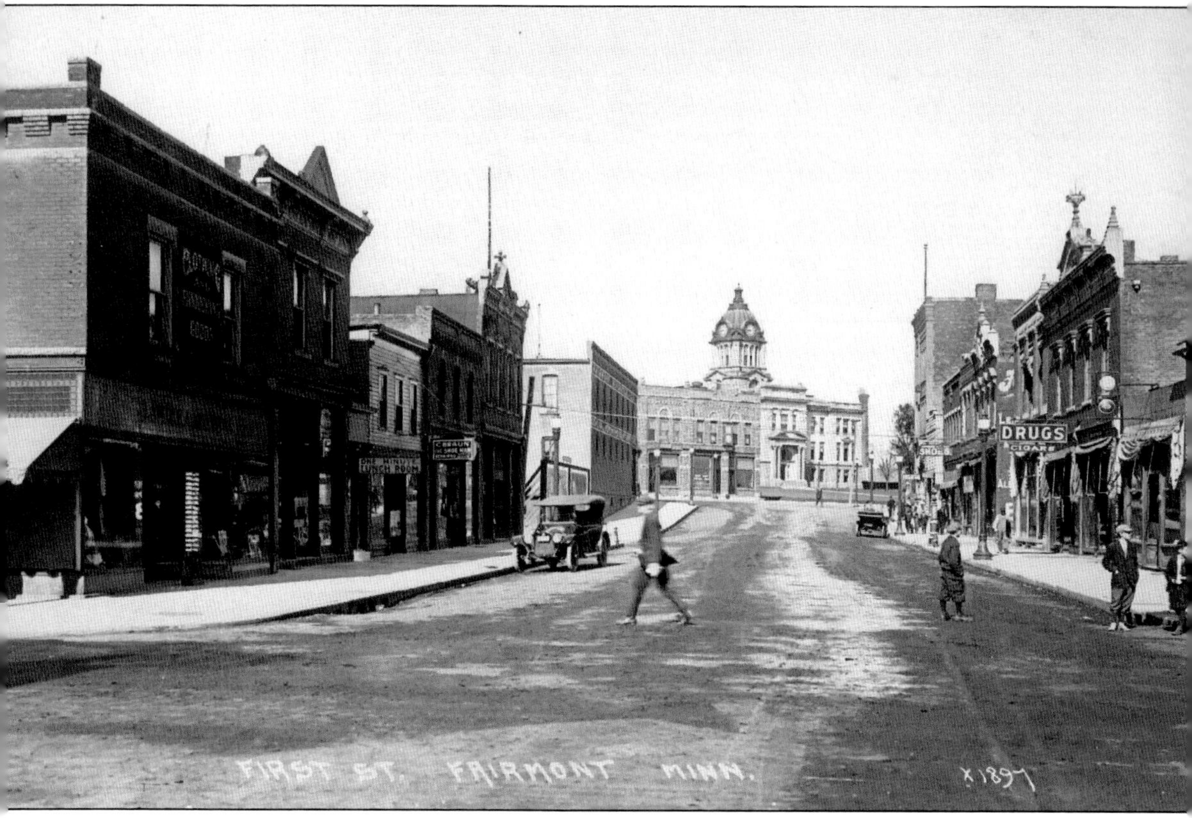

This was taken between 1915 and 1918 and shows West First Street. On the left is Lawler and Huntting Clothing Store, Fairmont Candy Kitchen (by 1918 it was H. E. Barto Drug Store), One Minute Lunch Room, Braun's Shoe Store, the Odd Fellows building (constructed in 1890, originally housing the Pioneer Meat Market, but by 1918, it was the G. T. Houseman Meat Market), Fairmont Mercantile Company (facing Main Street), and in the middle of the postcard in the same building are Houghtaling and Coult Hardware Store and the Martin County National Bank. The courthouse can also be seen. On the right, beginning from the front is the Charles Altenberg Jewelry Store, E. J. Edwards American Express and Drug Store, Sanitary Barber Shop, H. F. Rockwell Billiard Hall with the Serle Ice office on the second floor, Leemhuis and Teskey Shoe Store (by 1918 this was the A. W. Day and Sons shoe store), the Sweet Store (Sweet Shop) with the Cosmos Club on the second floor, C. N. Petersen Real Estate/Insurance, and the post office (in the tall structure). This was known as the Feustal Block, which was built in 1895.

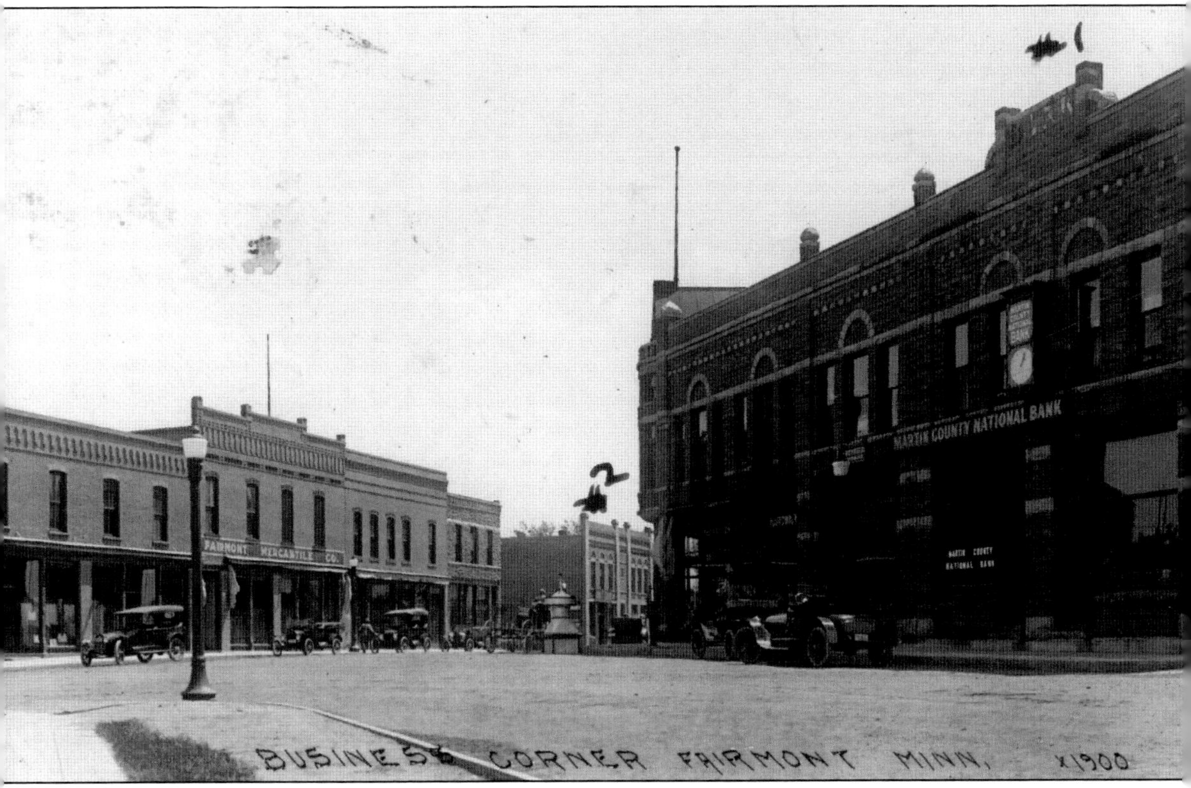

This is the intersection of Lake, First, and Main Streets. The first two buildings on the left are the Fairmont Mercantile Company, once known as Ward and Cadwell. They were built in 1895 at a cost of $4,000. The third building is H. C. Jones Furniture and Undertaking with the Acme Cigar Factory on the second floor. Michel Brewing Company is the fourth structure, and the Ward Machine Company is identified with a number two over it. A. L. Ward had this building constructed in 1894 for $7,000. He wanted to show respect to the entire city of Fairmont by having all four sides finished with the same brick and ornamentation. It was razed in 1941 to widen the road, where Chubb Park and the curve in the road are now. The building on the right was known as the Pipestone Block. It was built in 1895 at a cost of $10,000. This housed the Martin County National Bank, now called Profinium Financial, and Houghtaling and Coult Hardware Store.

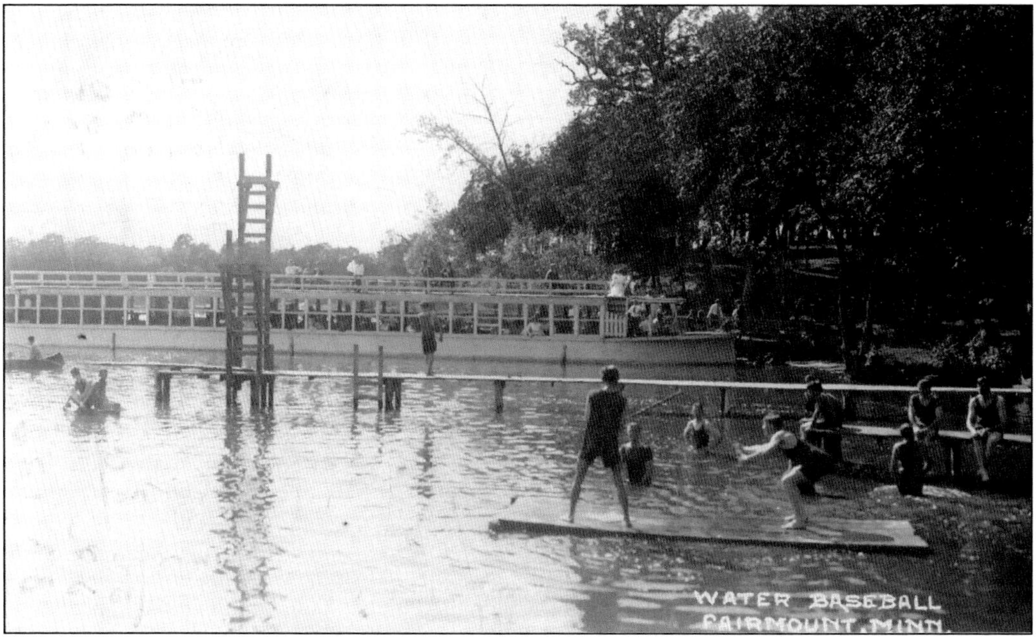

Water sports have always been a popular entertainment in Fairmont. Here the children are playing a game of water baseball in Lake Sisseton near Sylvania Park in the second decade of the 20th century. The *Concord* is docked behind them.

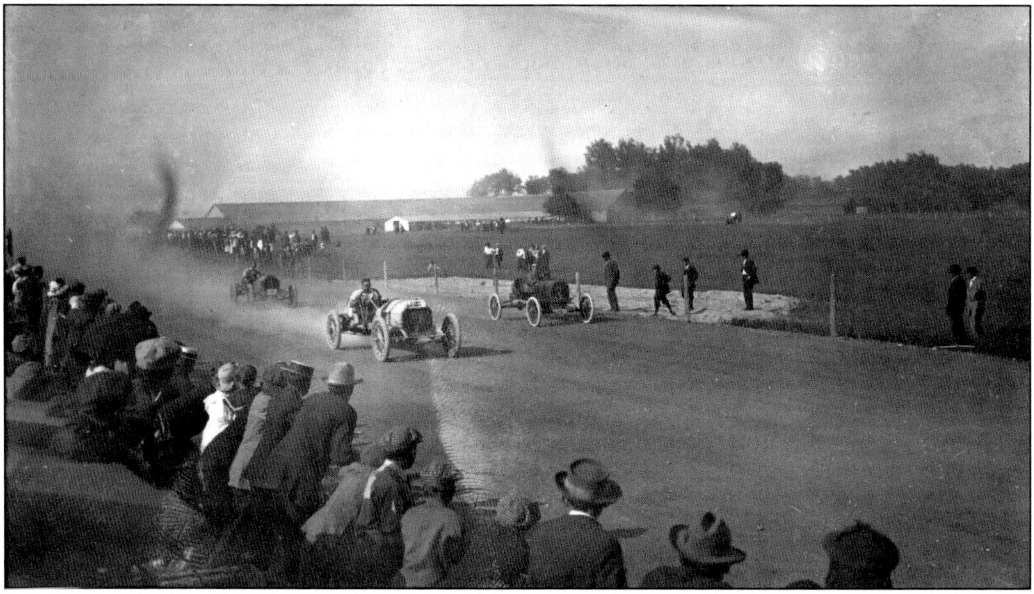

Pictured is the three-mile stock car race on the fairly new racetrack at the Martin County Fairgrounds in 1913. The buildings in the rear were constructed in 1912. The Martin County Fair is one of the oldest in Minnesota. The first fair in 1865 was so small it only took up one room in the courthouse. The fair found a new home when land was purchased for $500 in 1877 on the corner of Blue Earth Avenue and State Street. It remained there until 1964 and moved to its present location in 1965.

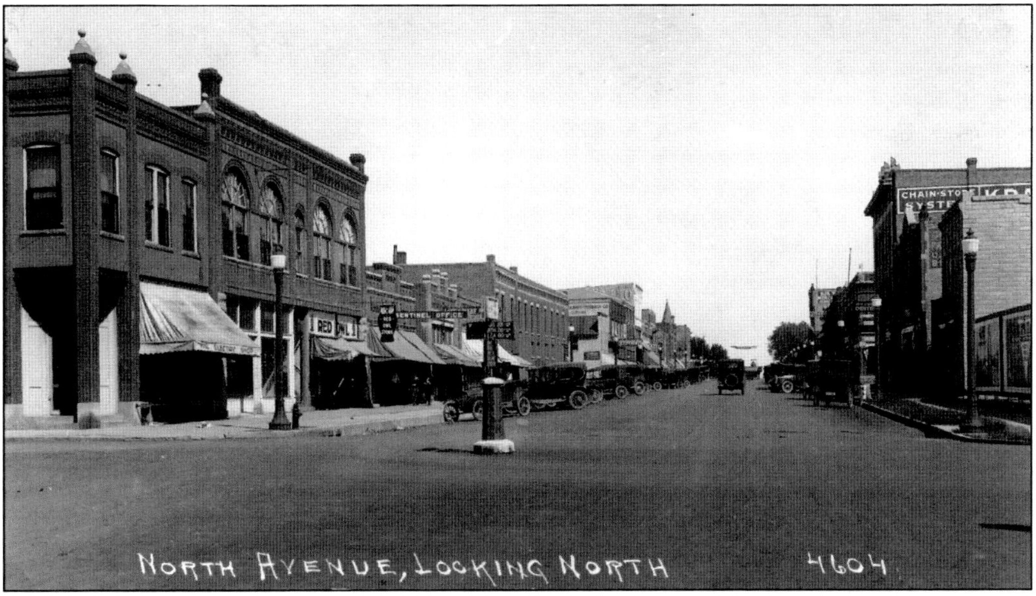

This is now the first block of Downtown Plaza. When this photograph was taken in the 1920s, it was known as the 100 block of South North Avenue. The businesses in 1921 on the left are City Electric Company, Cheney Motor Company, Red Owl store, the Fairmont Daily Sentinel office, City Meat Market-Mouritsen Brothers Proprietors, G. F. Stromberg Wallpaper and Paints, Flo Studio, and the Lawler and Huntting Clothing Store facing First Street. On the right, notice the billboards where the Old Post Office is now, John Krumholz Flour and Feed, J. H. Gorman Implement Company, and Kraft-Misbach Clothing Store. This postcard was mailed on August 5, 1924.

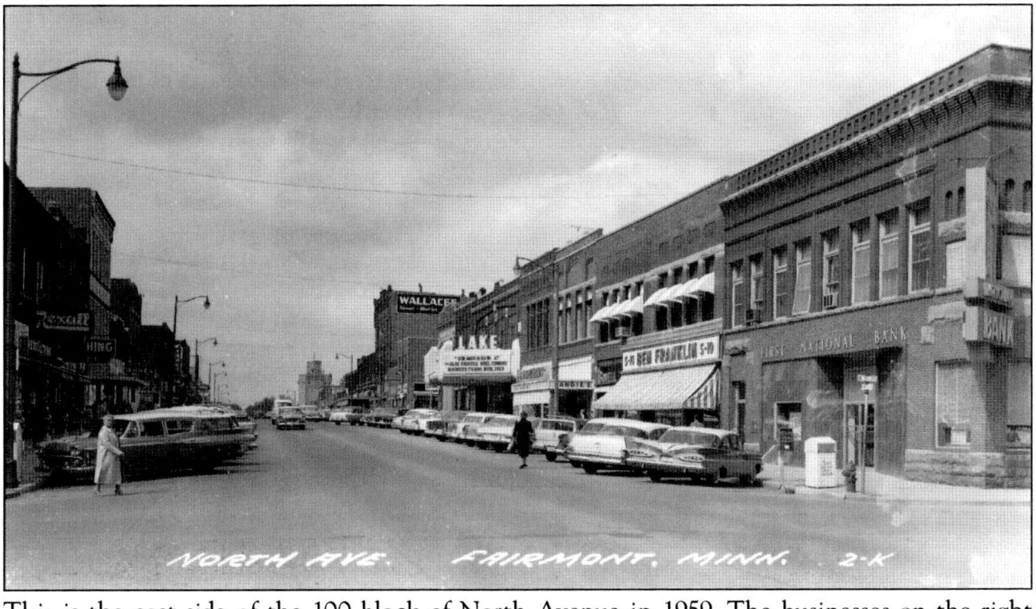

This is the east side of the 100 block of North Avenue in 1959. The businesses on the right are the First National Bank of Fairmont, Ben Franklin's, Sovell Jewelry, the Sweet Shop, Mahowald's Ace Hardware, Lake Theater (razed in 1988), Gardner's pharmacy, and the Fairmont National Bank.

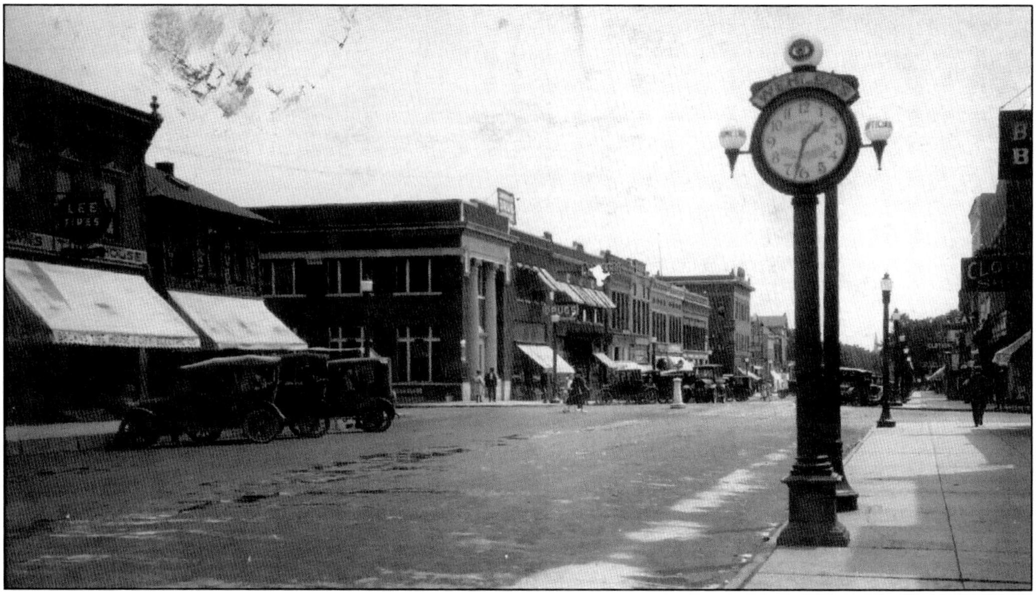

This postcard shows what is now Downtown Plaza looking south. The first building on the left housed both Brown's Tire House and the City Electric Company. Down the street are Burton Brothers, the Citizen's National Bank (now Bank Midwest), Canright Brothers Drug Store, the Strand Theater, Shrailberg's Quality Grocery, the Sweet Shop, Crooker Jewelry, Seihl Hardware, and the First National Bank of Fairmont. On the right side is Wehler's Jewelry Store's clock out front. This postcard probably dates from the early 1920s.

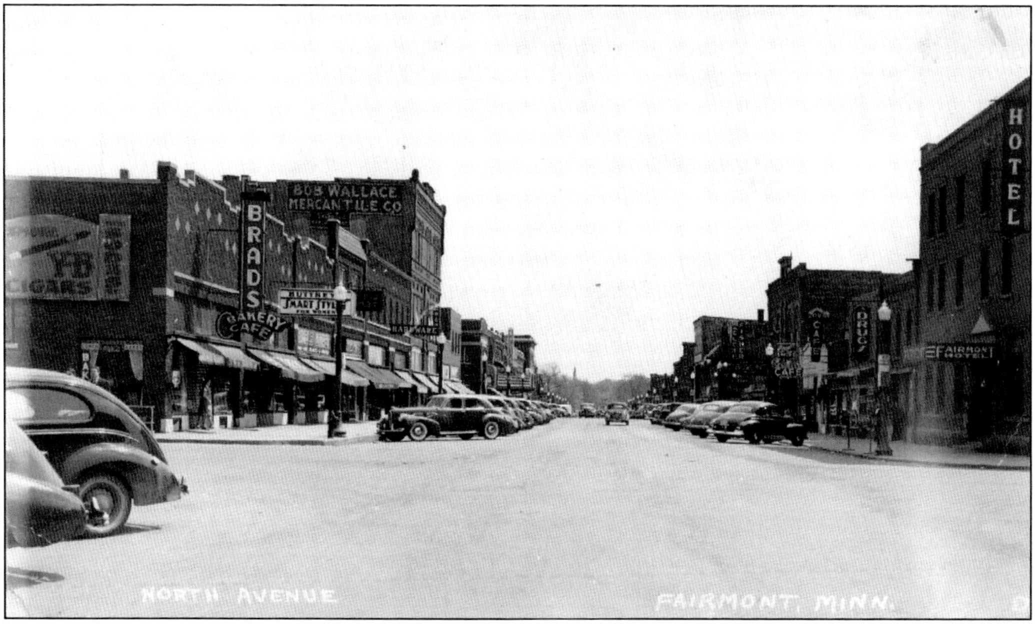

This is North Avenue (Downtown Plaza) sometime in the 1940s. The signs of the following businesses can be seen on the left: Brad's Bakery, Buttrey's Smart Styles for Women, Gamble Stores, a hardware store, and the Bob Wallace store. On the right are the Augusta Hotel, a drugstore, Lou's Cafe, Searles Cafe, Chase Wilson Bowling and Billiards, and Fishers and Laskers Clothing Stores.

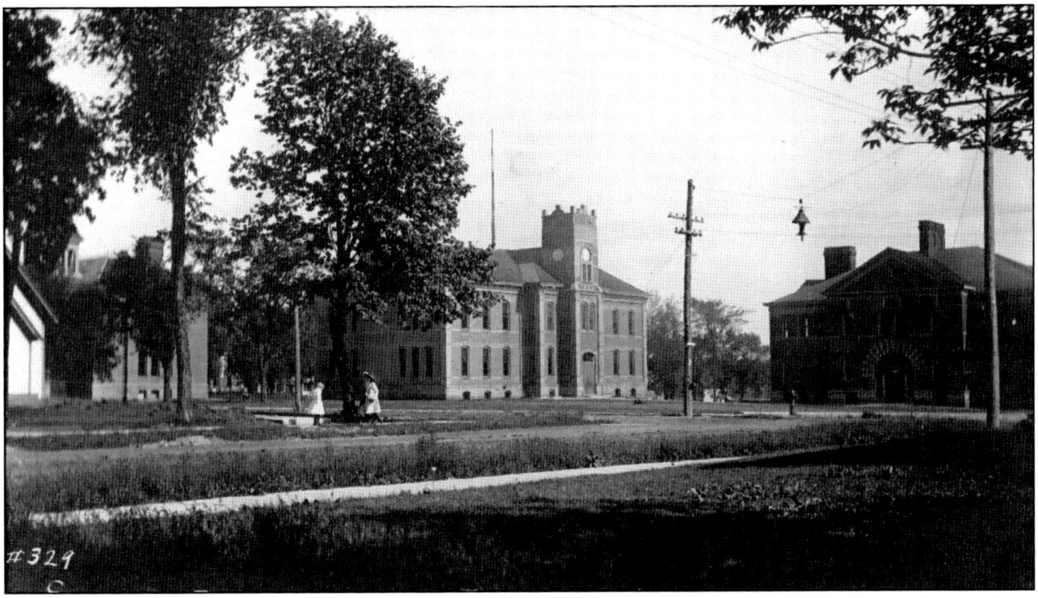

This view is from about 1907 shows three Fairmont schools in one block. They were located on the property where the Presentation College is now. From left to right are the primary school, built in 1895; the old central school, built in 1886; and the senior high school, built in 1900. By 1928, all three of these schools had been torn down. Fairmont's first school was organized in 1860 and stood where Profinium Financial is today. The "famous class of '89" was the first class to graduate in 1889.

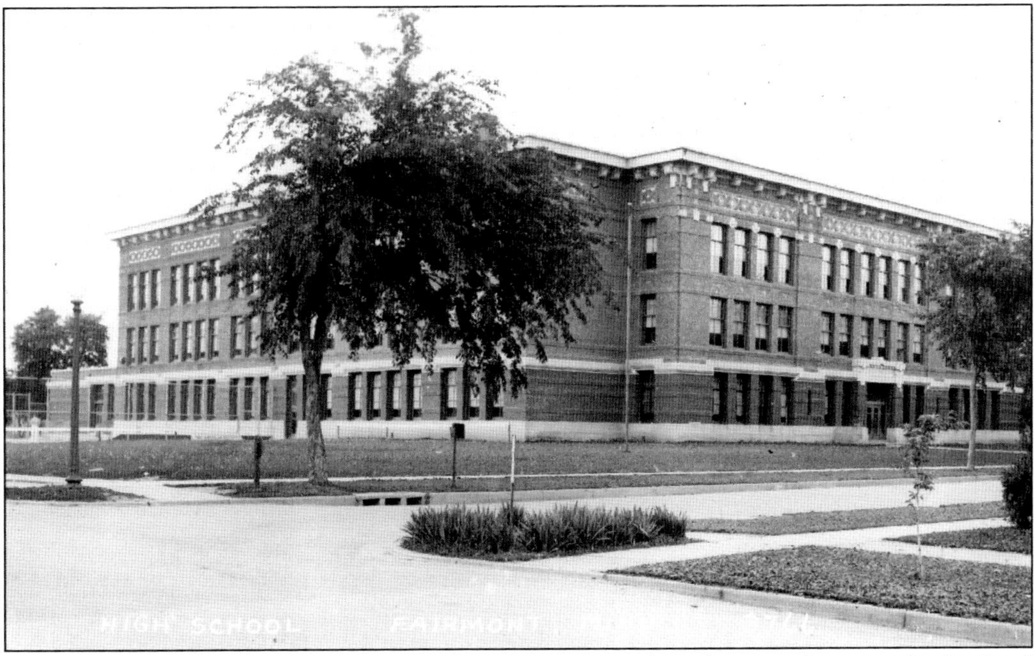

This was originally Fairmont High School, built in 1915. It later became the junior high school around 1952. On September 22, 1969, a fire was discovered that partially damaged the school. Again on September 29, 1969, fire struck the school. This time it nearly destroyed the building. A 13-year-old boy admitted to starting both fires because he thought a new school was needed.

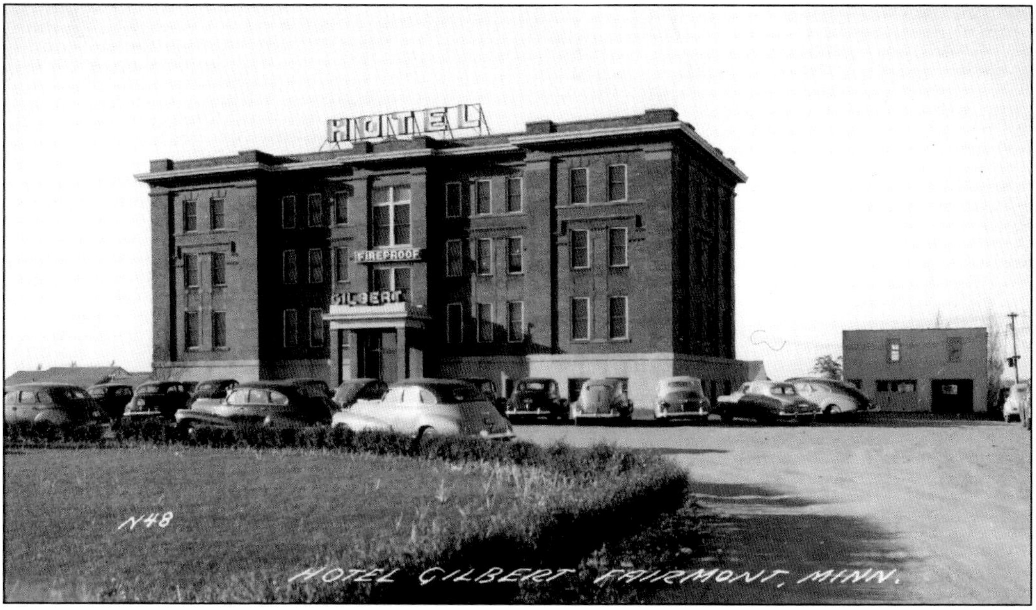

Harry Gilbert purchased this structure in 1940 and remodeled it into the Gilbert Hotel. The building was originally constructed in 1916 as the Ward Home for Dependent Children. This venture was given up by A. L. Ward about 1921, and the structure stood empty (except for caretaker Leo Krueger) until Gilbert purchased it. Krueger had until March 1, 1941, to get out. When the building was constructed, it cost $160,000, and no expense was spared; it even had three kinds of water—hot, cold, and soft. Along with two other buildings, it was razed in 2007 to make room for Kwik Trip.

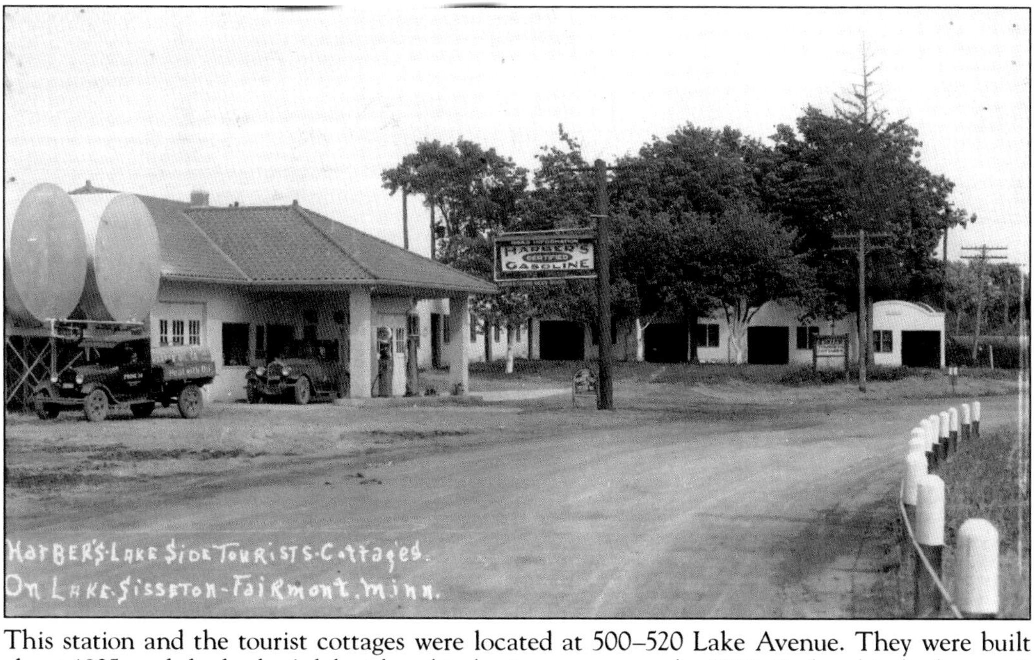

This station and the tourist cottages were located at 500–520 Lake Avenue. They were built about 1935, and the harbor's lakeside cabin business was gone by 1970. Each cabin had a state's name, including Colorado, Nebraska, Illinois, Wisconsin, and Ohio.

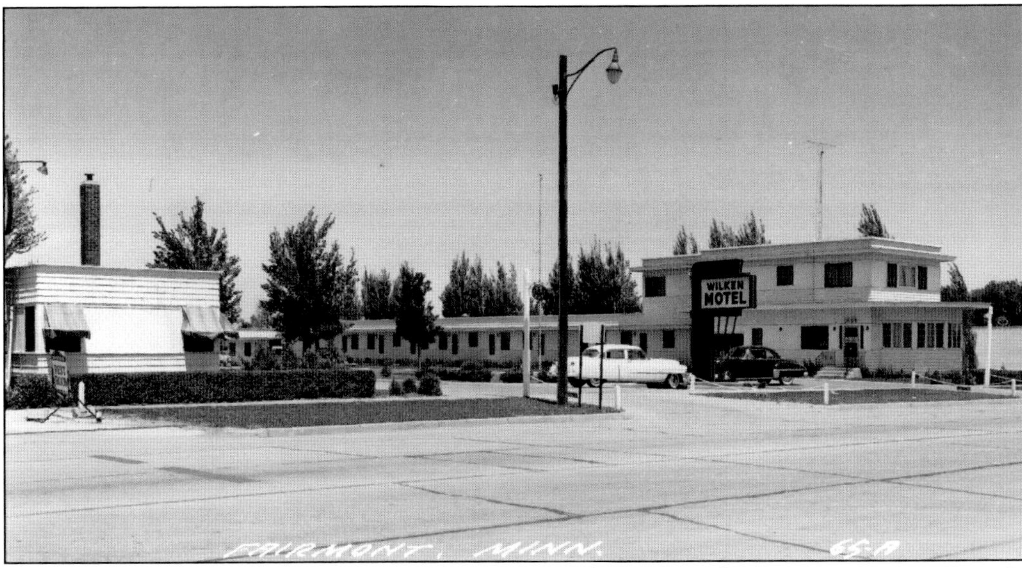

When Alvin Wilken built Wilken Cabin Court in the spring of 1941, it was way out in the country, and the only other building nearby was the Gilbert Hotel. It boasted that the cabins were "modernly equipped with electric lights, running water and gas for cooking." It was sold to Leo Gardner in 1961, and after Interstate 90 opened, the business slowly declined. Gardner's wife eventually sold the property to developers of the Checker Auto Store chain. The motel was razed, and the Checker Auto Store was built. That store has since been razed and replaced by Walgreens in 2004.

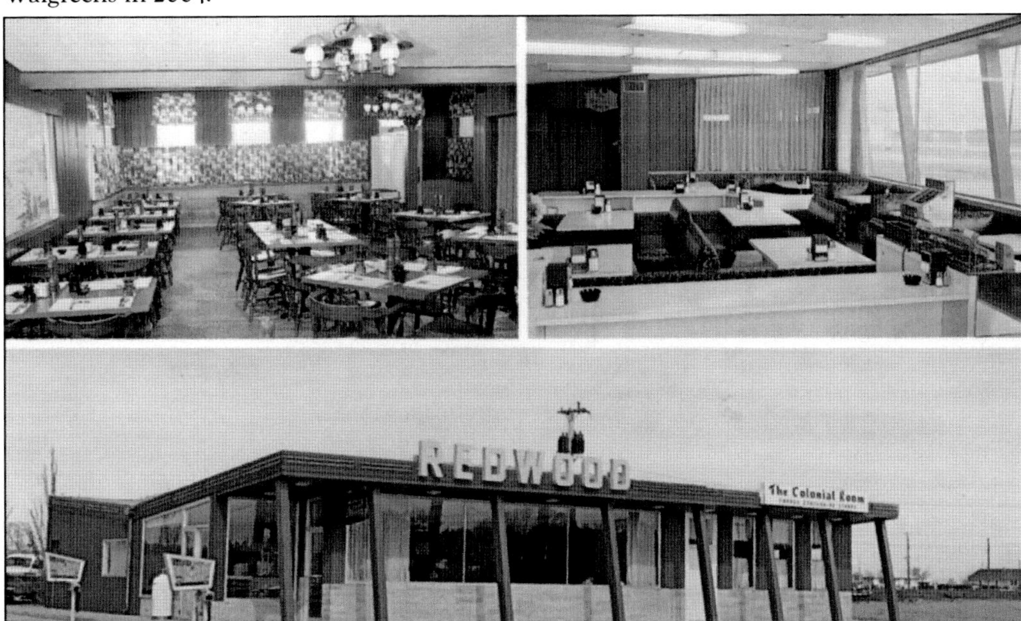

The Redwood Restaurant was built by John Watters in 1959. It was first a drive-in café and was known as "the finest drive-in in the northwest." It later became one of Fairmont's finest restaurants. Along with the Drive Inn Theater, it was torn down about 1989 to make room for K-Mart, which closed in 2009.

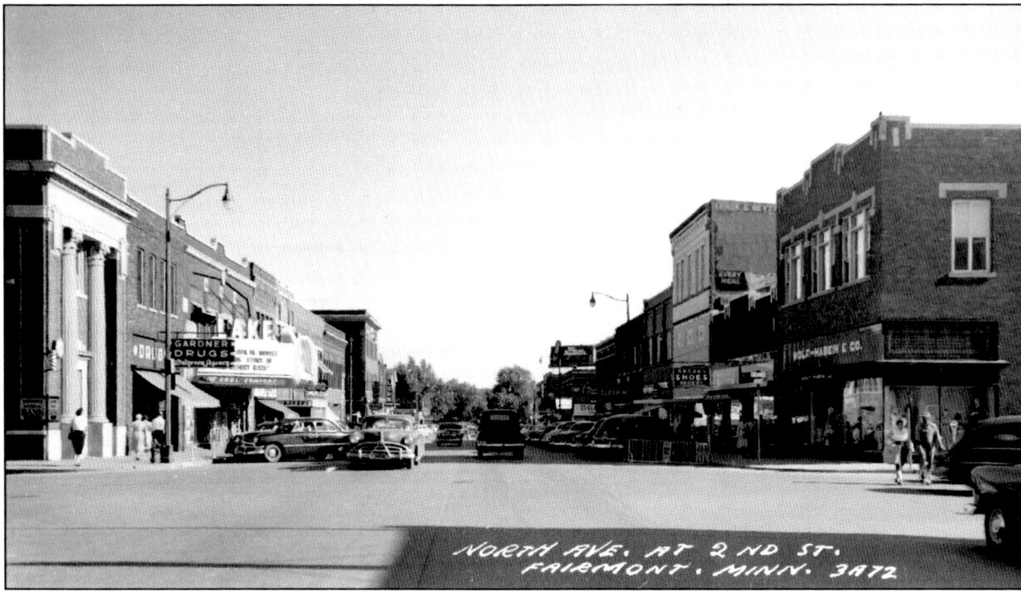

This is Downtown Plaza looking south in 1953. On the left are Fairmont National Bank, Gardner drugstore, Lake Theatre (the movie *Desert Rats* is playing), Mahowald's Hardware, the Sweet Shop, Sovell Jewelry, Woolworth's, and First National Bank. On the right are Wolf-Habein Department Store, Singer Sewing Machine Company and Braun's Shoe Store (in the same building), Foster Furniture Company, Flora's Ready to Wear, Grewe's Jewelry, Rosewalls Clothing Store, and Paulson's Pharmacy.

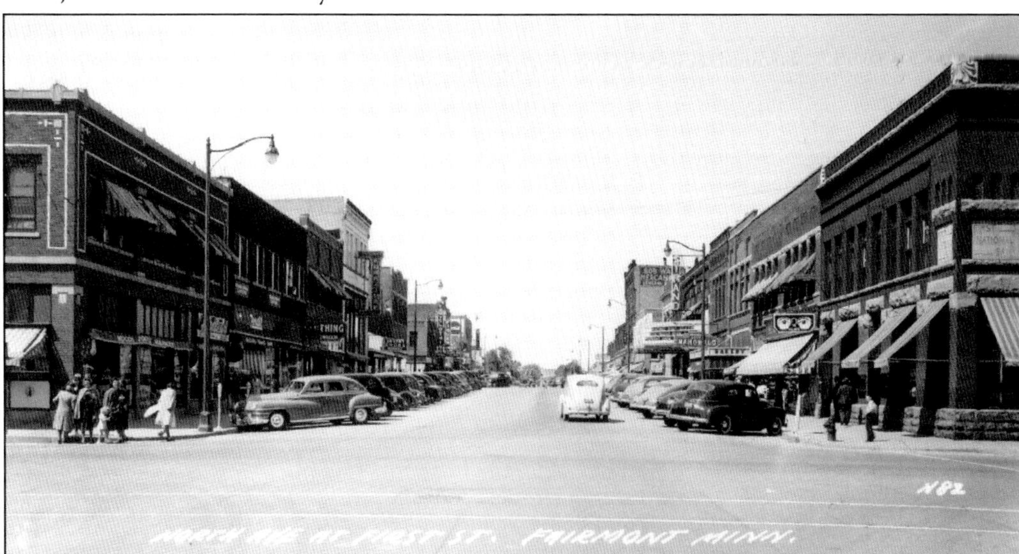

This is North Avenue looking north in 1947. The businesses on the left are Mocol's Grocery (built in 1928), Landhuis Jewelry, Paulson's Pharmacy, Rosewalls Clothing Store, Grewe's Jewelry, Flora's Ready to Wear, Forster Furniture Company, Braun's Shoe Store, Singer Sewing Machine Company, and Wolf-Habein Department Store. On the right side are the First National Bank, Dr. R. W. Palmer (optometrist), Woolworth's, A. G. Crooker Jewelry, Model Bakery and Sweet Shop, Mahowald's, Storkville, the Strand Theater, Gardner's pharmacy, and Fairmont National Bank.

Four

GRANADA AND IMOGENE

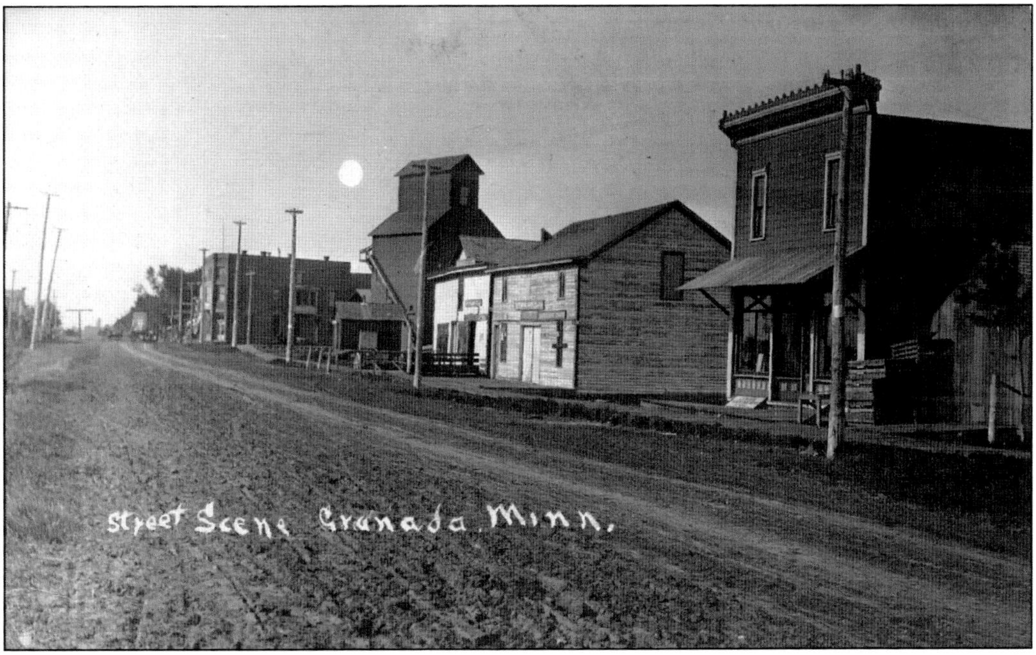

Albert Reynolds built the Handy Store in 1888, and Handy (now Granada) was born. Shortly afterward in 1889, Handy moved to its present site and Ed Anderson platted the town. Much to the chagrin of the locals the railroad renamed the town in 1891. The Field and Boston Hardware Store (on the right) was built in 1895. This building eventually became the Assembly of God church and has been substantially remodeled. It closed in 2003. (Courtesy of the Granada Historical Museum.)

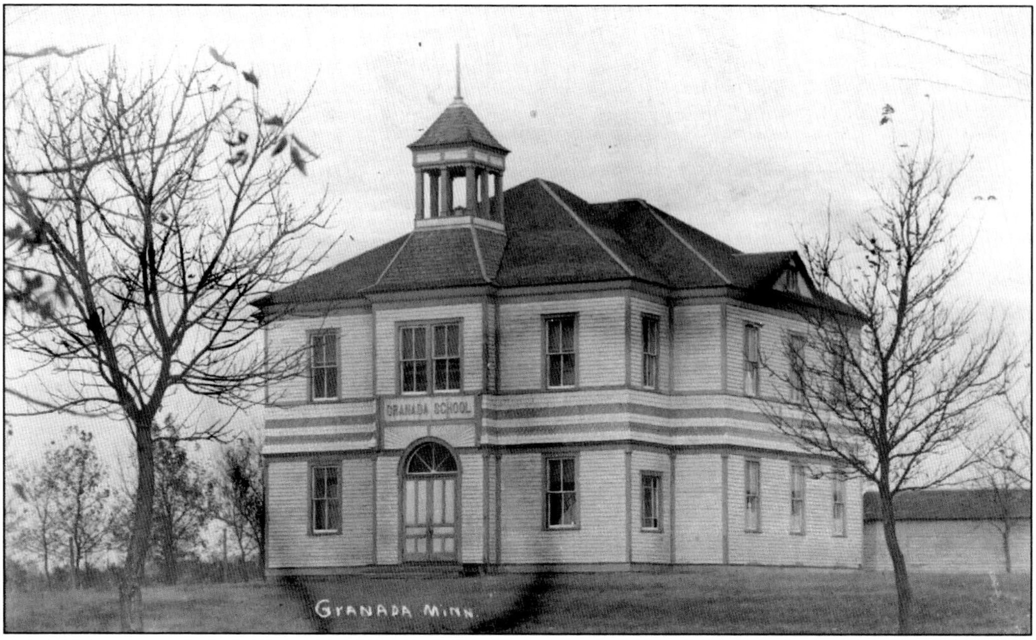

This is the Granada School building about 1910. It was built during 1895 and 1896 and finished with a coat of paint in April 1896. It cost $2,000 to build and was so big that only two rooms were used the first year and the third room the next. The fourth room was not used for school functions until a few years later. In the beginning, the Woodman lodge used it for meetings and functions. The town's people also used it as a dance hall for awhile.

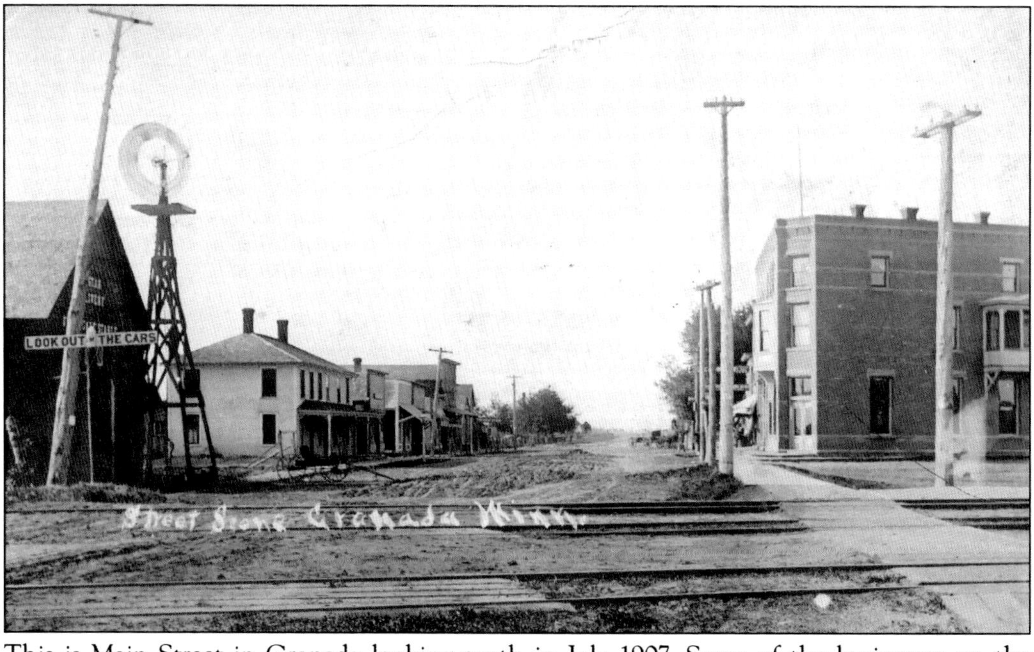

This is Main Street in Granada looking south in July 1907. Some of the businesses on the left include the Star Livery, Hodgman House (hotel), Granada Meat Market, City Restaurant, Granada Times, Harness Shop, W. E. Teskey General Merchandise, and Shields Blacksmith. The windmill on the left blew down in a storm in 1909.

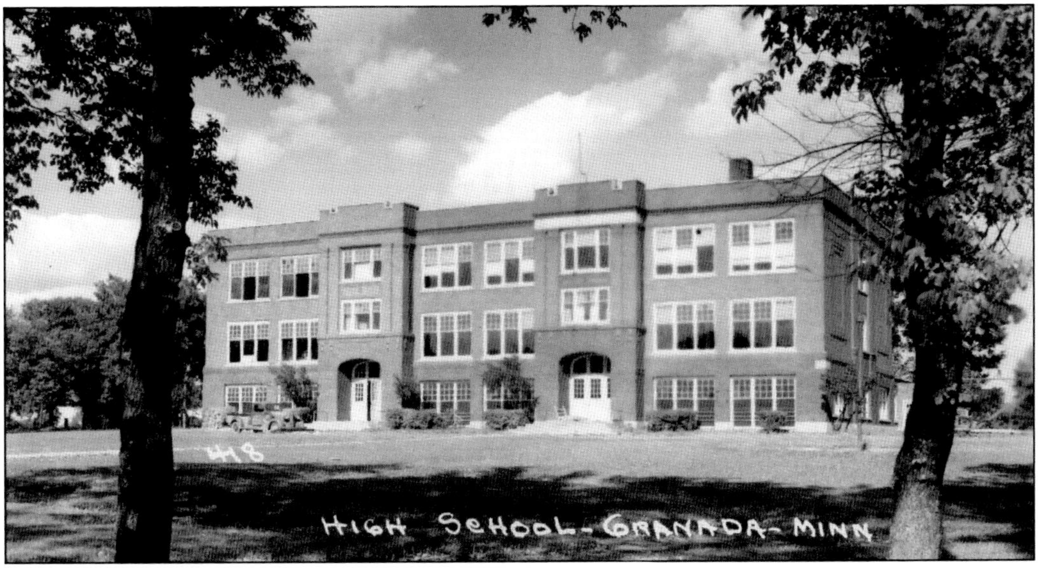

The Granada School was started by Charlie Chipman in 1866. He held the three-month school in his own home. School district No. 30 was organized on January 2, 1867, and it eventually became Granada-Huntley-East Chain High School. The first school building was 16 by 20 feet, and the lumber was hauled from Mankato. During 1888, the school was moved so many times across Center Creek that the students never knew where classes would be held. The school above was built in 1914, and a $15,000 addition was constructed in 1923. On September 19, 1966, fire destroyed this school. It is believed that faulty wiring in a third-story closet was to blame.

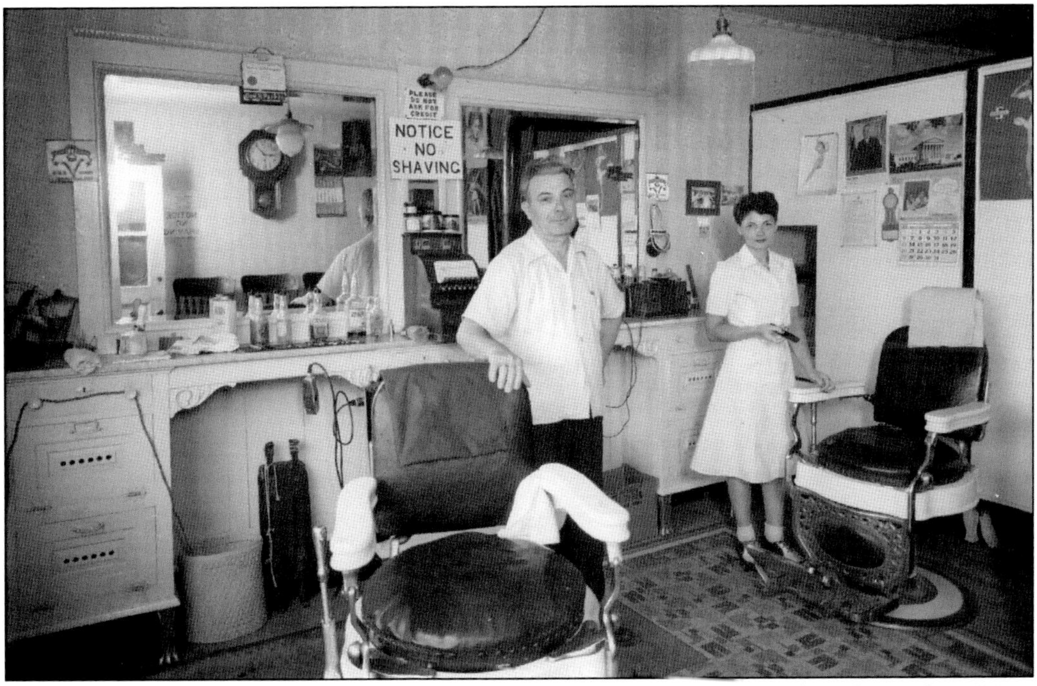

Pictured about 1950 are Dan Pappas and Mary Sehm in Dan's Barber Shop, located on Main Street. Pappas immigrated to the United States from Greece in 1912 and was Granada's last barber. (Courtesy of the Granada Historical Museum.)

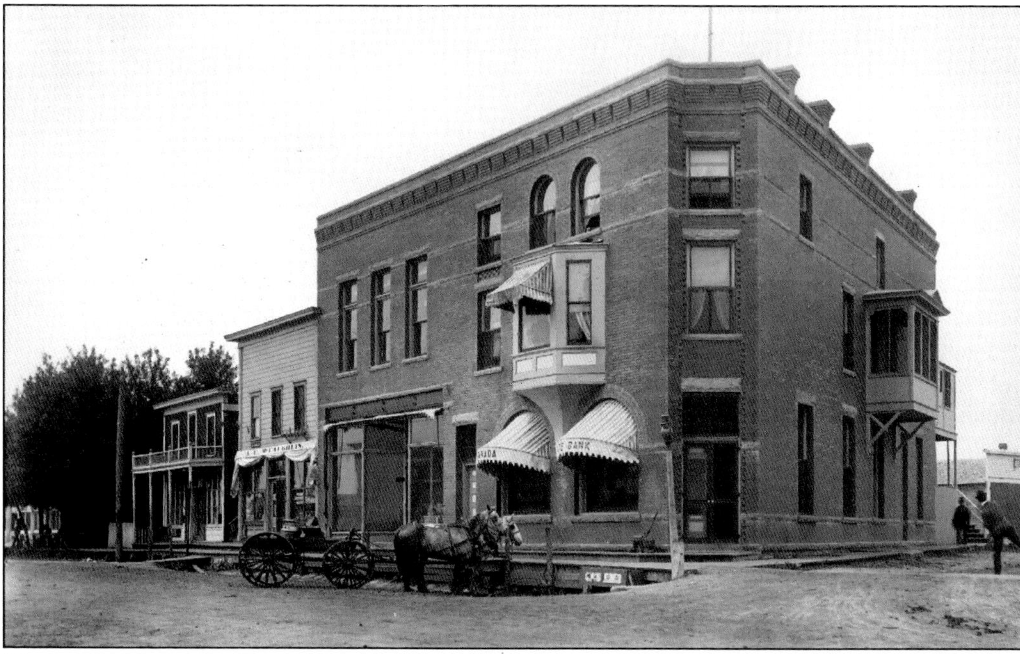

This is the Granada State Bank building about 1898. Notice how low Main Street was at the time. It appears to be three to four feet lower than it is today. The bank building was constructed in 1896 and over the years was occupied by a farm implement business, a café, a restaurant, a bar, and a museum. (Courtesy of the Granada Historical Museum.)

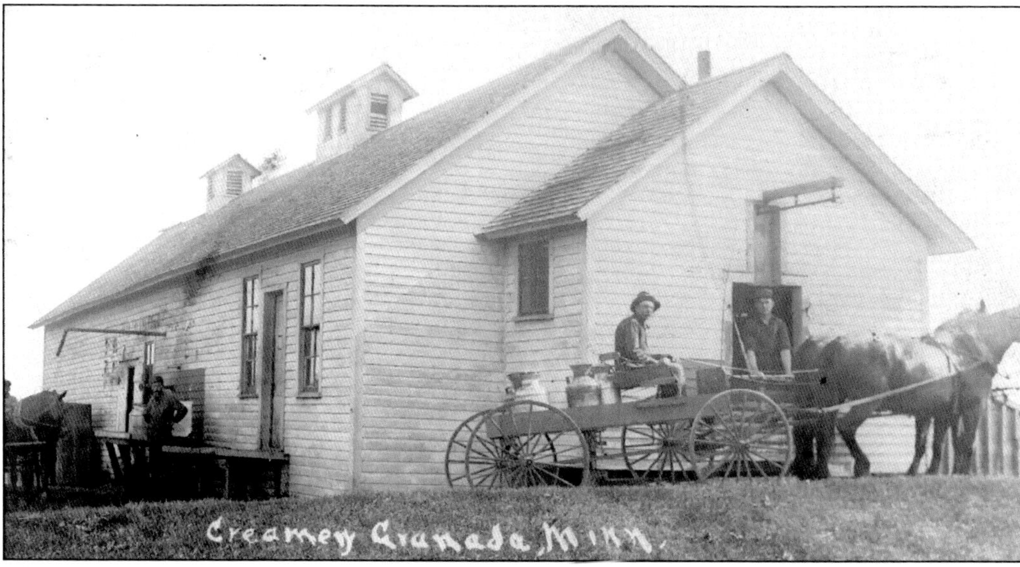

The Center Creek Creamery Company was organized in 1894. The creamery building was constructed in 1894 at 106 East Creamery Street and also added onto that same year. At the time this picture was taken in 1908, Art Anderson was president of the creamery. The chief buttermaker was A. J. Clapshaw, and the assistant was Ed Goerndt. Owner C. A. Nelson had no plans to rebuild the creamery after a fire destroyed it in 1931. At the time of the blaze, the Granada Fire Department had two fire trucks, a Model T Soda/Acid Fire Truck and a 1926 International Pumper.

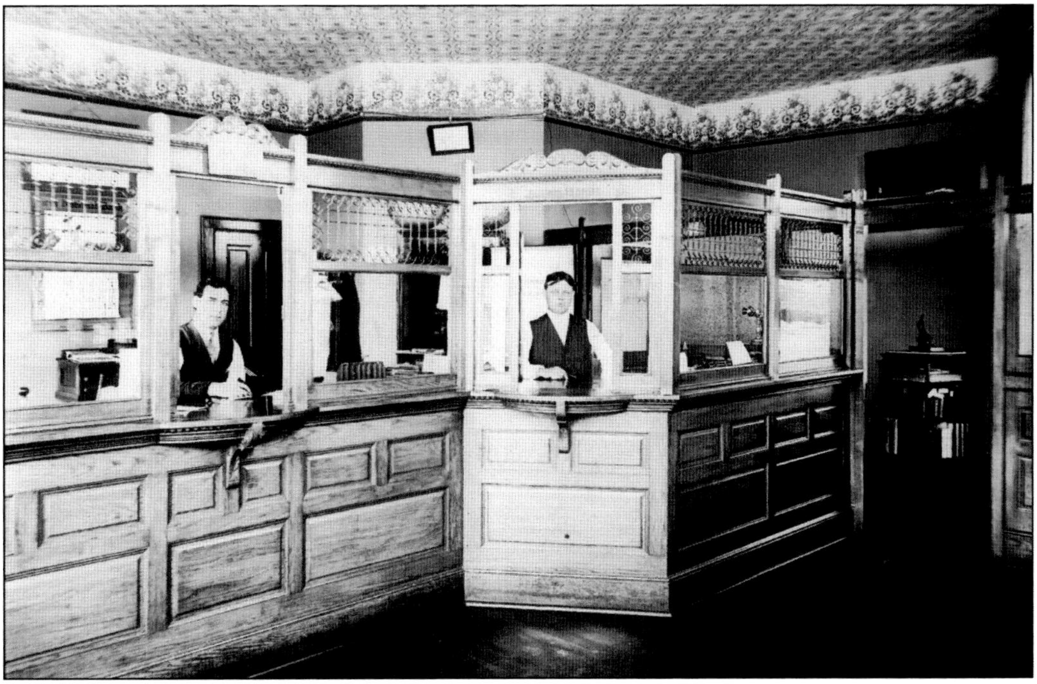

This photograph was taken about 1911 and shows the interior of the Granada State Bank. It opened on June 15, 1896, and closed on November 10, 1927, when a cashier was arrested on fraud charges. B. A. Burton (left) and Ben Eglin are pictured. (Courtesy of the Granada Historical Museum.)

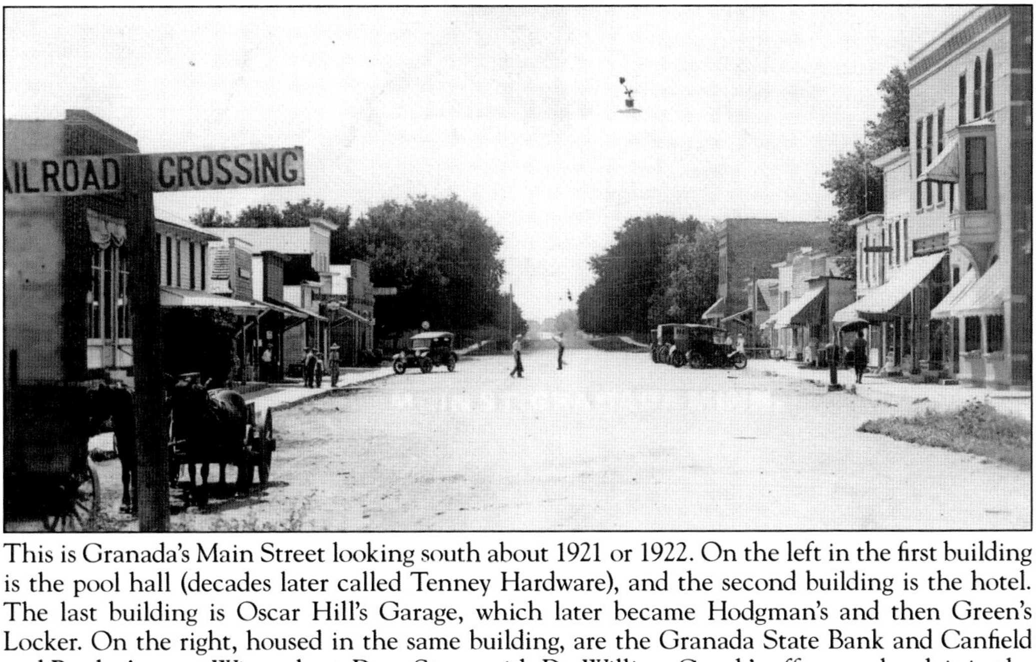

This is Granada's Main Street looking south about 1921 or 1922. On the left in the first building is the pool hall (decades later called Tenney Hardware), and the second building is the hotel. The last building is Oscar Hill's Garage, which later became Hodgman's and then Green's Locker. On the right, housed in the same building, are the Granada State Bank and Canfield and Barden's store. Winzenburg Drug Store, with Dr. William Gaugh's office overhead, is in the second building. The third building is the post office, and when Peggy Lutz was young, she lived on the second floor and had curtains for walls and a dirty, oiled floor. The First National Bank of Granada is the last building.

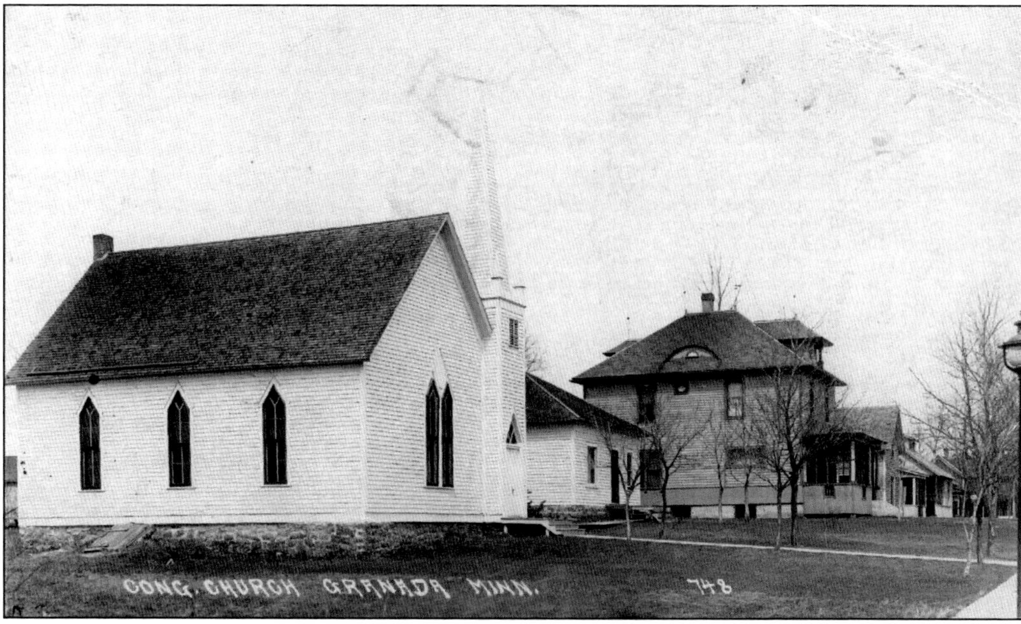

The Congregational Church of Granada was organized on November 1, 1892, and shown here about 1915. The church building was constructed in 1894 and dedicated to God on January 18, 1895. The parsonage next to it was built in 1897. The church has been remodeled several times, and the steeple has been removed. This church closed in 2007 and is now the Granada Getaway. The large house was Ben Eglin's home. It was later purchased by the Congregational Church and razed in 1975. (Courtesy of the Granada Historical Museum.)

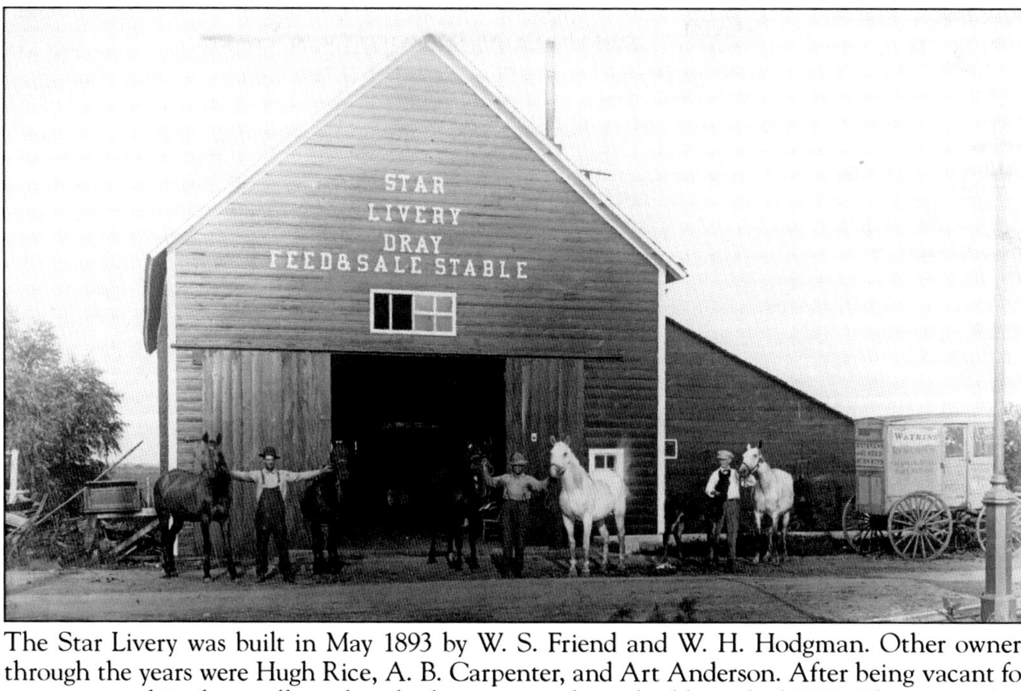

The Star Livery was built in May 1893 by W. S. Friend and W. H. Hodgman. Other owners through the years were Hugh Rice, A. B. Carpenter, and Art Anderson. After being vacant for many years, this place collapsed under heavy snow from the blizzard of 1975. The city park is here now. (Courtesy of the Granada Historical Museum.)

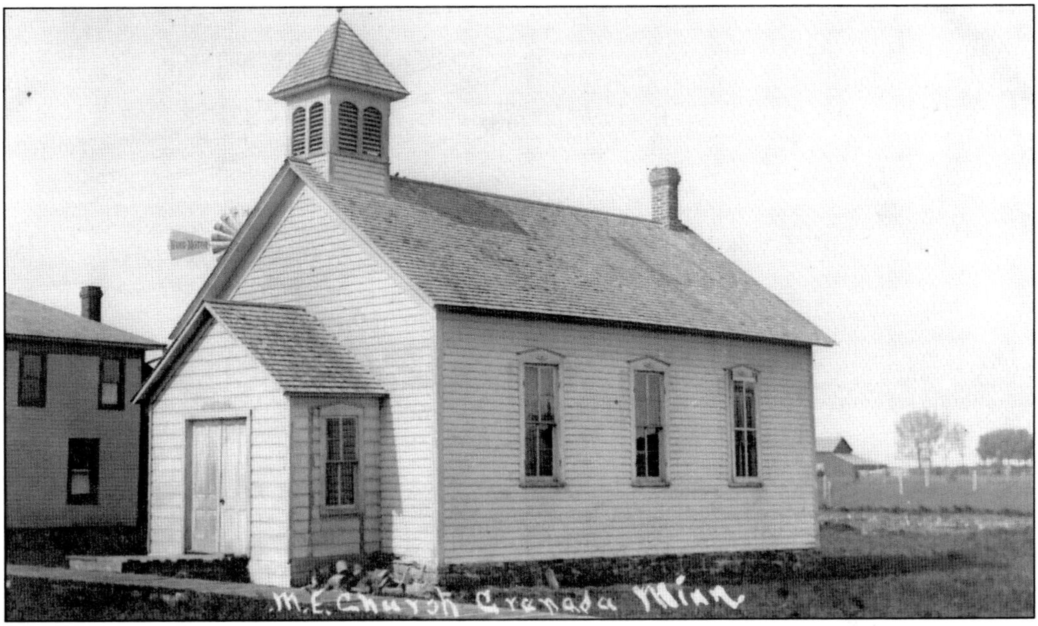

This is the first Methodist church in Granada. It was located at 213 South West First Street, north of Gordon and Donna Franzen's home. Originally this was the Granada School building, but the Methodists purchased it in 1896. It might be the school that was moved back and forth across Center Creek in 1888. After the Methodists built their new church on Main Street in 1907, this structure was remodeled into a parsonage and moved.

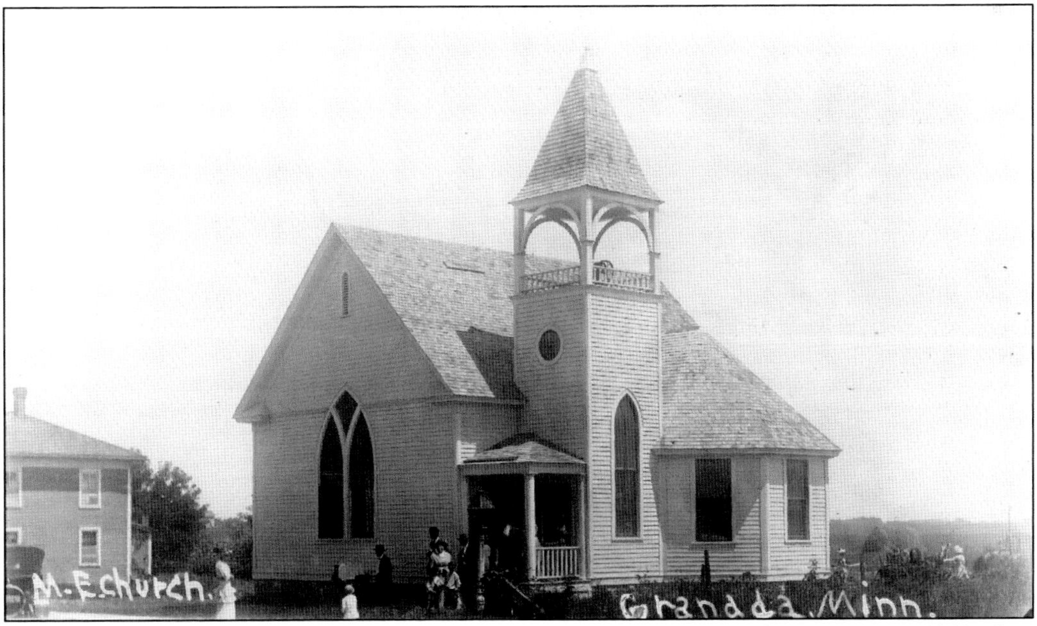

This is the Granada Methodist Church about 1910. One evening after service in 1910, they had "a fine view of Halley's Comet." The cornerstone was laid on July 24, 1907, and dedicated with the new steeple on November 3, 1907. Originally the 16-foot steeple was not included in the building plans. This church closed on September 24, 2000, and now houses the Granada Historical Museum.

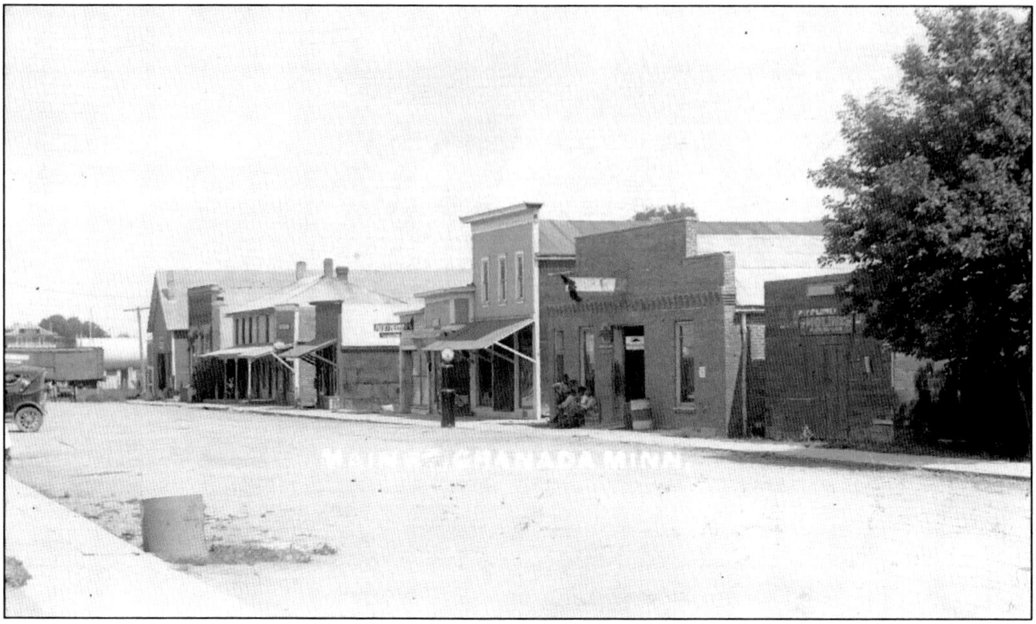

Shown here is the east side of Granada's Main Street looking north about 1923. From the right are unidentified, Oscar Hill's Garage (later Green's Locker), Teskey's Store (later turned into a garage for Earl Snow, Oliver Bakken, and Gustav Borkenhagen), Greenstran Harness, an automobile repair shop (later Dan Pappas's barbershop), Art Anderson's restaurant, Prouty's Meat Market, a hotel, Frank Cowing's store, and the livery.

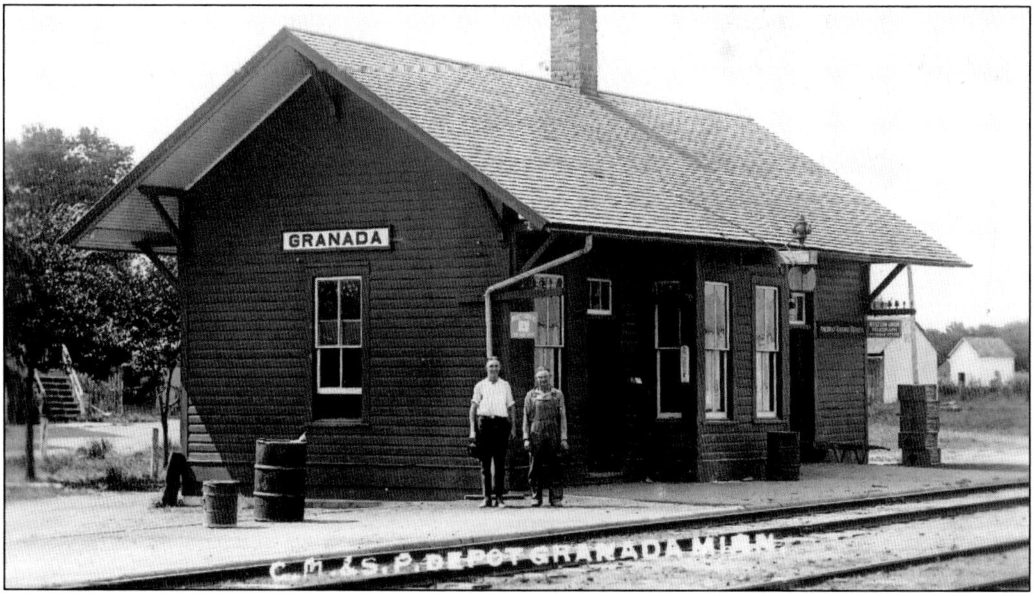

This is the Chicago, Milwaukee and St. Paul Railway depot in Granada about 1923, with Stanley Potter on the left. The railroad promised to build a depot in 1892, but the promise was not fulfilled until 1896. The depot was a busy place; the Ku Klux Klan held a rally here in 1924, and at one time, there were four passenger trains a day. Passenger service ceased about 1957, although freight continued until about 1959. After being vacant for many years, this structure was moved to Butterfield in 1977. (Courtesy of the Granada Historical Museum.)

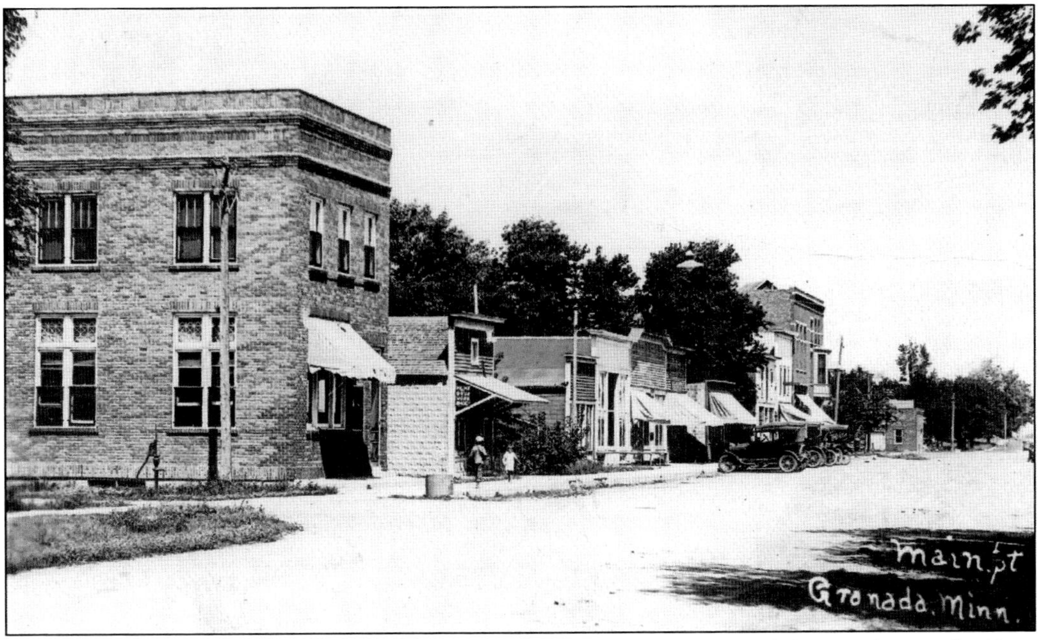

This is the west side of Main Street looking north about 1923. From left to right are the First National Bank, Greenstran's Shoe Repair, unidentified (possibly a barbershop), Ole Hanson's Café, W. W. Doty Store (two buildings), Eli Boudrye Hardware, the post office, Bert Colton Drug Store, Canfield and Barden, Granada State Bank, and city hall. The town pump can be seen to the left near the first window in the bank building.

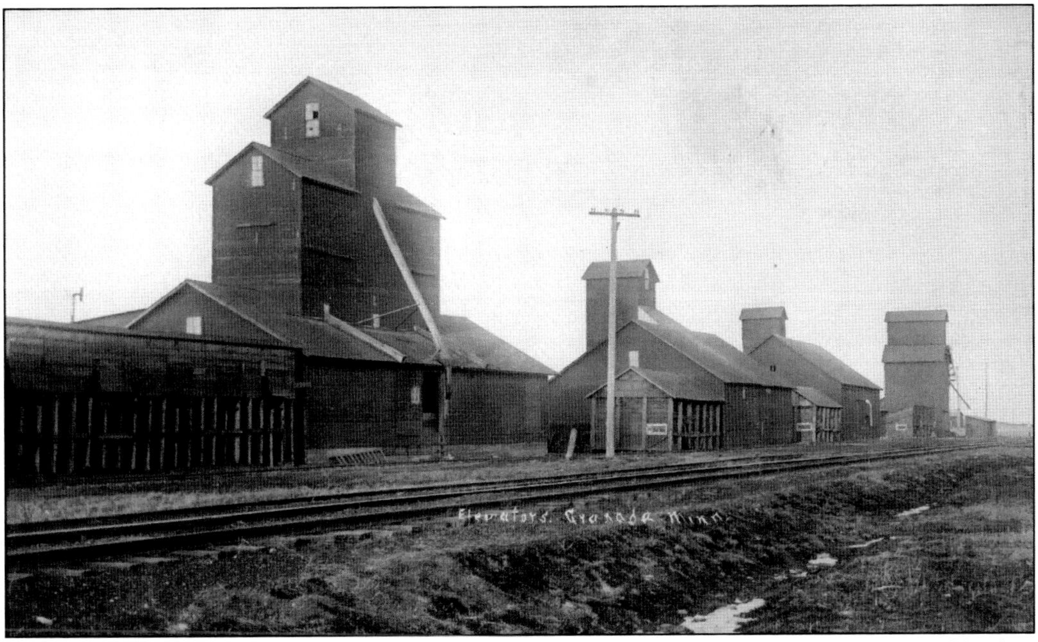

Here are the four elevators in Granada. Two of them are thought to have been destroyed by fire. The last one standing, at far right, was torn down in 1999. Many people will remember Herb Rotunda, who managed this elevator for many years. The first three were gone by 1923.

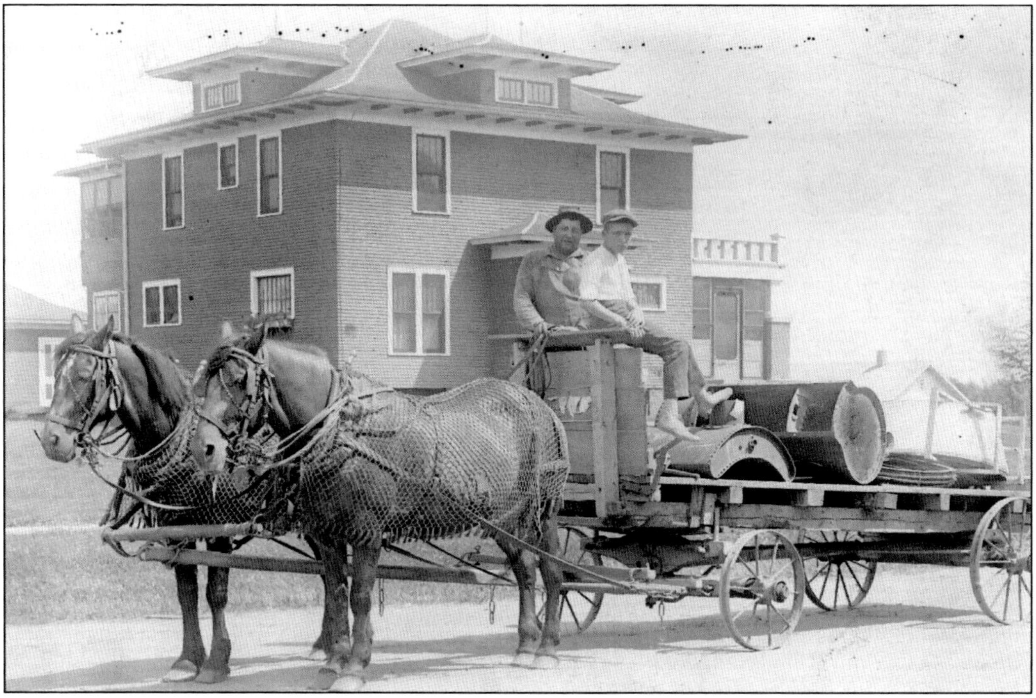

Fran Mortensen currently lives in this home on North Main Street. The home was nicknamed the "bankers house" after the profession of its previous owners. It was built about 1918 for B. A. Burton, a banker, and later A. C. Gray, who was a cashier responsible for the closing of the Granada State Bank, lived here. The large man is believed to be Jack Smith, who ran a dray line for Art Anderson. (Courtesy of the Granada Historical Museum.)

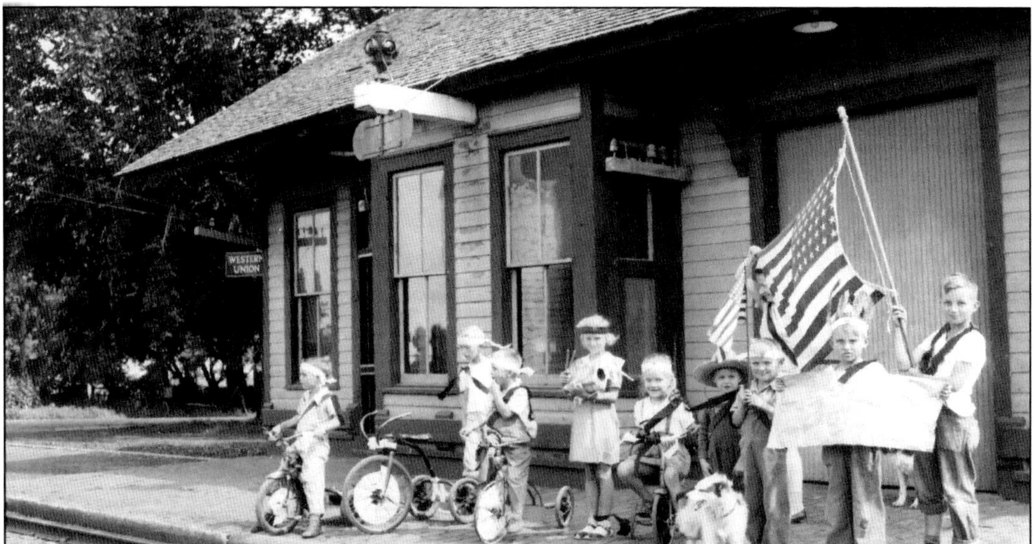

This is a Victory Day parade celebration in the mid-1940s, with (from left to right) Don Schneider, Duane Findley, Jerry Anderson, Sandra Anderson, Donna Weber, Phillip Tenney, Sonny Bakken, Rodney Prafke, Dean Findley, Hazel Tenney (behind the flag), and Spotty the dog at the Granada depot. (Courtesy of the Granada Historical Museum.)

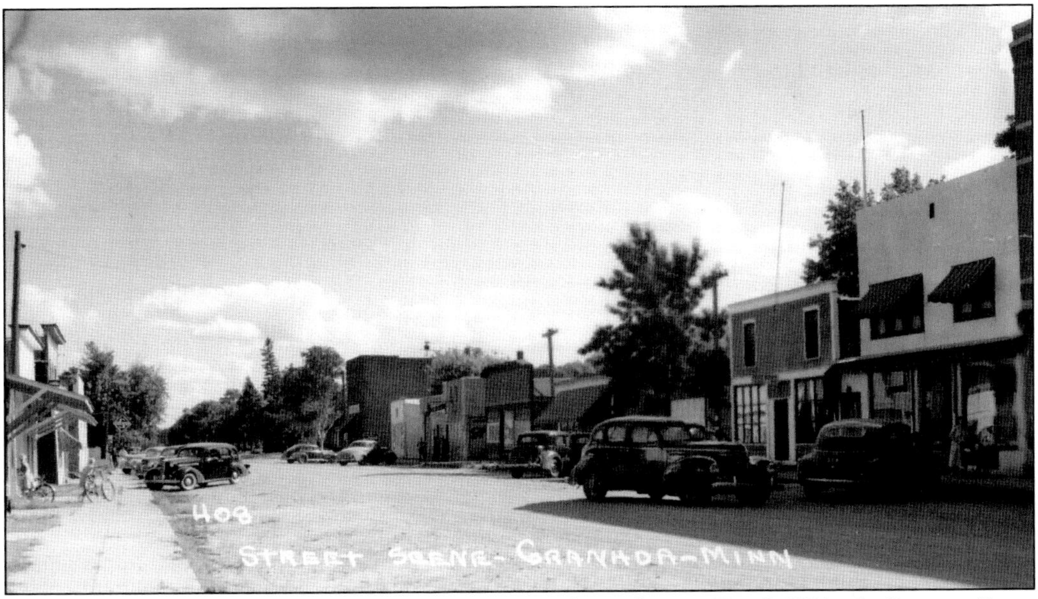

This is Granada's Main Street about 1948. From the right are Frank Weber's Grocery Store (later Marv's Grocery Store, which closed in 1977), the post office, Eli Boudrye Hardware store (later Ernie's Hardware), Carp's Place (later Rehse's Café), Willard's Café, a storage building for the Skelly station (at another time it was Mike Broviak's station), and Worden's Grocery (later Franzen's Grocery).

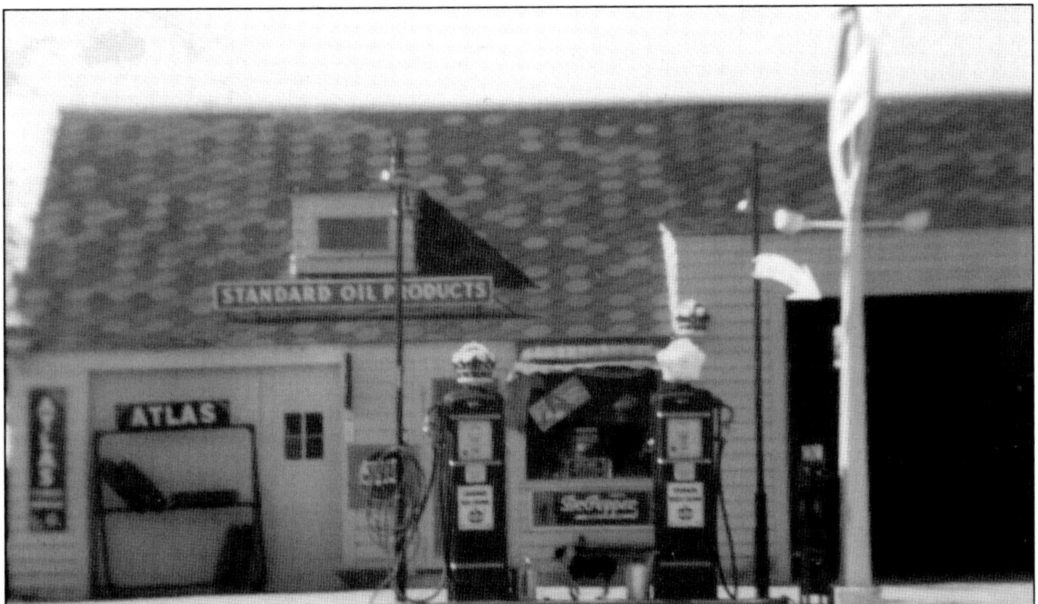

This is Paul's Standard Service Station when it was first located on the west side of Main Street in Granada. Note the gasoline pumps, which were right on the street. The McClearys purchased this about 1933, and when the station across the street became available, they bought it and remodeled this one into their home in the 1950s. (Courtesy of the Granada Historical Museum.)

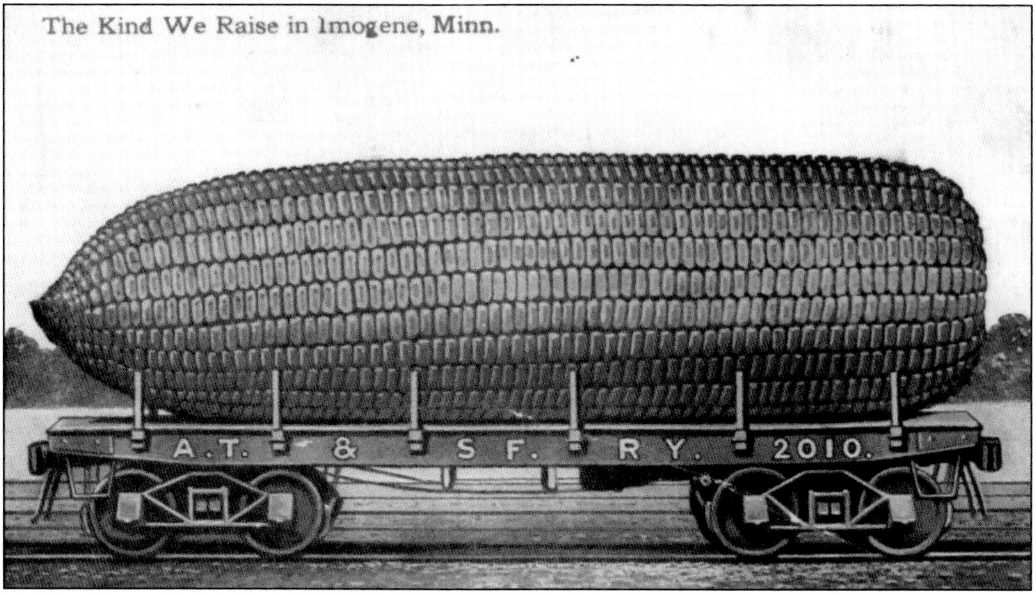

Imogene was platted in 1899 as Cardona. When the post office was established on March 28, 1901, the name was changed to Imogen (later Imogene). The post office closed on June 30, 1913. Curiously this is the only surviving town that never had a bank or church. Apparently the farmland near Imogene was very favorable for growing corn, as this postcard from about 1920 boasts.

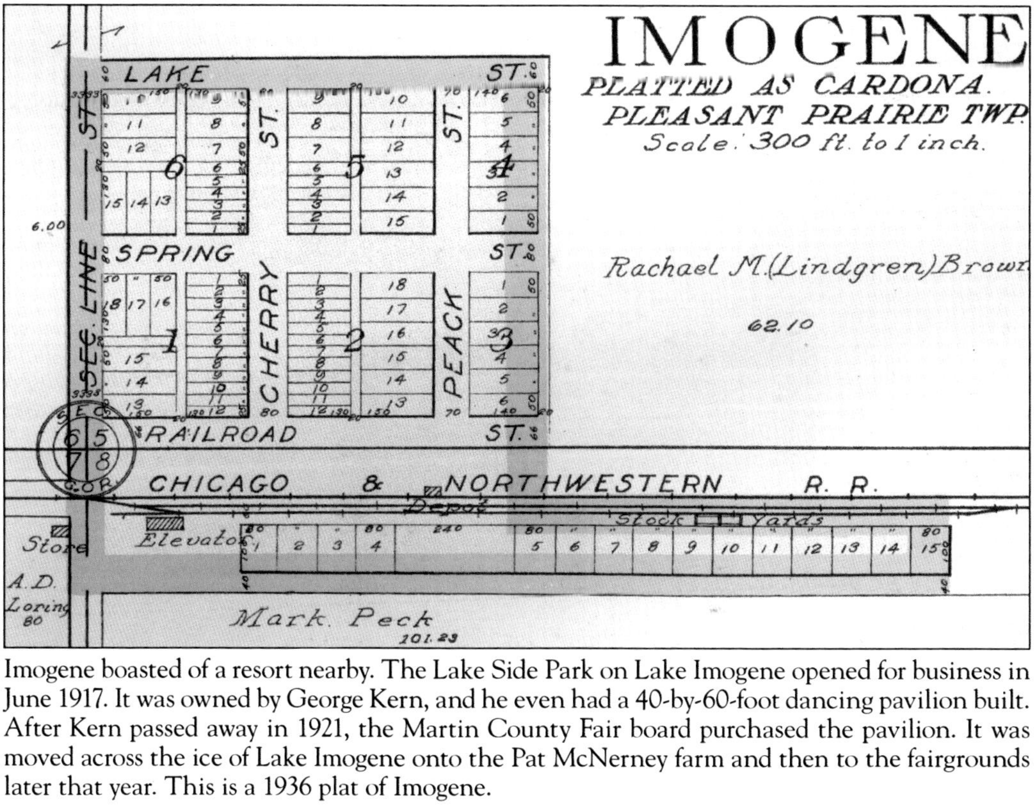

Imogene boasted of a resort nearby. The Lake Side Park on Lake Imogene opened for business in June 1917. It was owned by George Kern, and he even had a 40-by-60-foot dancing pavilion built. After Kern passed away in 1921, the Martin County Fair board purchased the pavilion. It was moved across the ice of Lake Imogene onto the Pat McNerney farm and then to the fairgrounds later that year. This is a 1936 plat of Imogene.

Five

NORTHROP AND ORMSBY

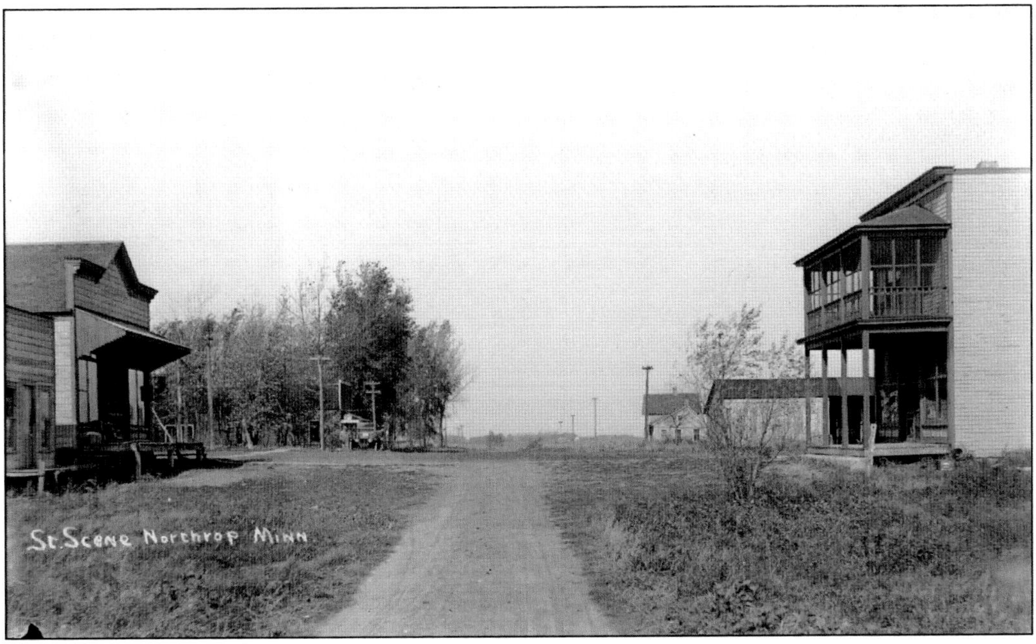

The village of Northrop came into being when the Omaha Railway built an extension in 1899 and named it after Cyrus Northrop, president of the Minnesota University. Locals wanted the post office to be named after Civil War veteran Charles Snyder, but the railroad won. The post office was established on February 1, 1900, and has been in the same location since 1915. The first small (partially visible) building on the left is currently the Northrop Post Office, but in this photograph, the post office was farther down the street.

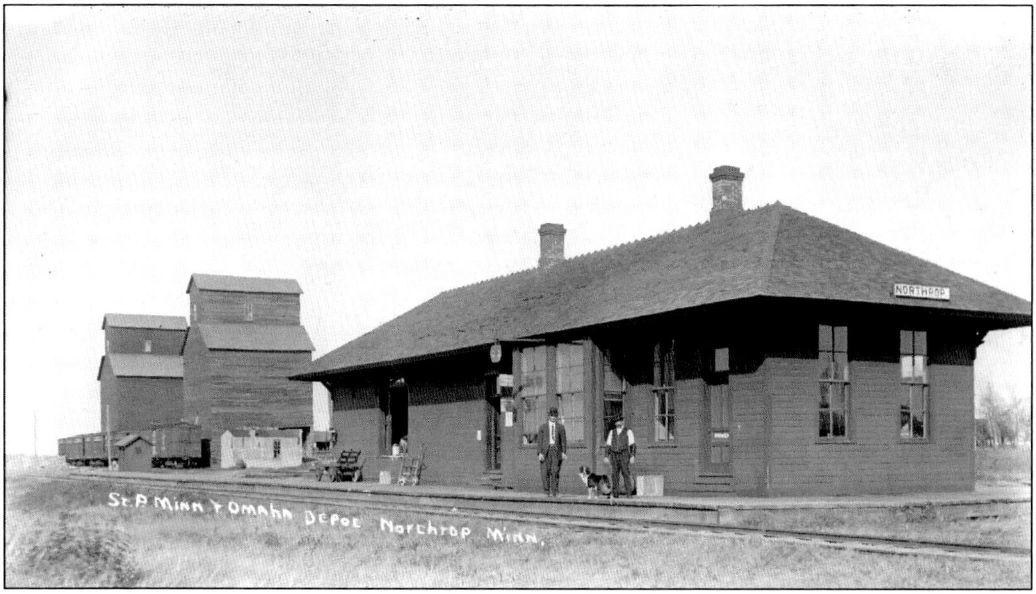

Isaac N. Stone was the first agent of the Northrop depot. The Becker Grain Company was started in 1912 by Gus Becker. He sold it to his son Ed "Windy" Becker in 1945. Windy built an elevator in 1959 only to see it burn to the ground in 1971. He sold the business to the L. H. Grain Company in 1981. It is currently owned by Watonwan Farm Service.

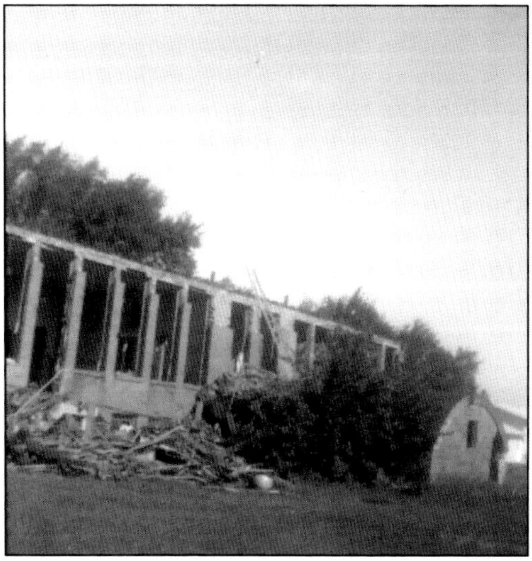

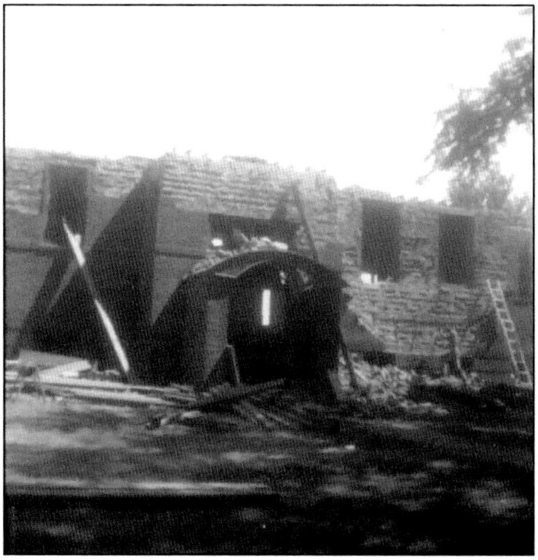

These two snapshots show the Northrop Public Schoolhouse being torn down in August 1972. The St. James Lutheran School was established in September 1895. The first schoolhouse was built in 1903 and later moved into Northrop in 1940. A new school was built in 1948 and torn down in 1972.

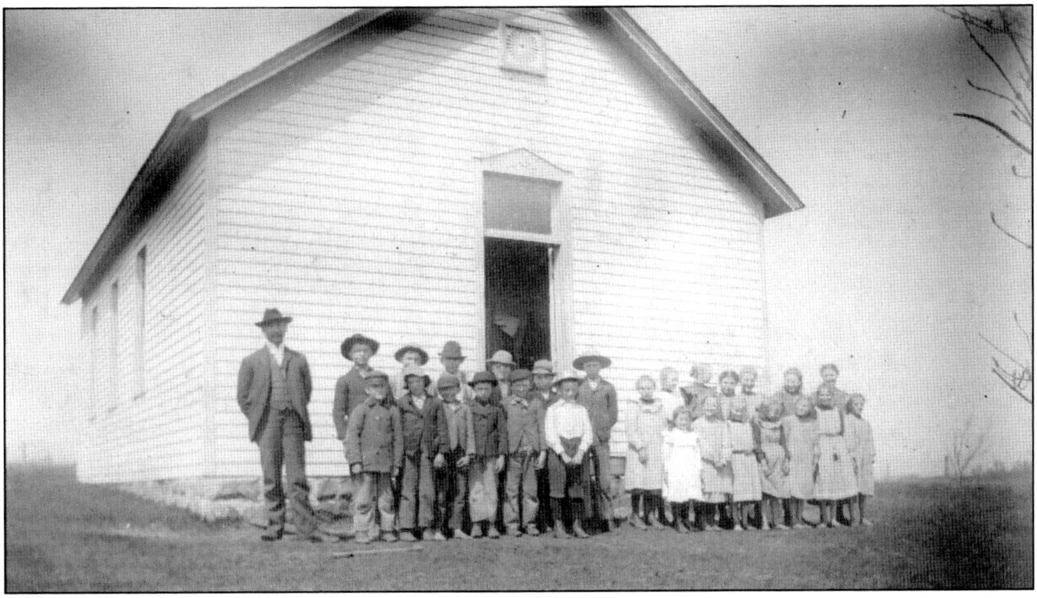

This is the White Lily School, which is district No. 31. It was located northeast of Northrop and organized in 1867. The school building was constructed in 1881 and closed in 1949. When Rev. A. Kohollof was the pastor and teacher, he taught in German in the morning and in English in the afternoon. The girls are (first row) Lydia Kohloff, Edna Anders, Elsie Kading, Hattie Wolter, Ella Kading, and Clara Kueke; (second row) Hulda Hartmann, Cora Rehberg, Emma Hunte, Tillie Wolf, Ella Walter, Bertha Bokelman, and Lydia Albert.

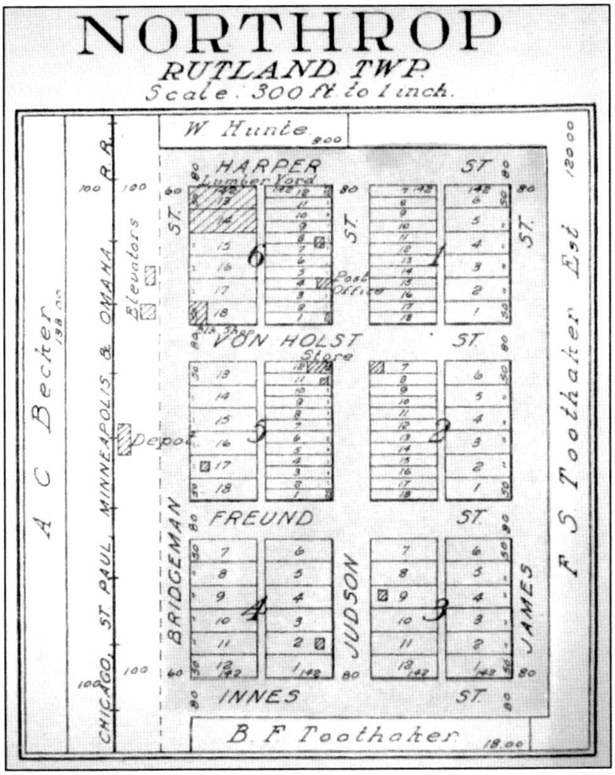

On this 1911 plat of Northrop, some of the businesses are visible.

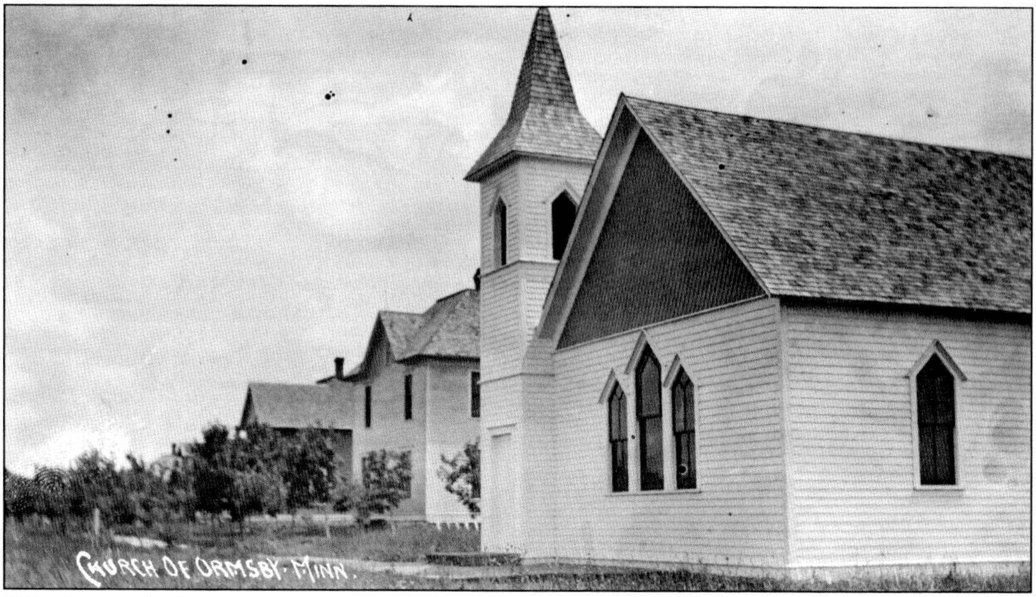

"The biggest little town in two counties" is the motto of Ormsby. An oat field became Ormsby when it was platted on October 14, 1899, and named after Edwin Ormsby, whose bank helped bring the railroad through the area. The Church of Ormsby was built in 1900 and 1901 and operated by the Baptist, American Union Sunday School, Methodist, and Lutheran faiths. Only two weddings were held here, and the first was in 1906. In 1947, the church closed and everything was sold.

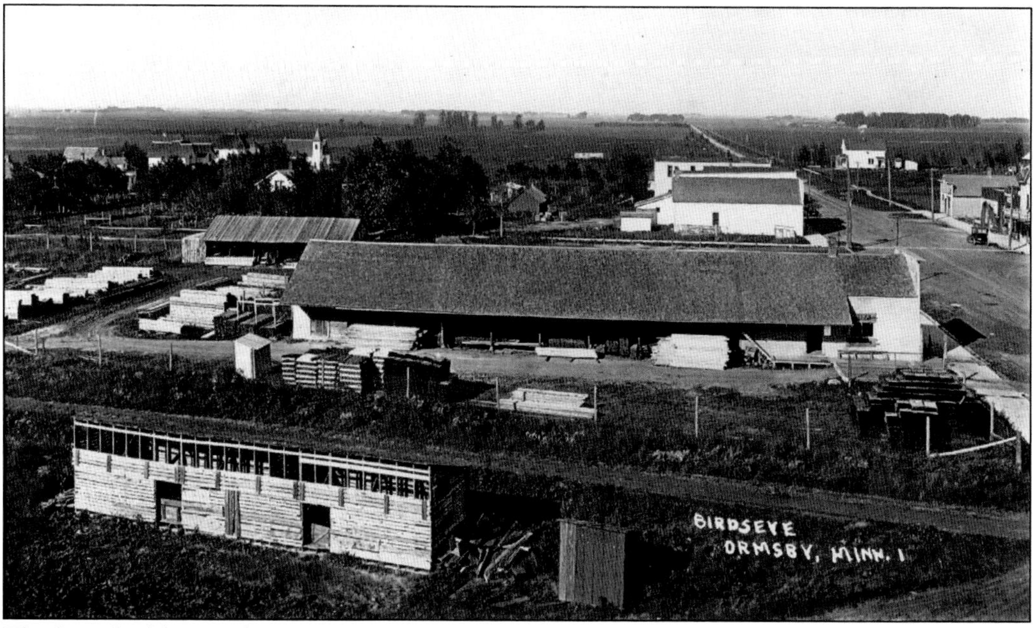

The large building in front was originally the Farver Lumberyard. The lumberyard and Samuel Faver's Land Agent office were the first businesses in Ormsby, in 1898, even before the town was platted. At the time this postcard was made about 1917, the lumberyard was probably owned by J. H. Queal. About 1920, this became the Thomas-Halverson Lumber Company and later the Watonwan Enterprises Building Supply.

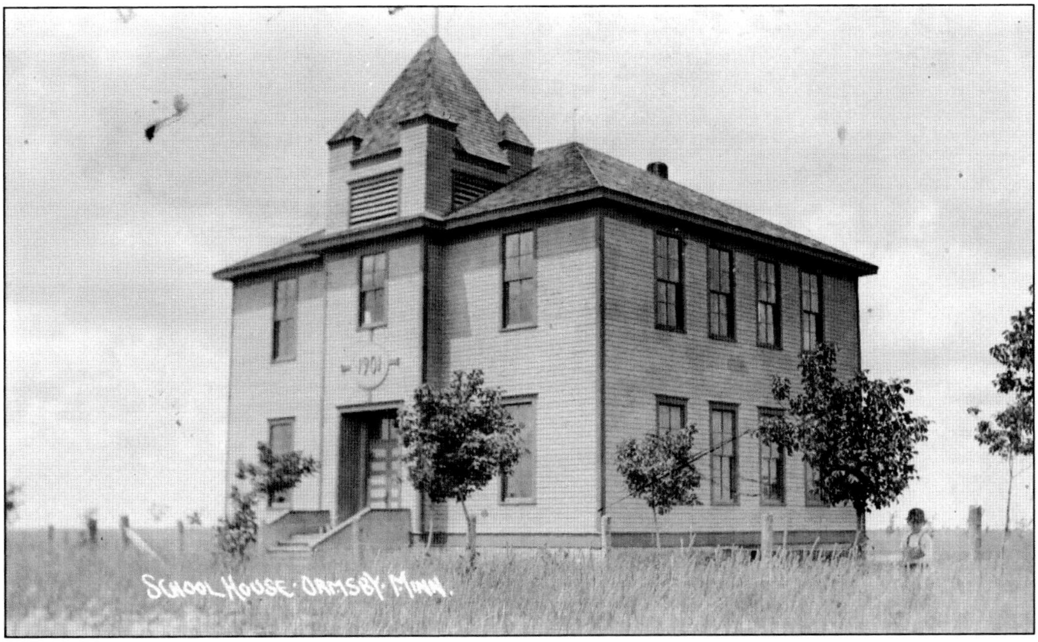

On July 8, 1901, the Ormsby School was organized and the large wooden school building erected. There was only one teacher until 1911, when two teachers were hired and only two rooms were being used. The upstairs rooms remained unused until 1917. The high school curriculum was from about 1917 to 1927. A new school was built in 1960 for the first through sixth grades. The old school was sold and has since been torn down. The Ormsby School district closed in 1977 and is now part of the St. James School District. This card is postmarked August 21, 1910.

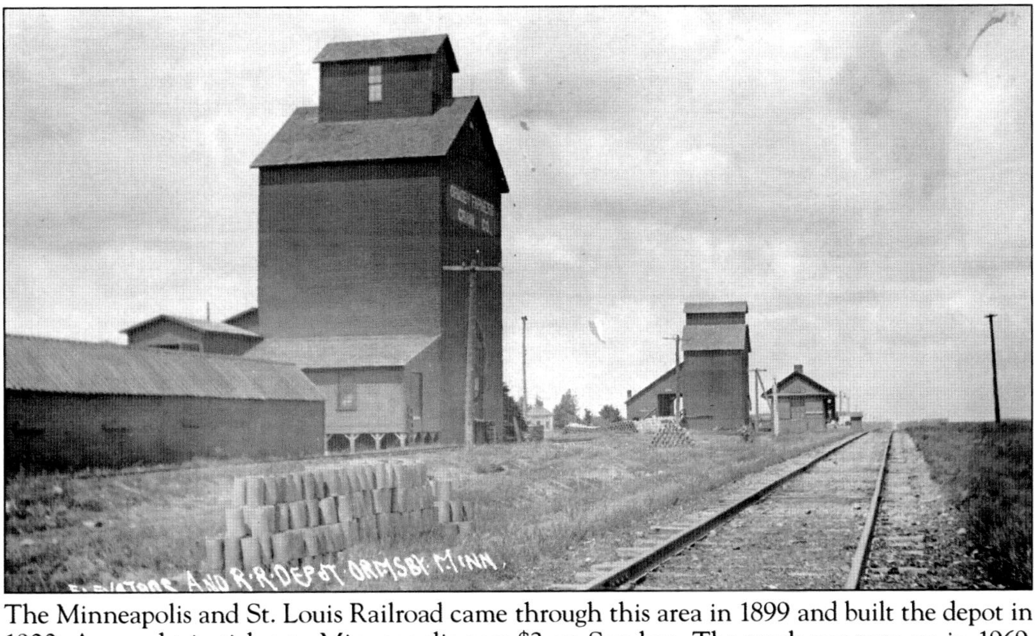

The Minneapolis and St. Louis Railroad came through this area in 1899 and built the depot in 1900. A round-trip ticket to Minneapolis cost $2 on Sundays. The track was torn up in 1969. This photograph shows the elevators and depot around 1915.

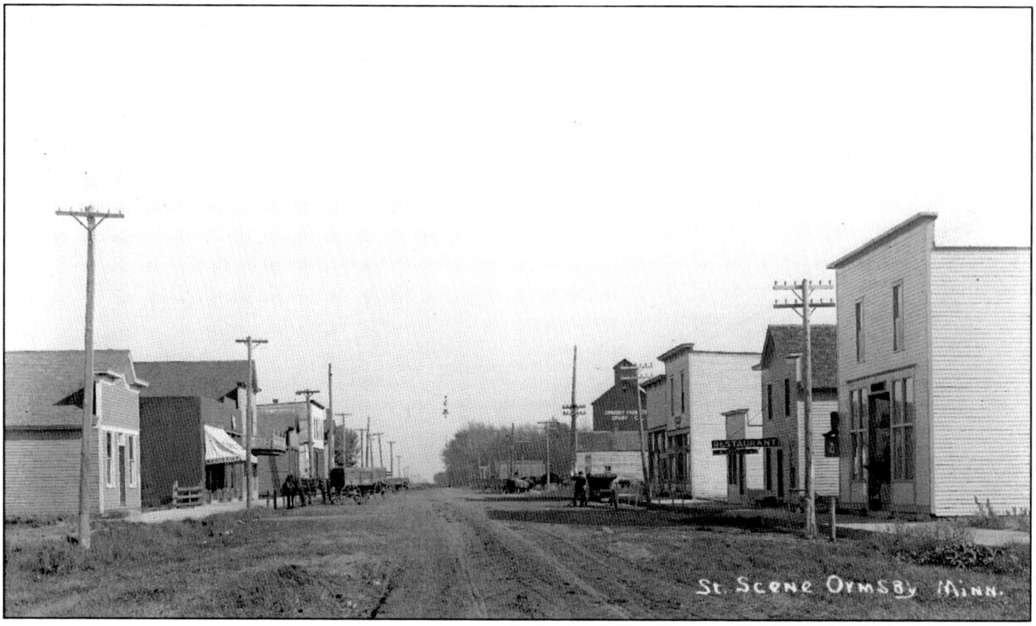

Pictured here is the Main Street of Ormsby looking east before 1914. The first building on the right appears to be a shoe store—note the large shoe for a trade sign. The next building is the Ormsby Restaurant. This originally was the first hardware store, but it became a restaurant about 1905. The fourth building is the Dammann Store and post office. It was built in 1901 and destroyed by lightning and a resulting fire in 1918.

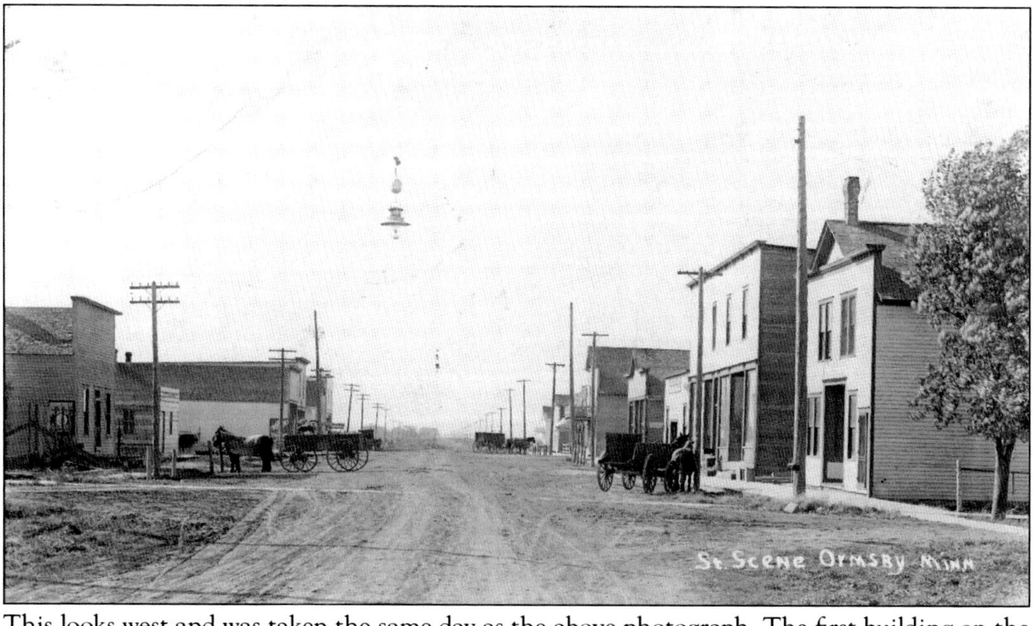

This looks west and was taken the same day as the above photograph. The first building on the right is the Ormsby House. It was built in 1901 and torn down in the 1980s. Sisters Anna and Bertha Mueller managed the hotel and offered a very fine meal with trimmings for 25¢. The third building is an implement business and later housed the Koch Drug Store from 1920 to 1941. The fourth building is the pool hall.

Six

Sherburn and Fox Lake

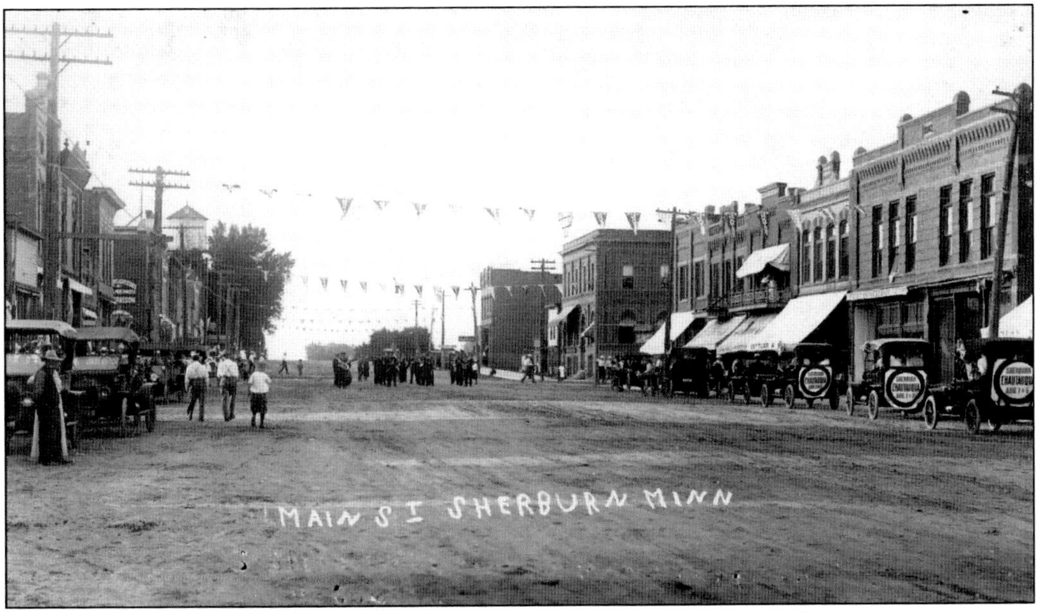

This is the chautauqua assembly that was about to begin in June 1915. Chautauqua was a time for people to gather and listen to lectures on education and speeches on enlightenment along with parades and many entertainments. Some activities for the children to receive an "Honor" were bouncing a rubber ball 100 times, an Indian Club Race, cleaning one's teeth, and swatting 25 flies each day! The chautauqua avoided political affiliation, and Teddy Roosevelt said that it was "the most American thing in America."

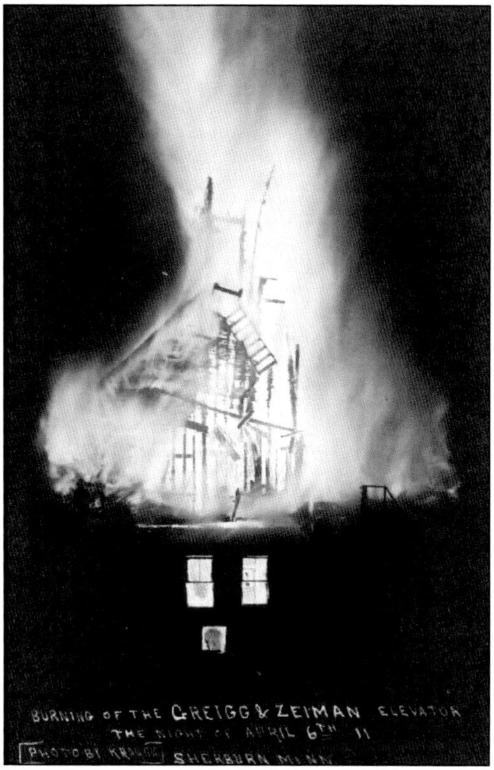

This fire happened on April 6, 1911, and destroyed the Greigg and Zeiman elevator. Sherburn was not having a good year, as this was the second fire to strike. It was first known as the Old Packard Elevator before Greigg and Zeiman of Estherville purchased it. Over 3,000 bushels of oats were lost in this fire. The first fire that year also destroyed an elevator owned by Alliance Elevator and Milling Company. The town of Sherburn was then left with only two elevators. The postcard photograph was taken by Allen Krause of Sherburn.

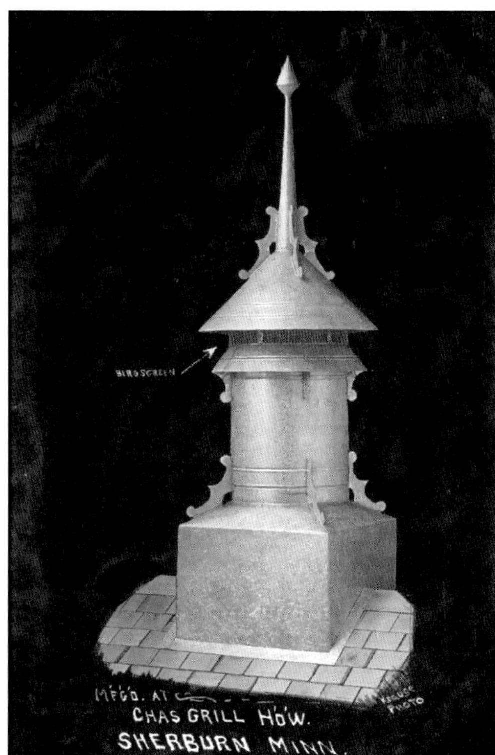

This fancy cupola was manufactured and available for purchase at the Charles Grill Hardware store. His store was a nice brick building on Main Street in Sherburn with the canopy on the second story (see page 75).

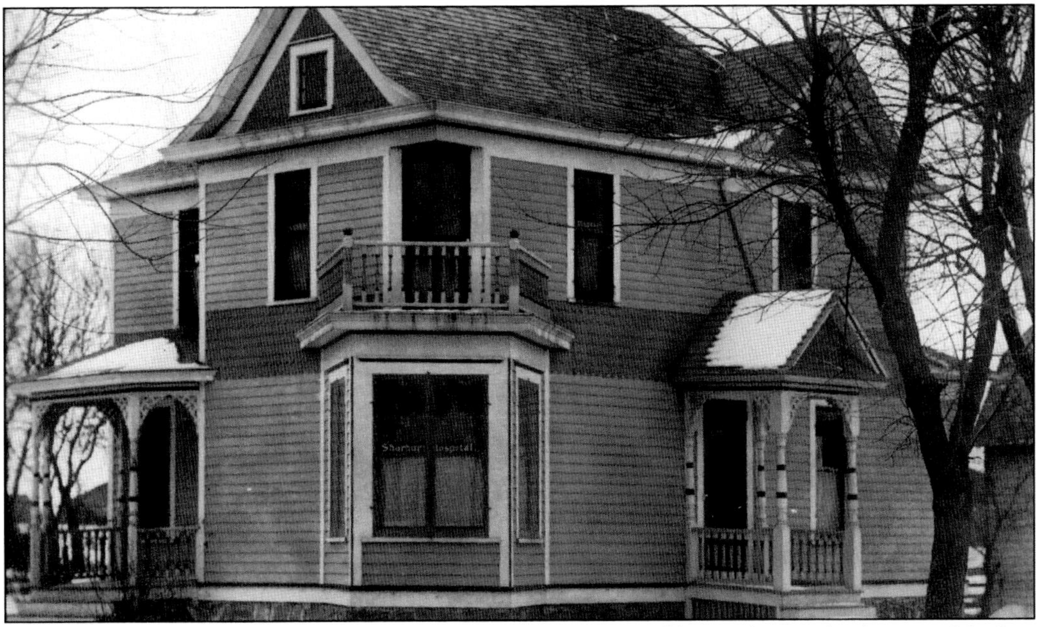

Dr. Malcolm J. Farrish came to the Sherburn area in 1892 and began his medical career. His first hospital was called the Kensington and was located in Jay Township on the Bettenhausen farm. He was joined by his brother Dr. Robert C. Farrish in 1901. That same year, they moved into Sherburn and established a hospital within the city limits. After a fire in 1904, they purchased this home, and it became Sherburn's second hospital. Dr. Robert C. Farrish and Dr. William Gaugh of Granada are reputed to have not lost a patient during the influenza pandemic of 1918. Dr. Malcolm J. Farrish passed away in 1915.

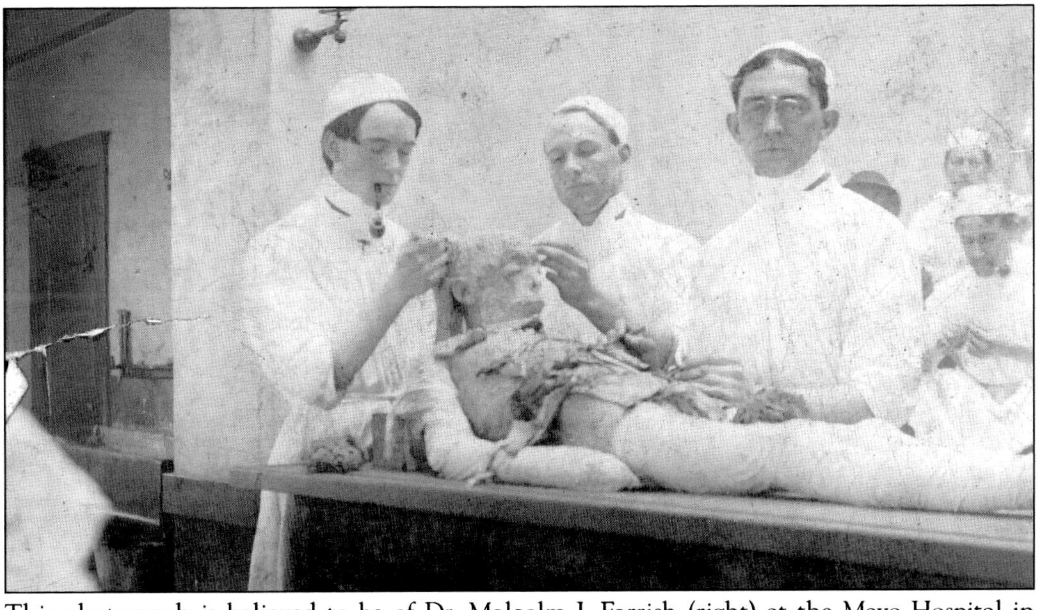

This photograph is believed to be of Dr. Malcolm J. Farrish (right) at the Mayo Hospital in Rochester where both he and his brother received their educations. The three men are dissecting a cadaver. At first glance, it appears to be a dummy corpse, but upon close examination, it is possibly a real human cadaver.

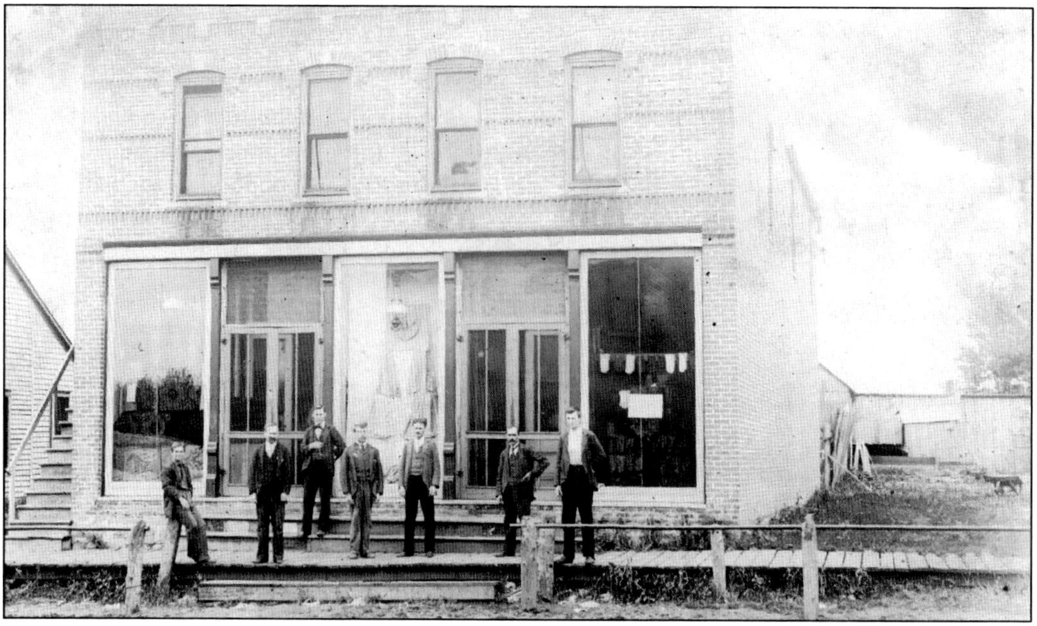

This is an early-1900s image of Tim Sammon's One Horse Store in Sherburn. The One Horse Store was founded in Monterey in 1901 and moved to Triumph in 1908. Sherburn became Sammon's new home in 1914. He took the quip "one-horse store," uttered by a rival, and turned it into his trademark name. It is well known that Santa Claus stopped by for the children for several Christmases.

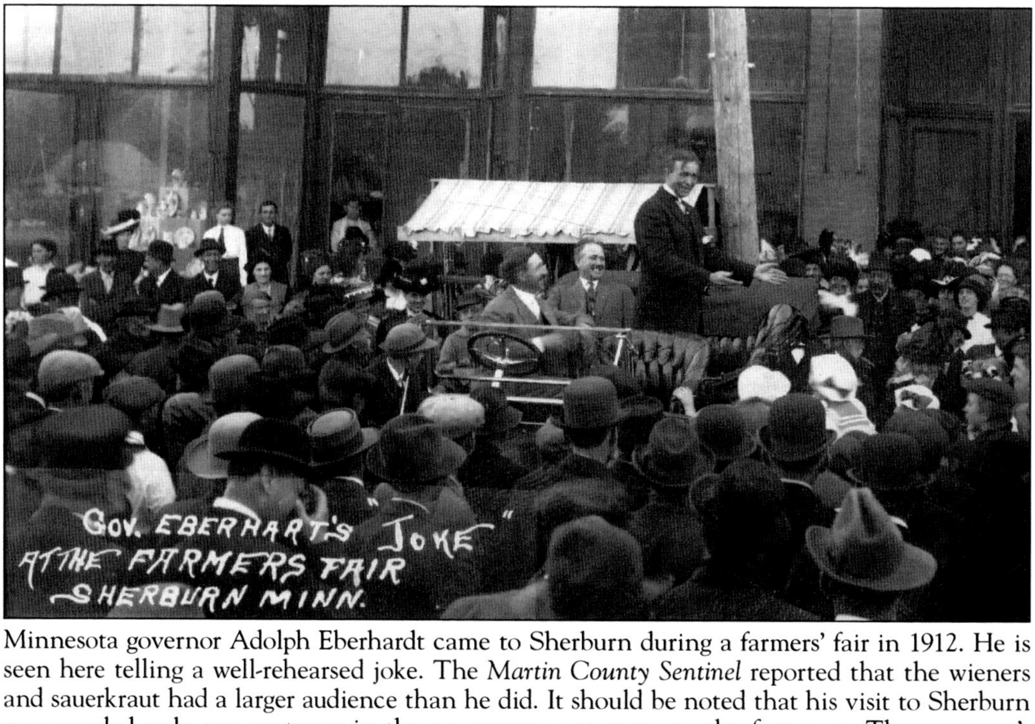

Minnesota governor Adolph Eberhardt came to Sherburn during a farmers' fair in 1912. He is seen here telling a well-rehearsed joke. The *Martin County Sentinel* reported that the wieners and sauerkraut had a larger audience than he did. It should be noted that his visit to Sherburn commanded only one sentence in the newspaper, not even on the first page. The governor's opponent, however, received full front-page articles.

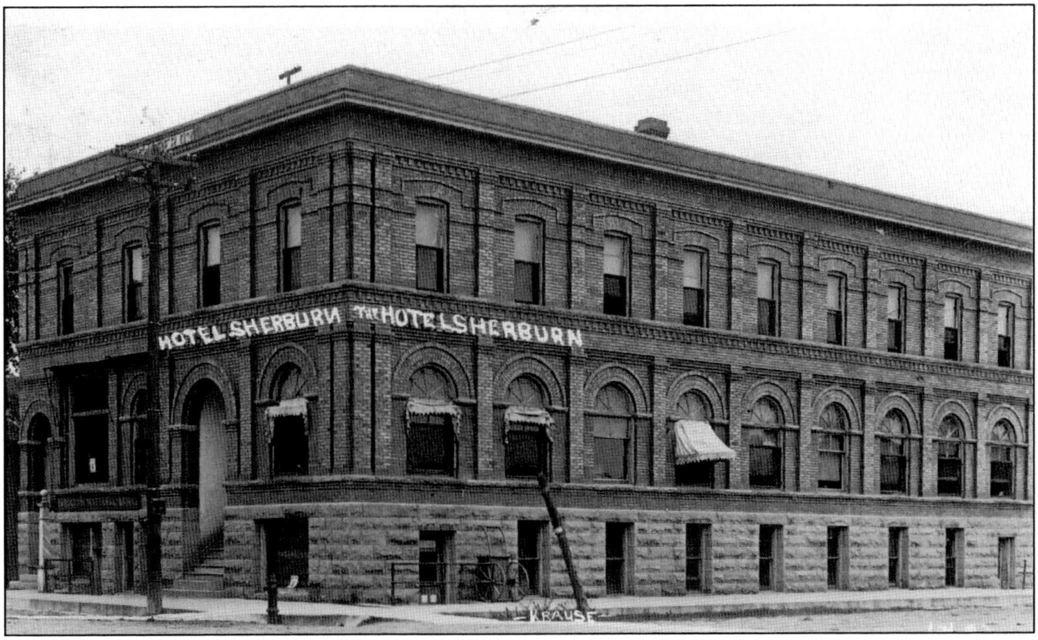

This photograph is of the Haber Hotel, which was built in 1903. It is referred to here as the Hotel Sherburn. In the 1950s, it was transformed into an apartment complex and then sat vacant for many years. Gordon Bute purchased it in 1998 in hopes of restoring it and finding a home for the Sherburn Historical Society. However, in 2003, it partially collapsed and was torn down. The Sherburn Museum has also since disbanded.

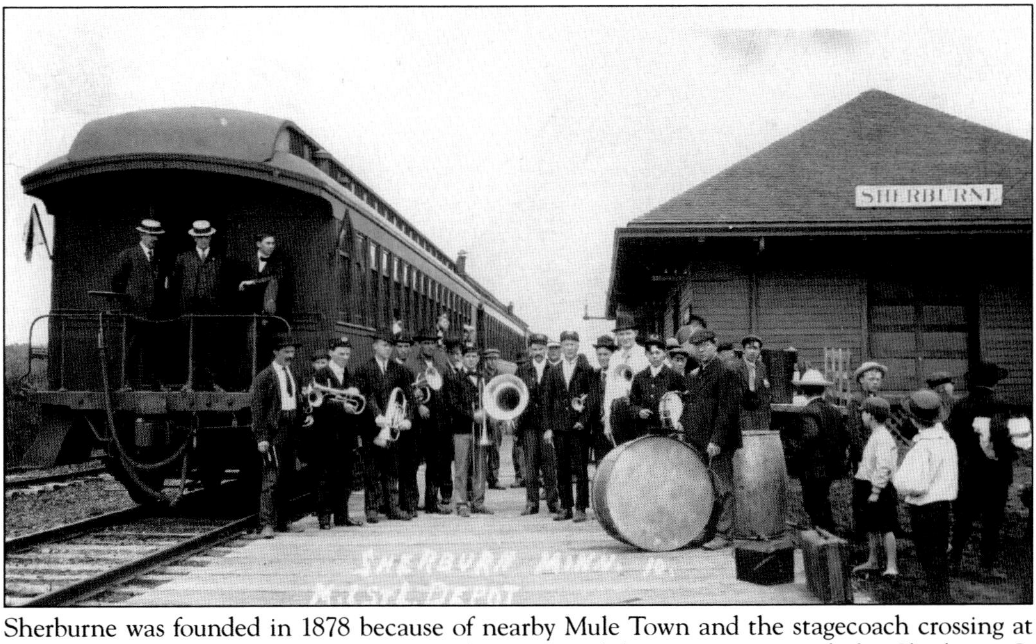

Sherburne was founded in 1878 because of nearby Mule Town and the stagecoach crossing at George Archer's sod tavern. It incorporated in 1879, and the town was named after Sherburne S. Merrill, a general manager for the railroad. In 1902, the spelling of Sherburne was changed to Sherburn. This photograph was taken in 1908, and note how they haven't changed the depot sign to the new spelling.

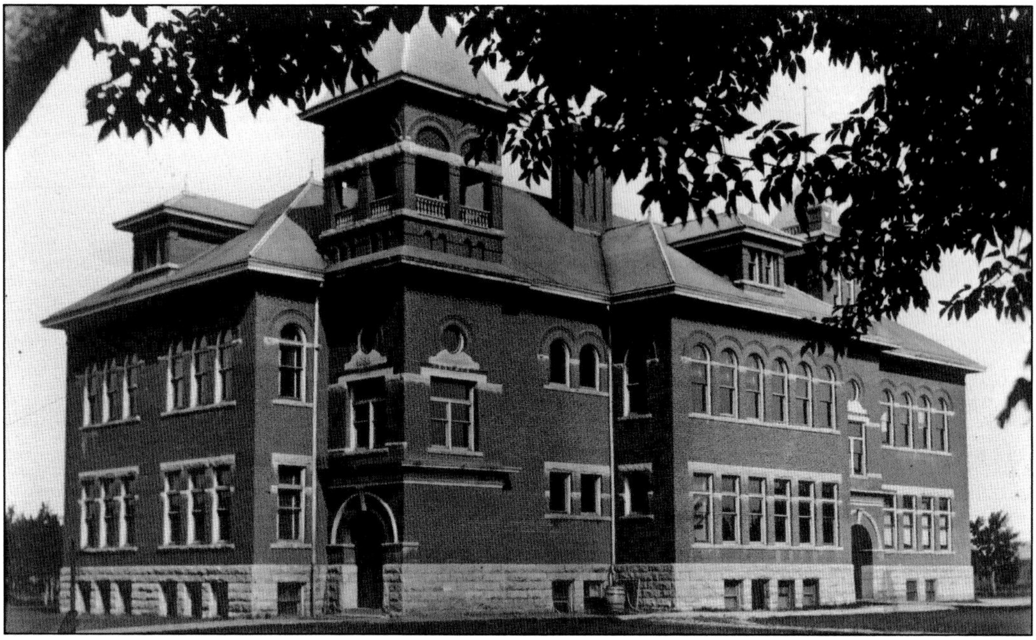

This is Sherburn's second schoolhouse, built in 1898. It housed elementary classes, and by 1901, it became an accredited high school. The class of 1901 became the first to graduate from Sherburn High School. Sherburn's first school was a one-story building constructed in 1879. It was known as District No. 68, and in 1884, a second floor was added. It has since been moved and remodeled into a home on Main Street. A new high school was built in 1921 and finished in 1922. By 1955 or 1956, another new high school was built, and the old one was remodeled into the elementary school. The school building above has long since been torn down.

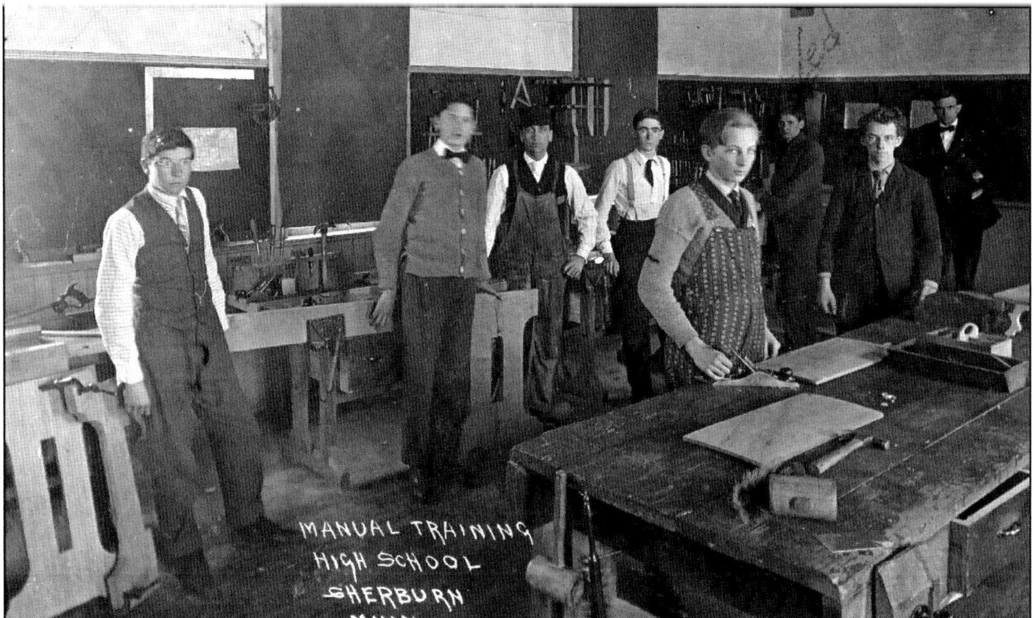

These are the students in a manual training class at Sherburn High School around 1910. Manual training must be what is now called shop or industrial arts class.

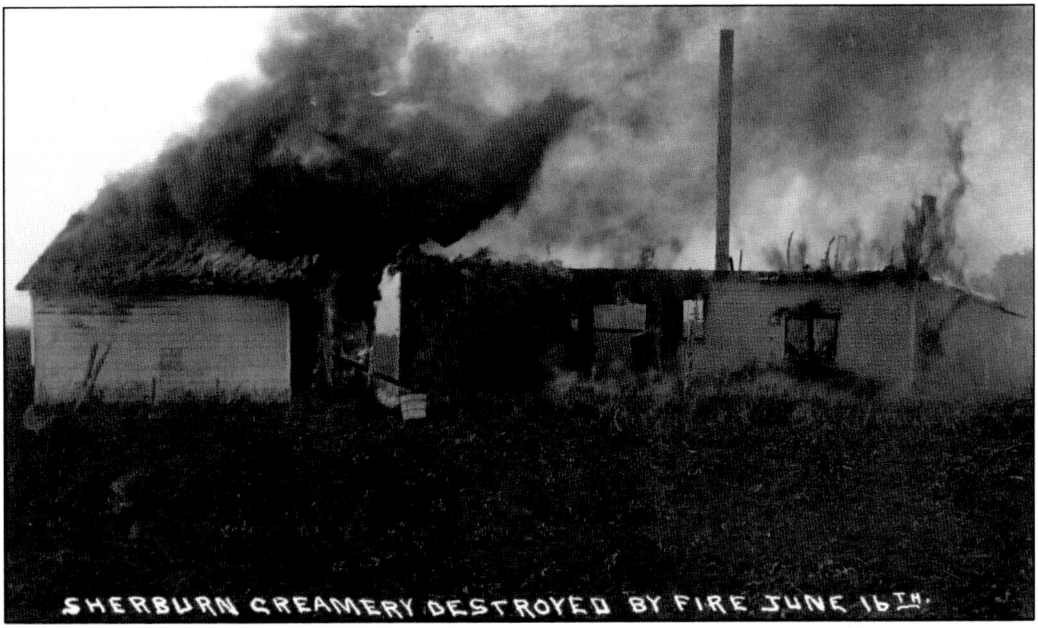

This creamery was originally built in 1893 after the farmers organized a cooperative in Jay Township. It cost $365 to build. By 1905, it had 85 patrons and was doing quite well. This photograph shows the fire that destroyed the creamery on June 16, 1913.

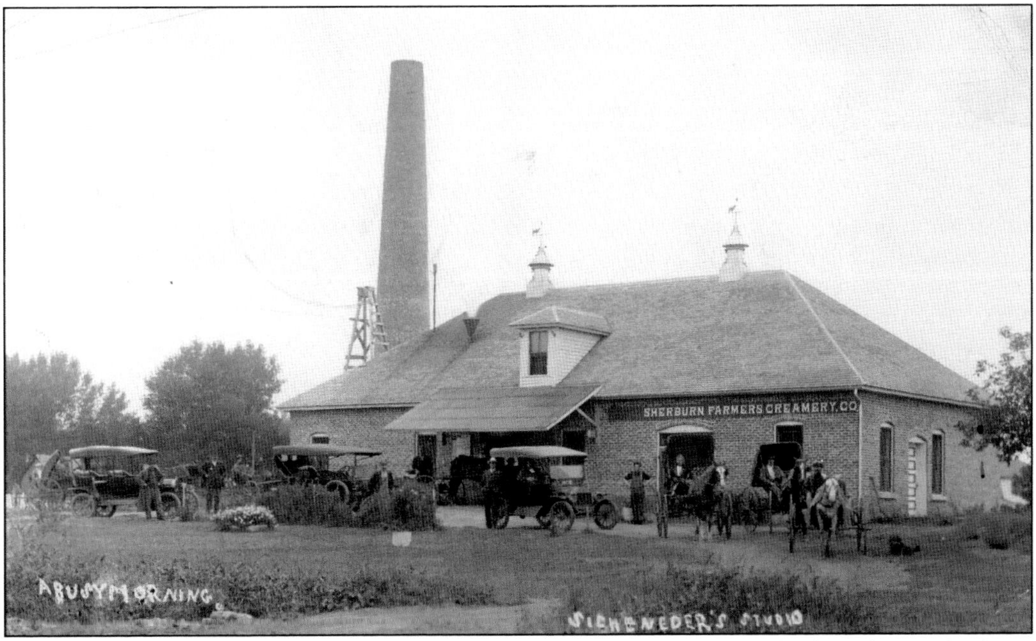

After the fire in 1913, the creamery moved into Sherburn. This shows the brand-new Sherburn Farmers Creamery Company building shortly after it was constructed in 1914. It closed in 1952.

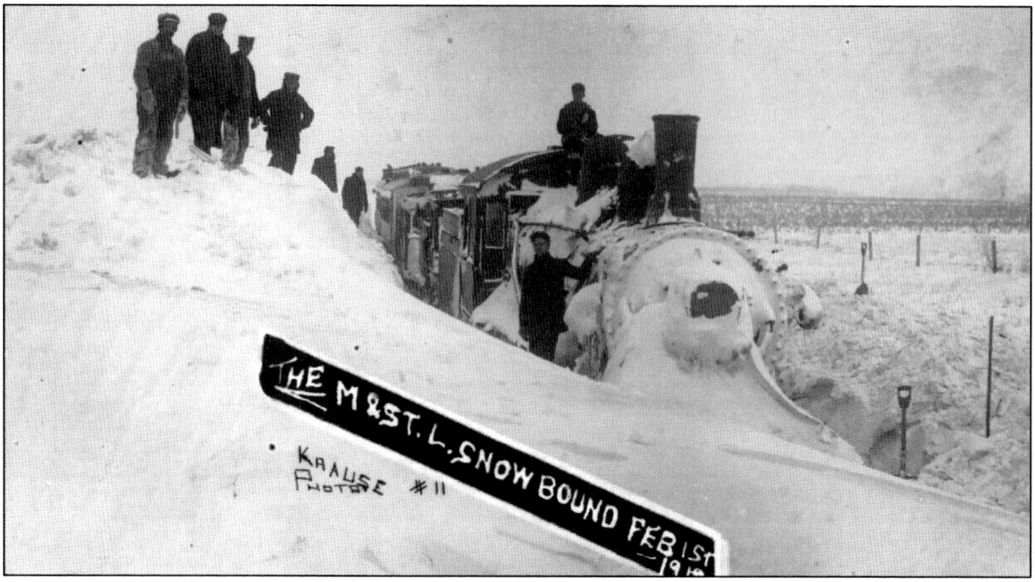

The Minneapolis and St. Louis Railroad train managed to get snowbound during the February 1, 1912, blizzard. This storm was not quite as bad as the previous ones in 1881 and 1909, but it still caused its fair share of inconveniences. The train pictured was at a standstill near Sherburn, and the photograph shows how deep the snow drifted in some areas.

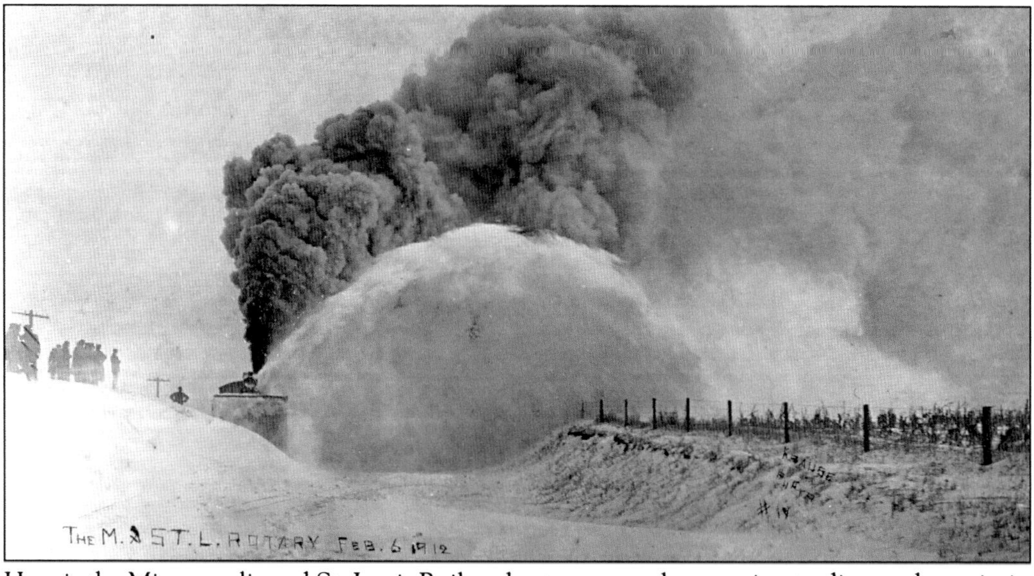

Here is the Minneapolis and St. Louis Railroad rotary snowplow coming to dig out the train in the postcard above. This photograph was taken five days after the last, on February 6, 1912. The rotaries were becoming more common by this period and made clearing the tracks a lot easier. Previously the trains would push the snow off the tracks if they were able to or ram into the snow hoping they would eventually get through. If the train could not get through, the railroad tracks were dug out entirely by hand.

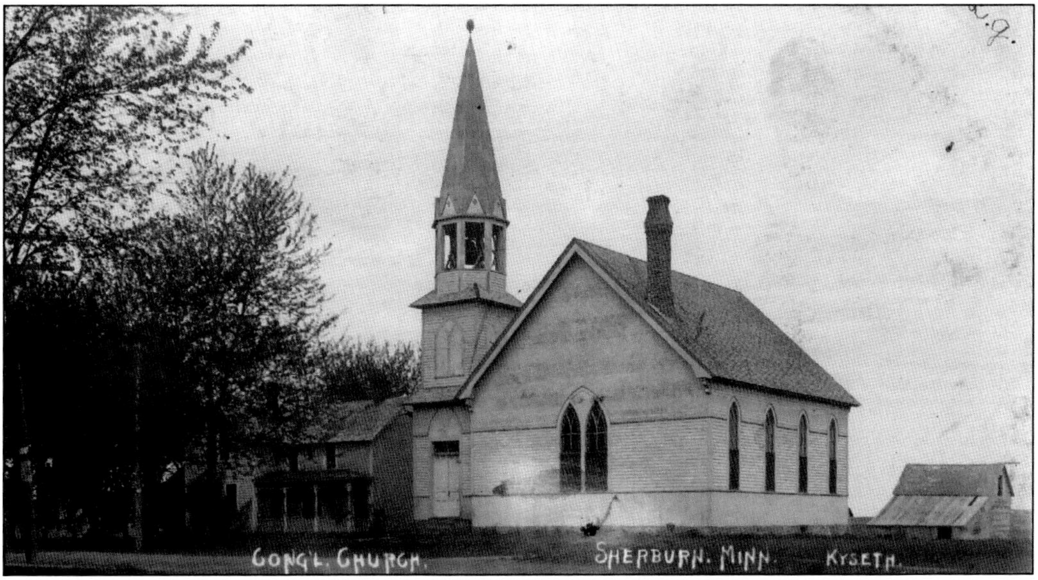

The Congregational Church of Sherburn was started in 1879. This congregation worshipped in members' homes until a church was built later that same year. The Sherburn Baptists also helped with the new church, but in 1881, the Congregationalists purchased the Baptists' share. A new church building, pictured above about 1907, was constructed in 1892. A message on the back, written by Rev. B. A. Warren, says, "This is where I put the Congregational people of Sherburn asleep."

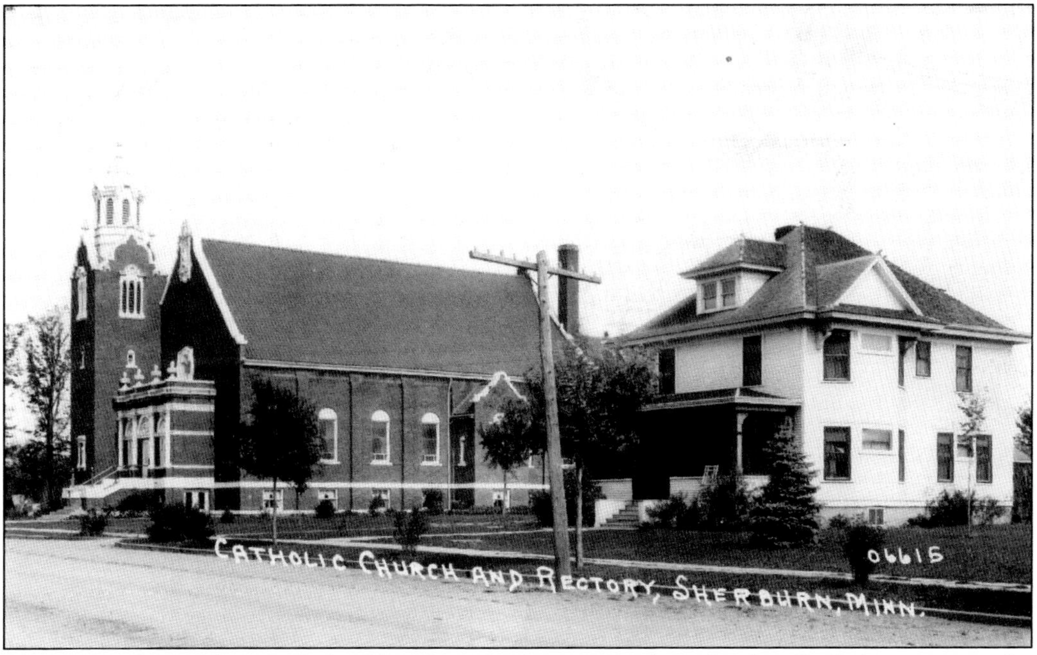

The roots of St. Luke's Catholic Church go back to 1868 when the first Catholics came to the Sherburn area. The first mass was held in 1875 at the home of Frank Rooney. The first church was built in 1888. It served until 1921 when this one, which cost about $50,000 to build, was dedicated. The rectory was built 1913 and was finished that October.

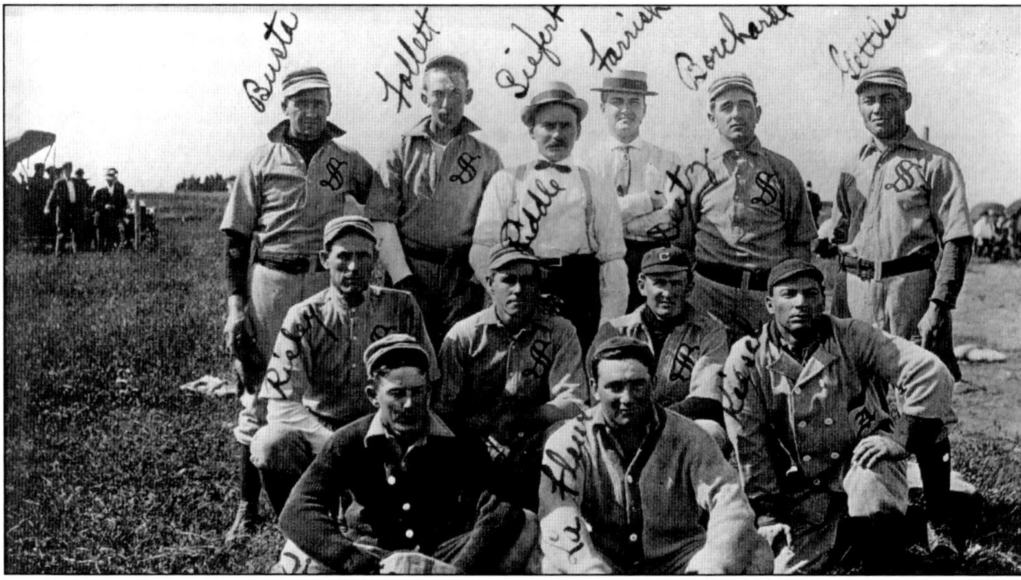

A note in a 1909 Sherburn baseball score book states, "In 1909 May 31 Sherburn had a base ball team. When Bill Borchardt got a single and our Ed Risely with another hit scored Sherburn only run against Delavan Minn nothing. This is what started the Base Ball in Sherburn." This postcard shows the team in 1909. They played the Colored Gophers of St. Paul on September 11, with a score of 3-2, and again on September 12, with a score of 3-0 (in 10 innings). Sherburn lost both times.

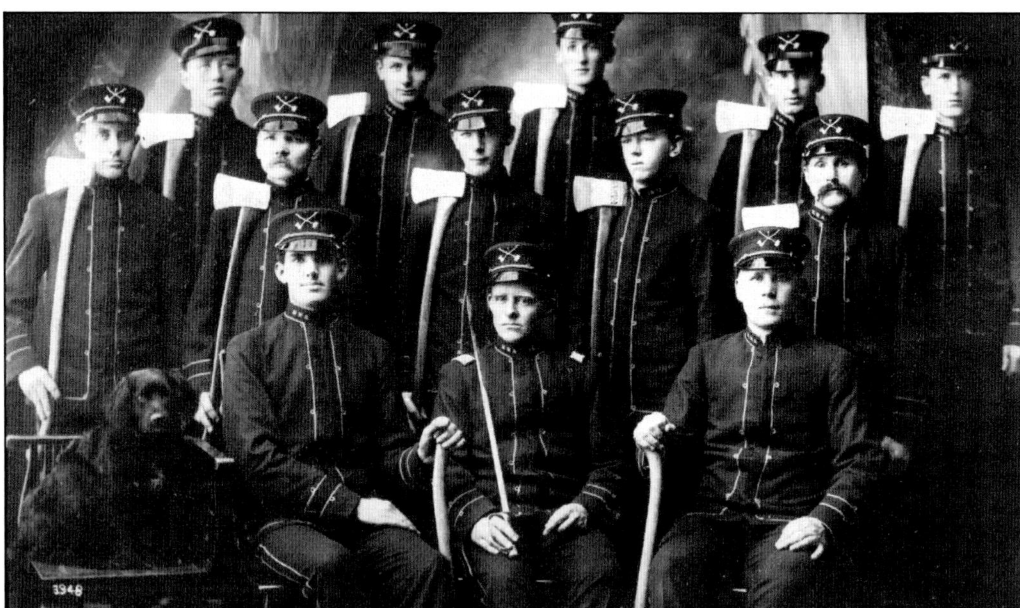

Here is a postcard of the Foresters, Fox Lake Camp No. 1973. This is part of the Modern Woodman of America lodge. The Foresters were a specialized drill team for parades and the like. They were popular from the 1880s until World War I.

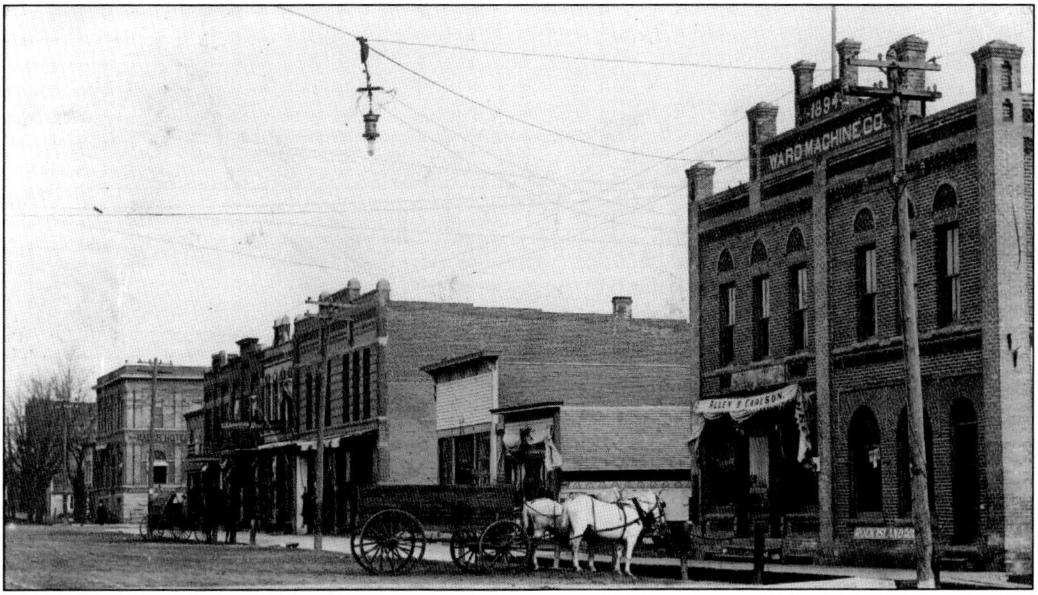

This 1907 view of Main Street shows the Ward Machine Company building that was constructed in 1894. It was a branch store of one in Fairmont. A. L. Ward had his business in almost every town in Martin County. The buildings in Sherburn and Welcome were almost identical to the one in Fairmont. In the same building is the Allen and Carlson Shoe Store. Five buildings to the left is the G. A. Sutherland Real Estate business.

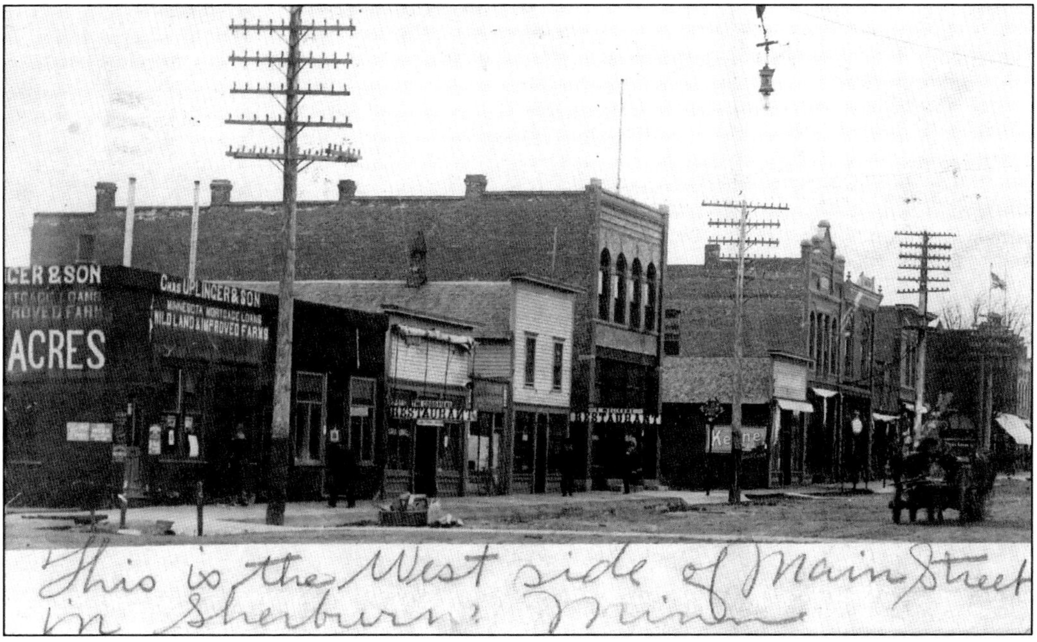

This is the west side of Main Street looking north. This postcard is postmarked April 13, 1908. From left to right, the businesses are Charles Uplinger and Son, who offered Minnesota Mortgage Loans, Wild Land and Improved Farms; unidentified; the Good Meal Restaurant; Double Wrapper (the tiny building); B. Wellcome Restaurant; and a saloon that has a Gund Beer sign outside.

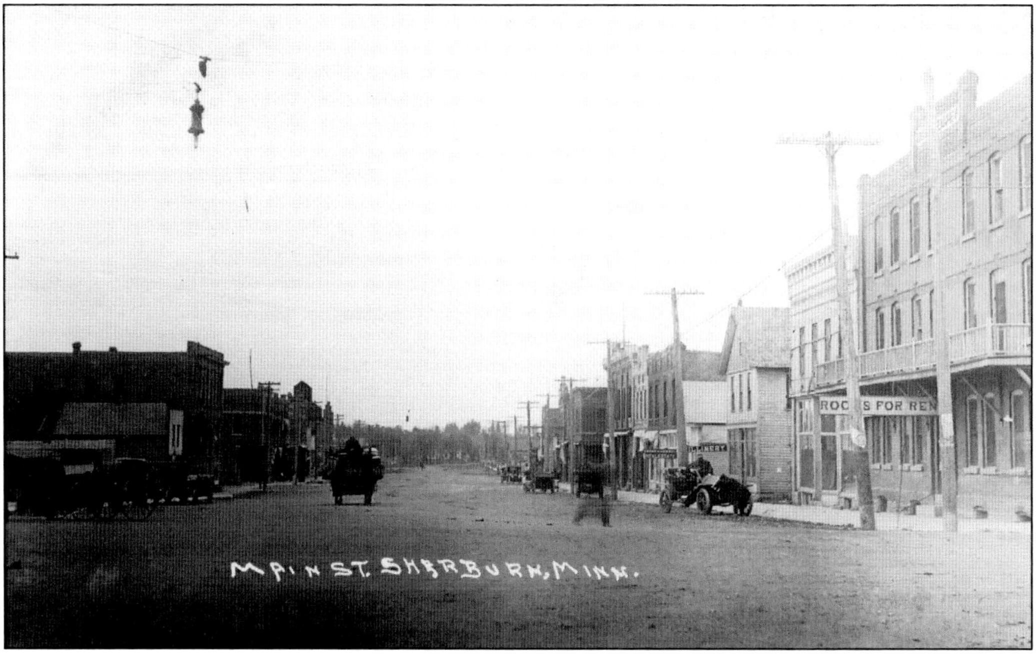

This is Main Street looking south in the second decade of the 20th century. Visible are horses and buggies and automobiles. On the right is the Smith Hotel, and three doors down is a millinery. The small wood structure next to it is the Cross and Gemmill Real Estate office.

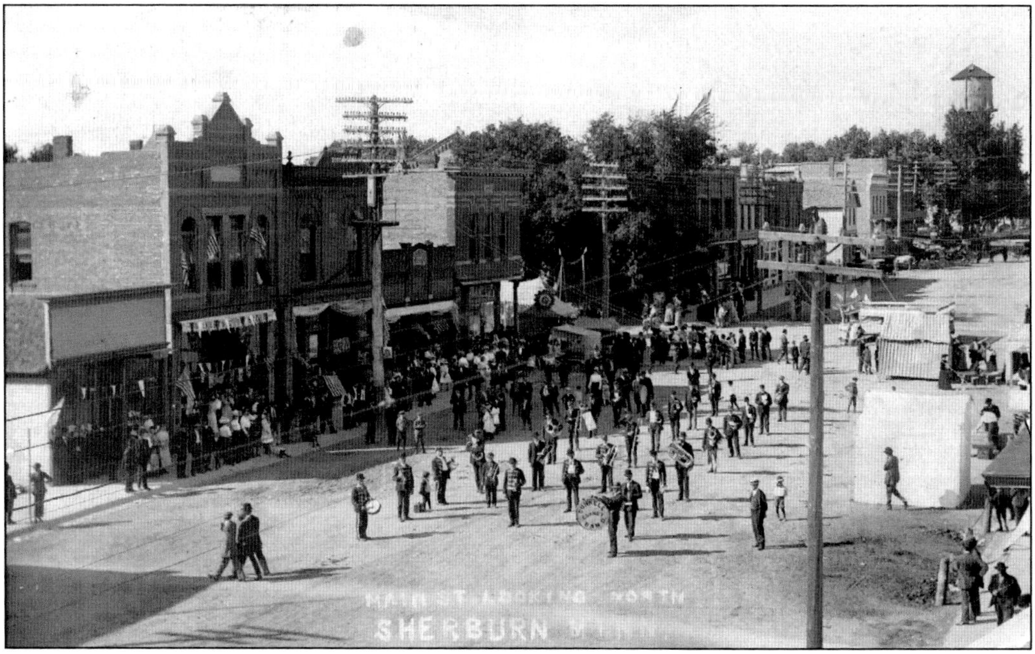

Here is Main Street looking north, probably for a July 4, 1909, celebration. This was postmarked in December 1909 and shows the Dunnell Cornet Band. The Dunnell Cornet Band must have been good; it shows up in quite a few old postcards. The first brick building is the Seifert Drug Store.

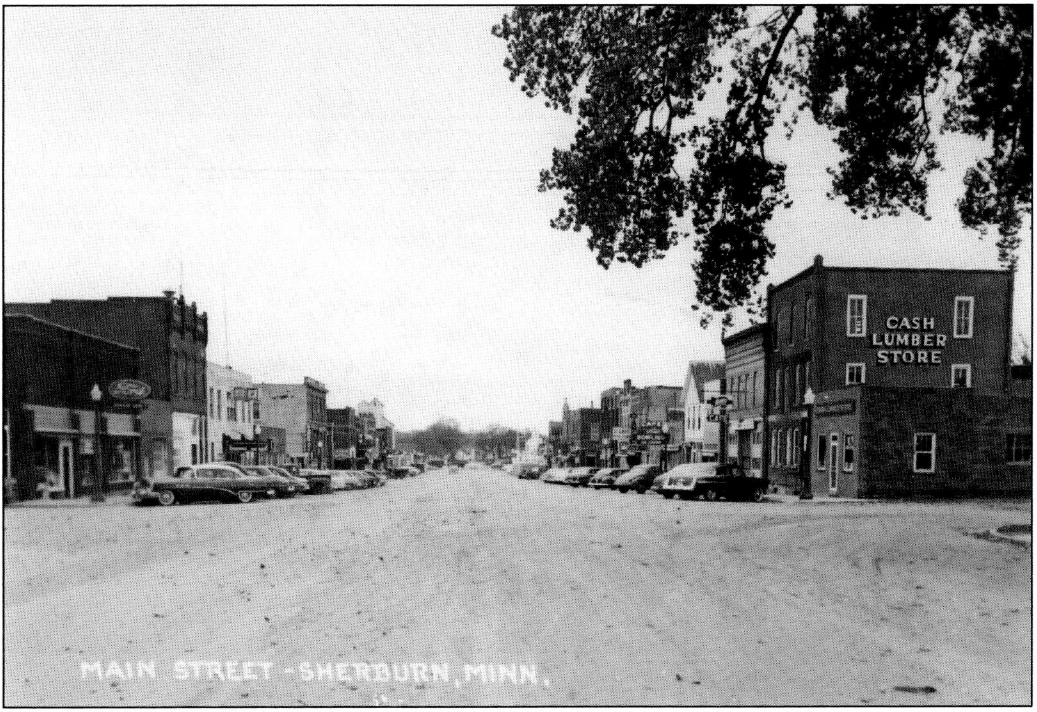

This is a much later postcard of Main Street, dated September 19, 1958. It was purchased by a traveler as a souvenir because they "Ate dinner in this town." On the left is the Ford garage, on the right in the first two buildings is the Cash Lumber Store, and the third building is a café.

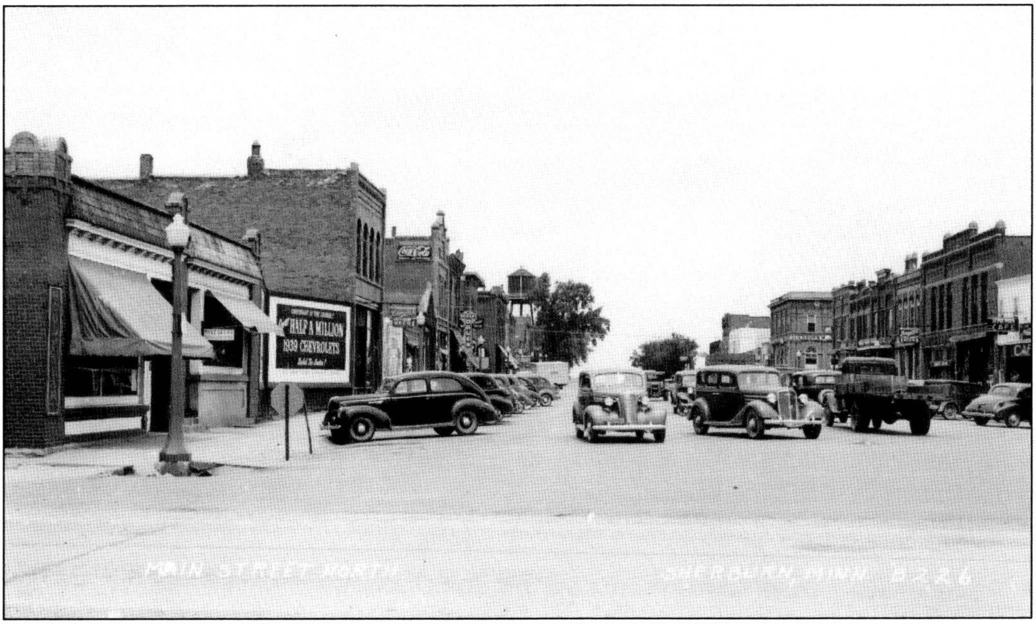

This is a 1939 view of Main Street when the post office was located in the first building on the left. The building to its right was a bar. A bar was also located on the right side in the first brick building. This was a thirsty and a busy town, as there appears to be three lanes of traffic.

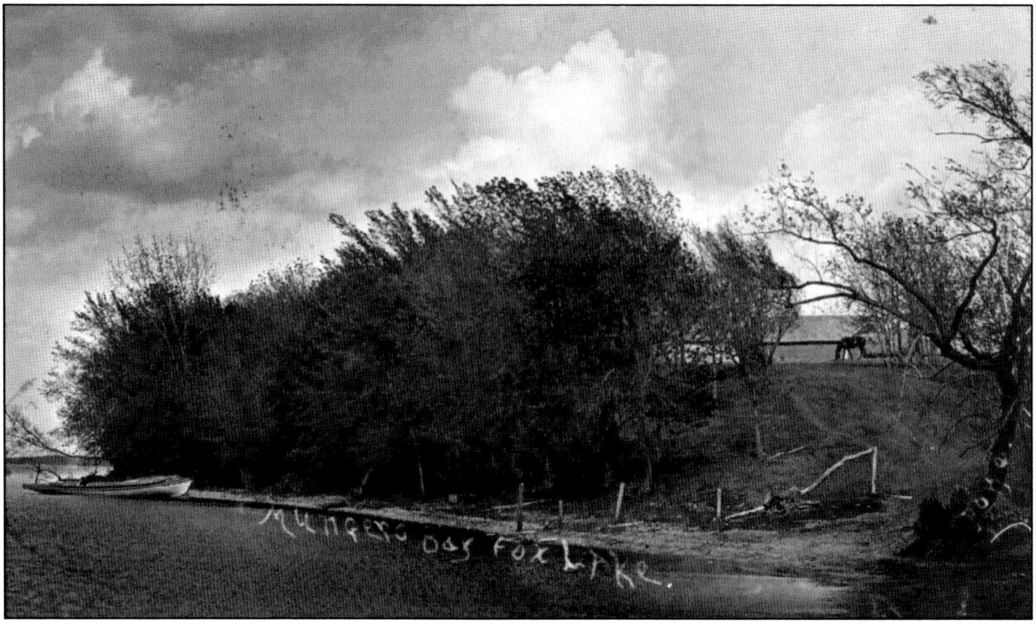

Fox Lake came into being when the Chicago and North Western Railway built a line in 1899 and named the town. The post office was established on May 13, 1901, and was the last one in the county to open. It closed in 1951 and then reopened as a rural contract station for five years. Mail was then assigned to Welcome. This is Munger's Bay before 1910. The boat on the far left is the *Maid of the Mist*.

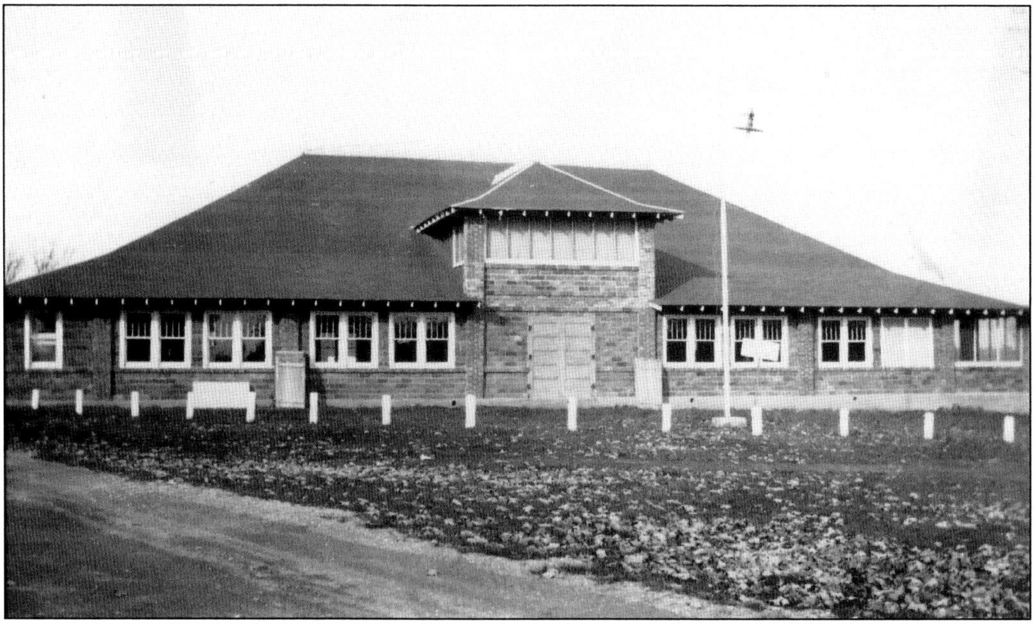

This is the pavilion at Fox Lake Park near Sherburn. According to an article in the *Sentinel*, it was built about 1928 and the photograph was taken in 1929. It was later known as the Fox Lake Ballroom. Toward the end of its life, it was purchased by Brian and LeeAnn Steen, who planned to raze it. They held a "last bash" party in the ballroom on October 22, 2005.

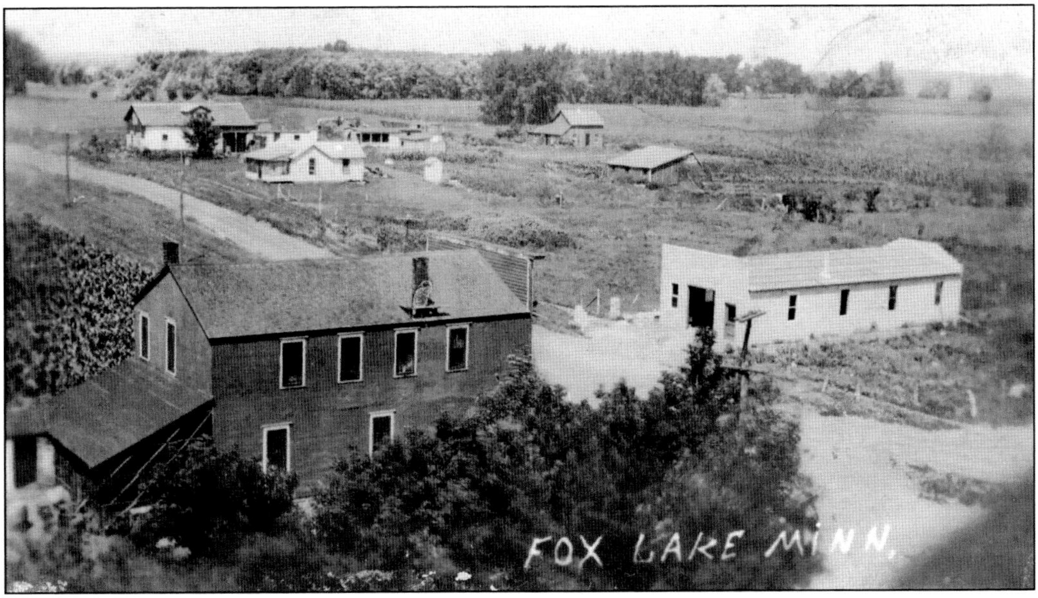

This is Main Street in Fox Lake. The building on the left is the Fox Lake Hotel. On the right is Harry Adam's Blacksmith Shop. The last building is the J. H. Queal Lumberyard built in 1916. Fox Lake was an amazing little town. It also had a bank, which opened in 1917 but closed shortly afterward in 1923. The Bingham Brothers Grain Elevator was built in 1916 but was moved to Manyaska in 1928. Some other businesses were the F. H. Oltman Dray Service, established in 1899; Tenhoff Restaurant, which burned in 1907; three saloons—Adams, Axtell, and McCartin; and Herman Schultz's Livery Barn (and he was Fox Lake's self appointed constable). There was even a steamer on Fox Lake owned by Valentine Ershfeld.

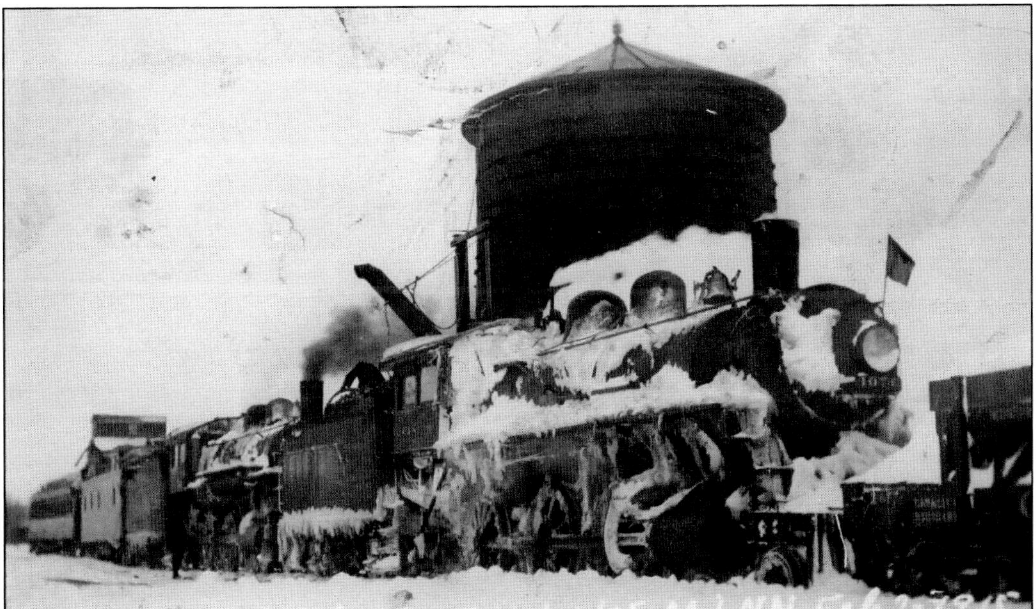

This shows the Chicago and North Western Railway snowplow at Fox Lake in 1915. A very similar water tank can be seen at Heritage Acres.

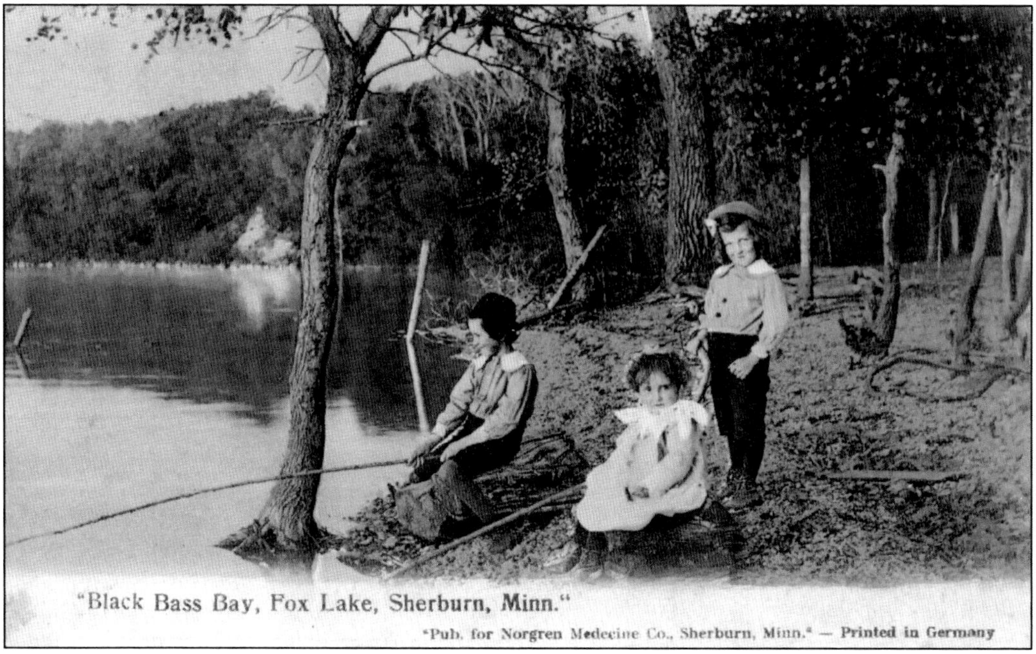

The Norgren Medicine Company of Sherburn had this postcard published around 1911. It was printed and hand colored in Germany and shows Black Bass Bay on Fox Lake.

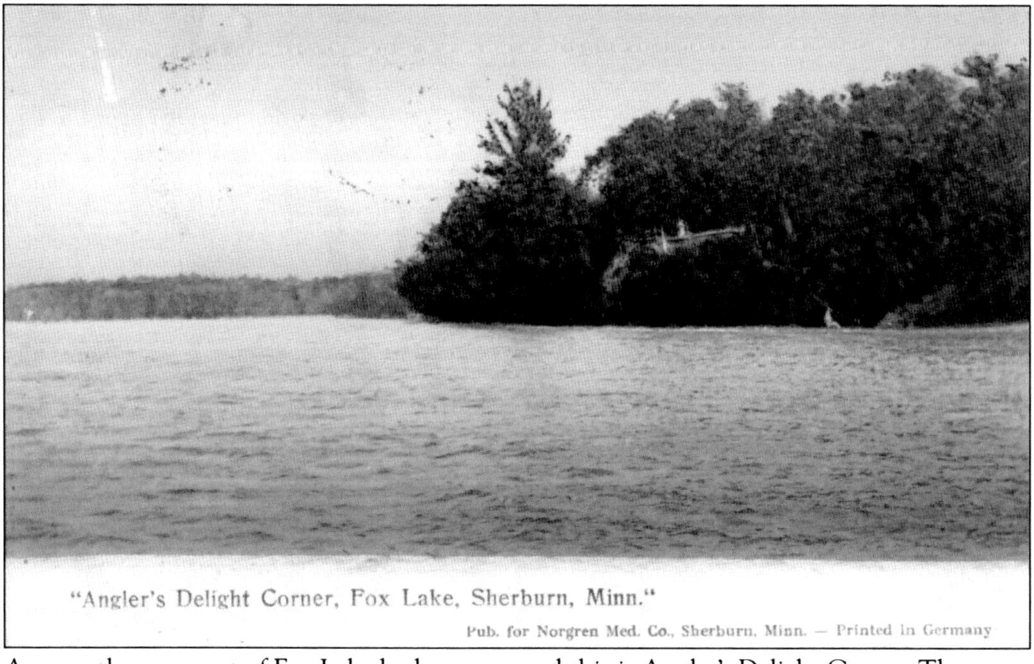

Apparently every part of Fox Lake had a name, and this is Angler's Delight Corner. There was also a Weber Island and a place called the Narrows on Fox Lake. This postcard was mailed on March 6, 1909.

Seven

SILVER LAKE TOWNSHIP

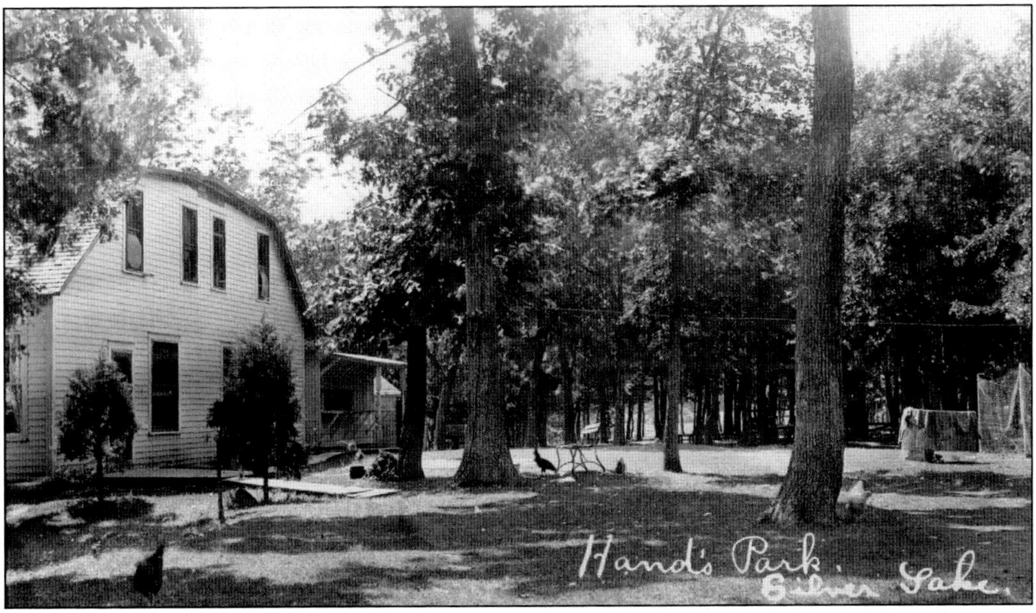

Ernest Hand opened Hand's Park in 1893 with two boats and a bathhouse. This is the main house, and the park, a landmark for more than 80 years, was just as popular as Interlaken. Silver Lake Township was also home to the village of Center Chain, West Side Summer Resort, and Fort Britt. Silver Lake was once called Precinct No. 1, along with four other townships. Its first real name was Fort Britt, but it was changed in 1860 to Nevada and again in 1863 to Silver Lake.

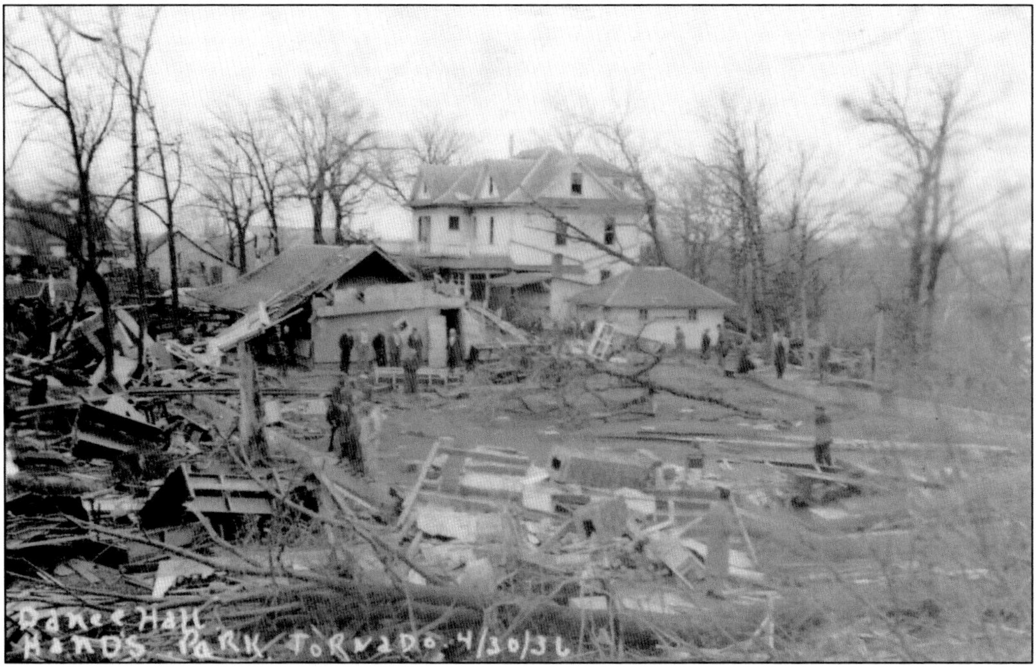

This photograph shows the Hand's Park tornado of 1936 and the remains of the dance hall, which was built in 1918. The tornado happened late in the afternoon around 5:00. It started in Sheldon, Iowa, and left a 20-mile-long area of devastation in Martin County. It went through Tenhassen, Silver Lake, East Chain, and Pleasant Prairie Townships and severely damaged over 100 farms. The National Guard was called out to keep the looters and souvenir hunters to a minimum. Raymond Schelmeski, Emmet Barnett, and Emma Detert were killed as a result of the storm.

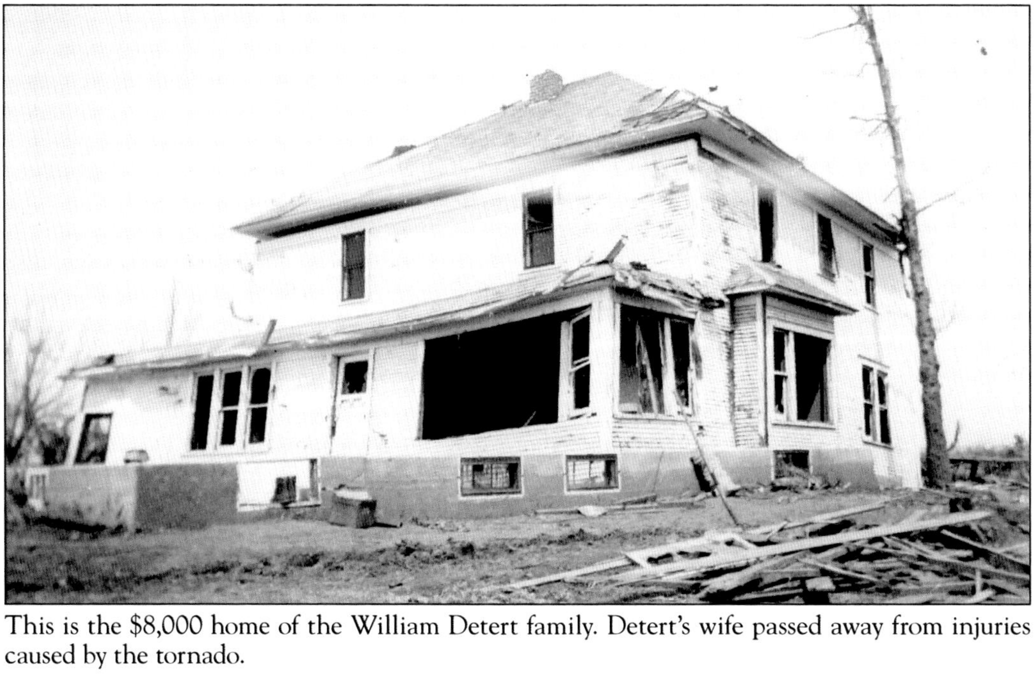

This is the $8,000 home of the William Detert family. Detert's wife passed away from injuries caused by the tornado.

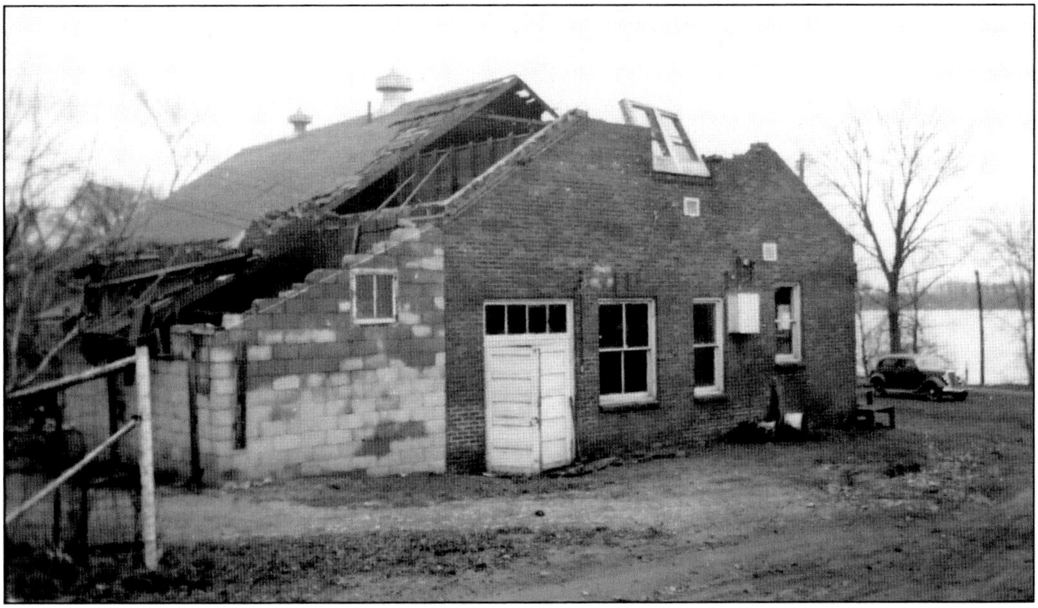

Here is the heavily damaged East Chain Creamery.

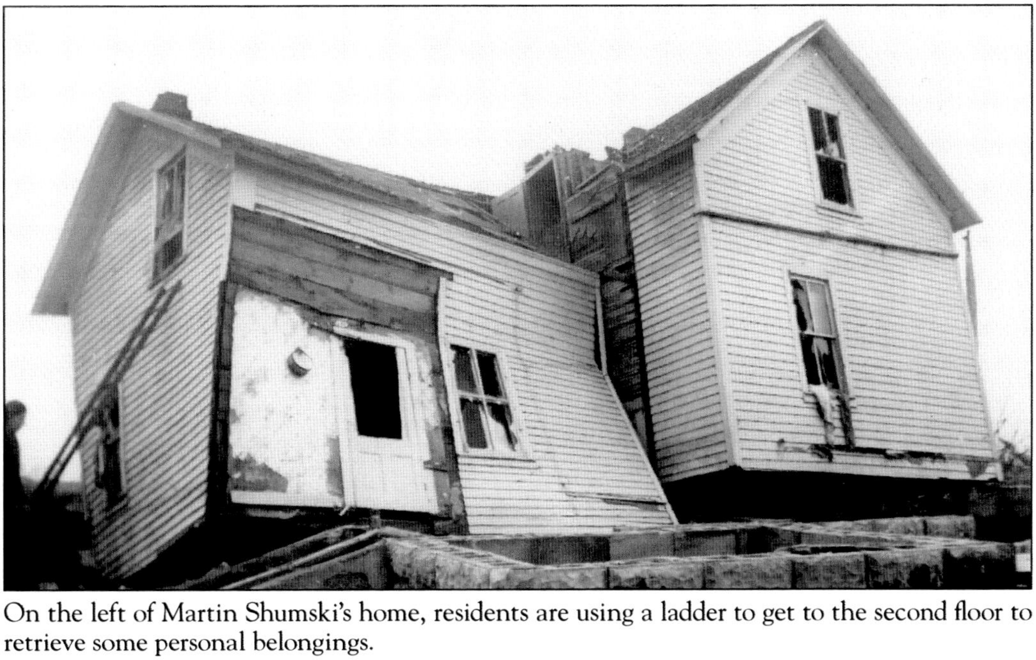

On the left of Martin Shumski's home, residents are using a ladder to get to the second floor to retrieve some personal belongings.

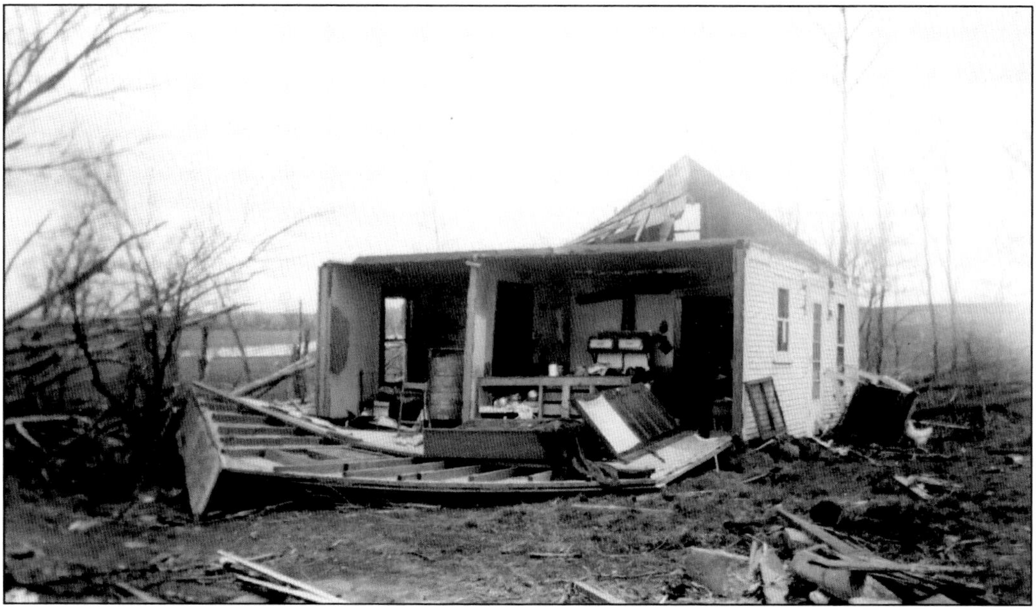

The Carl Sundberg family was in this house when the tornado picked it up and deposited it where a windmill once stood. The family tried to get to the cellar but was unable to due to the suction holding the door shut. Elsie Sundberg suffered the most with a broken collarbone and injured ankle, all while being five months pregnant. The family rebuilt, salvaging what they could.

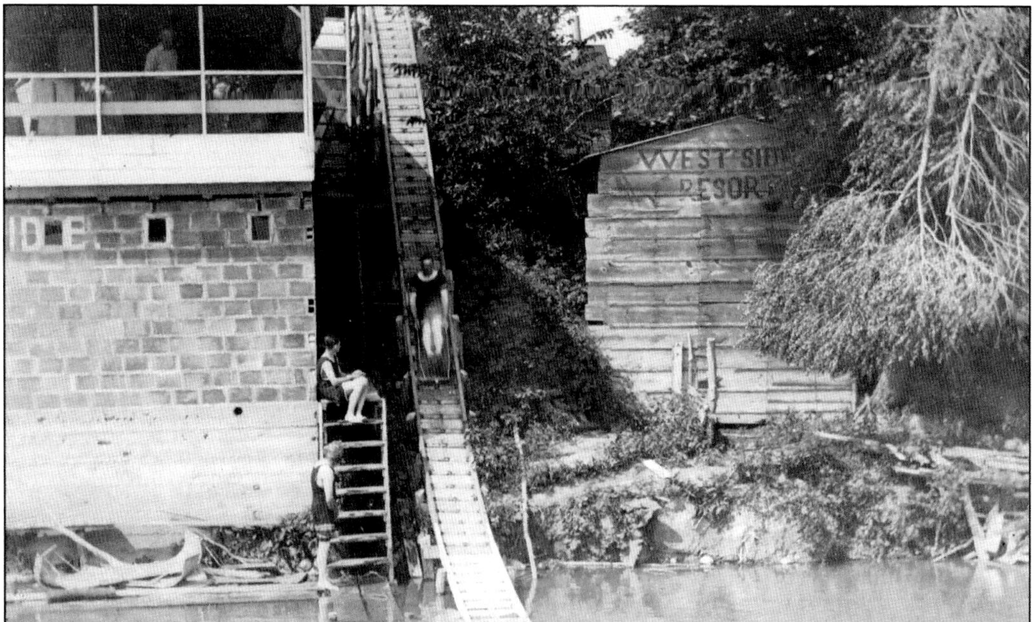

C. A. Personius was the proprietor of the West Side Summer Resort, which was located in section 31. One could have "Meals, Lunches, Candy, Cigars, Pop and Soft Drinks, Stable Room, Hay & Grain, Lodging, etc all at reasonable rates." Boats and free camping were also available, and visitors could play on the toboggan water slide. Personius was also a photographer and took many photographs of the Silver Lake area.

Eight

TRIUMPH AND MONTEREY

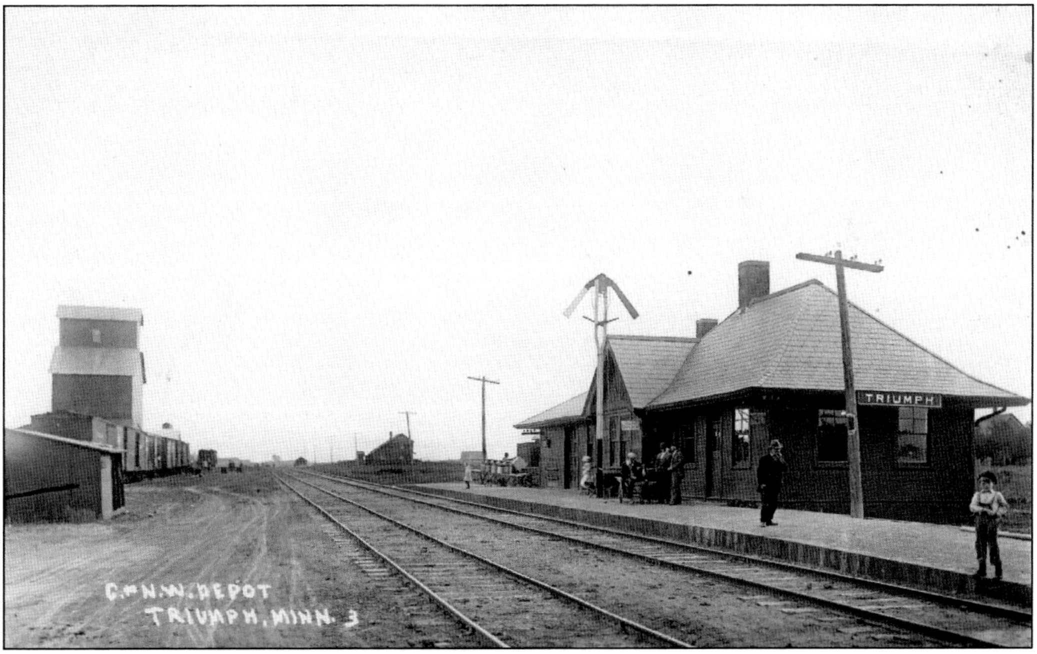

The boundaries of Triumph were first laid out on March 18, 1899, and the Chicago and North Western Railway depot (above) was built the same year. The first train was expected to arrive on July 28, 1899. Railroad service promptly began in earnest as by November Triumph had two freight and two passenger trains. Just a few months later in January 1900 the railroad began daily mail service to the new Triumph Station. By July 1900, this bustling new town had a newspaper, the *Triumph Progress*.

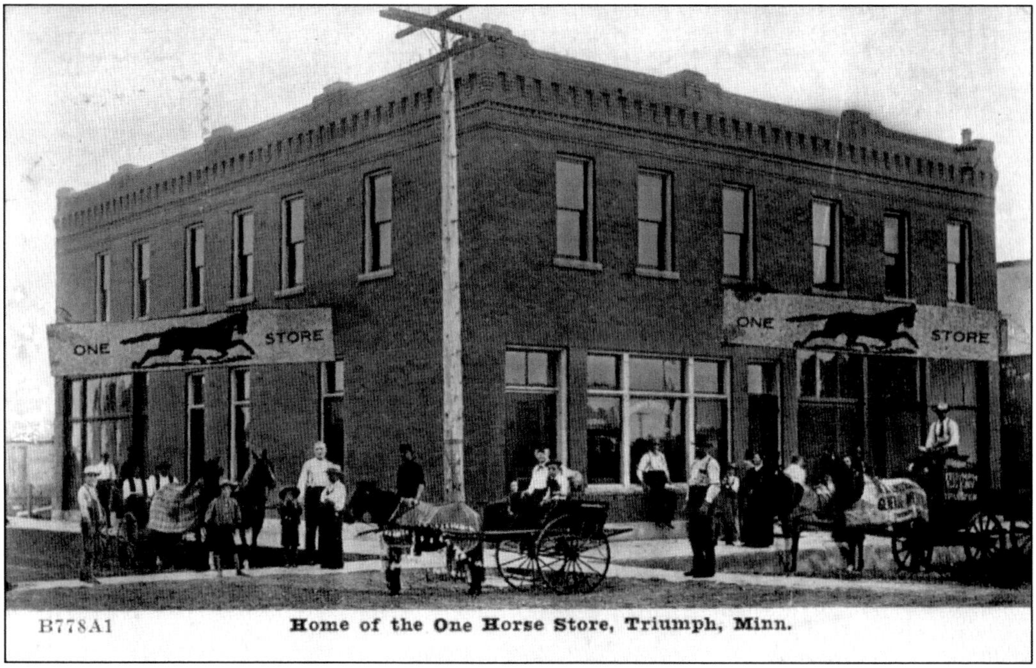

This postcard shows the Triumph State Bank and the One Horse Store. The bank was located on the left side of the building, and Tim Sammons's store was on the right. The One Horse Store first opened in Monterey in 1901, and Sammons moved the business to Triumph in 1908.

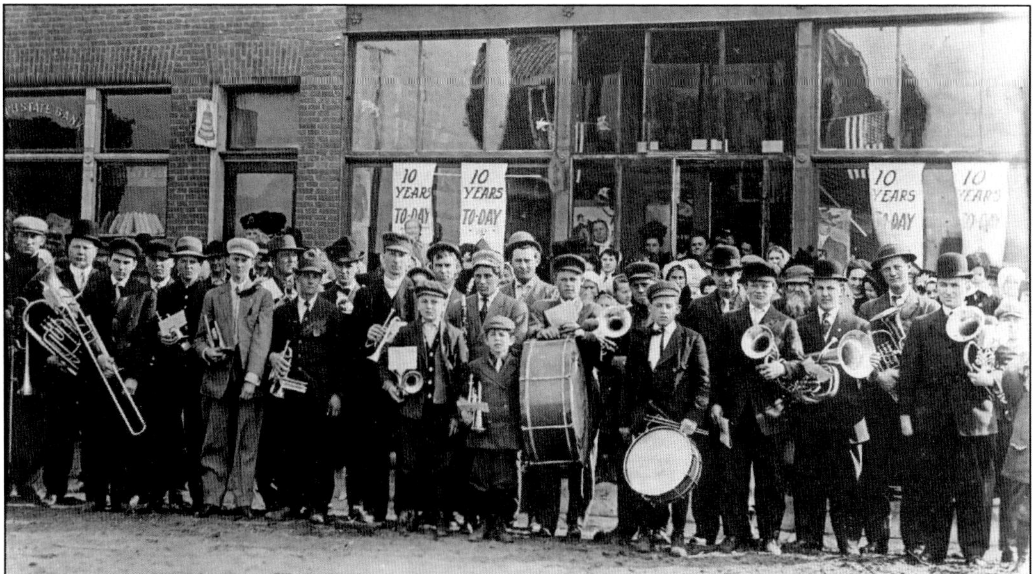

This is a souvenir postcard of the 10th anniversary celebration of the One Horse Store on March 25, 1911. From left to right are Jack Pixler, Ernest Holmquist, Arthur Pope, George Blomquist, Edward Niedorf, Marvin Pixler, Tory Peterson, Clarence Edhlund, Albert Umhoefer, Gus Bork, Cliff Umhoefer (front, center), Eskil Gradberg, Cecil Cole, Ted Pope (next to bass drum), George Krumwiede, Walter Larson, Casey or August Krumwiede, Percy Rippel (with snare drum), Arthur Uhrhammer, Aaron Rippel, A. H. Esse, Otis Olson, and Henry Bergesen.

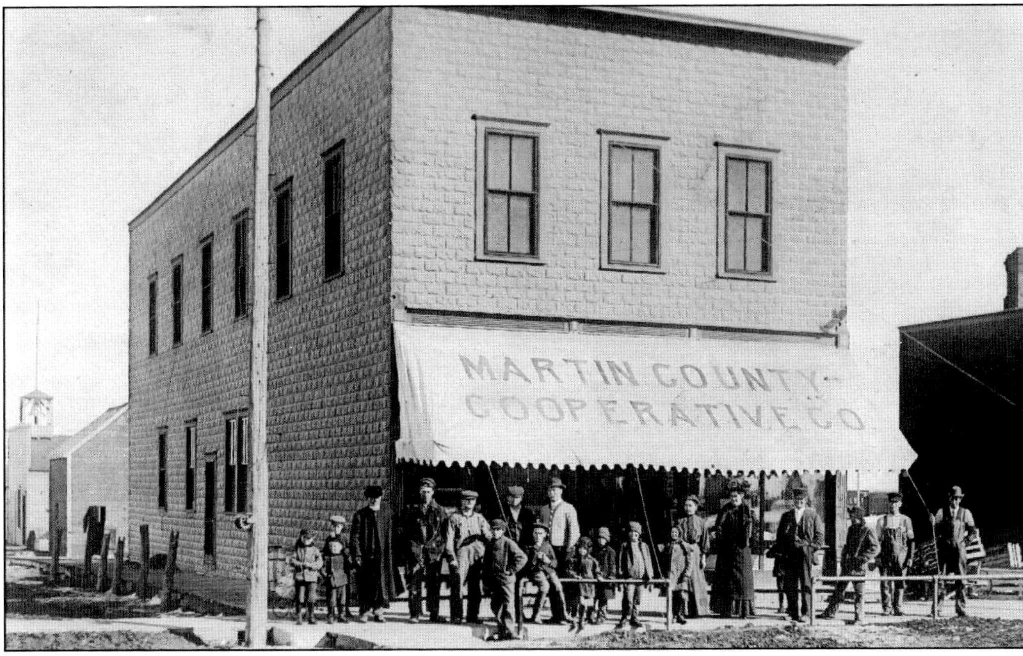

This is the Martin County Cooperative Company about 1908. The building doubled in size with an almost identical addition in 1909. The section shown here was built in 1900.

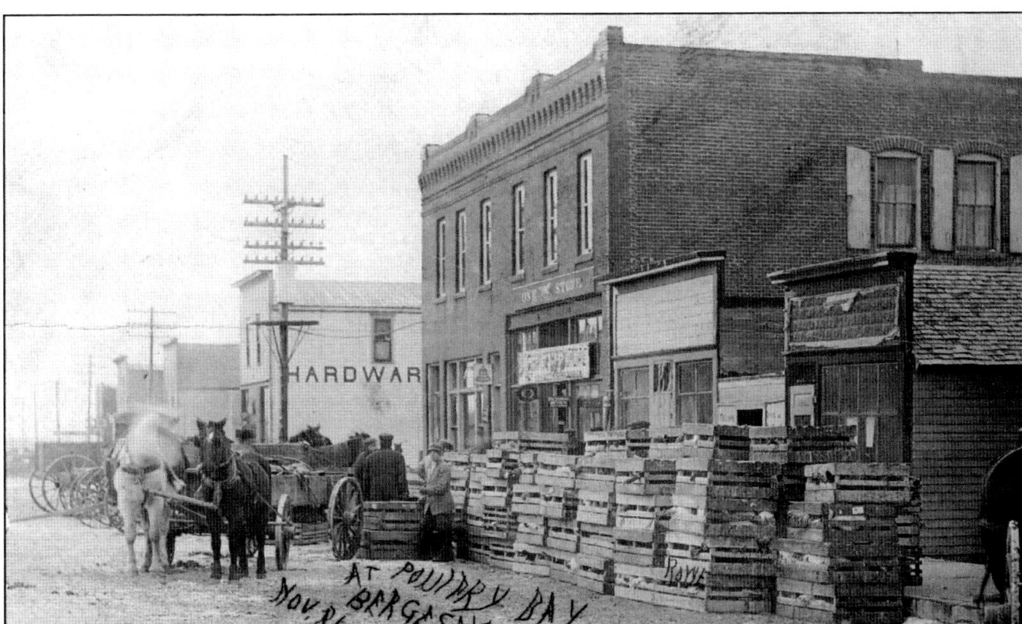

This is a photograph of Poultry Day at Bergesen's on November 18, 1911. The business was located in the first building on the right. The second (very short) building from the right is the Triumph Post Office. The brick structure housed the Triumph State Bank, which opened in 1901, and the One Horse Store.

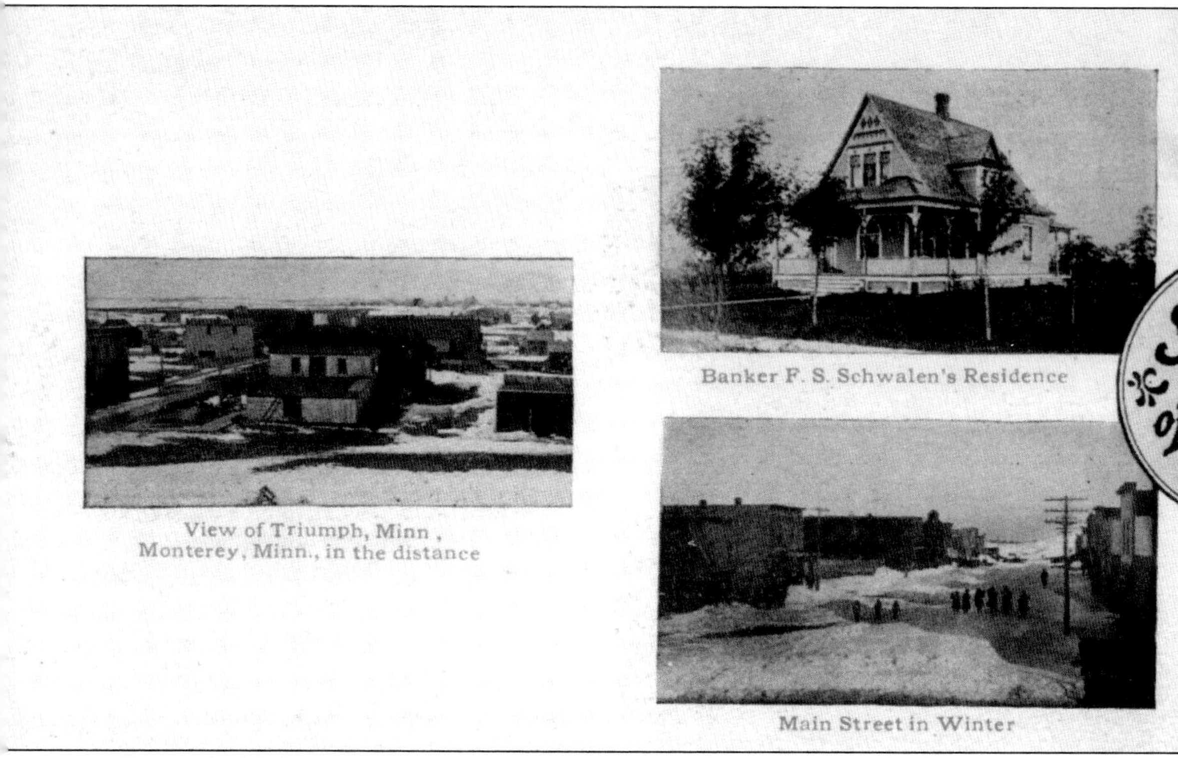

This is a double-length, hand-colored postcard postmarked on June 26, 1912, from the Monterey Post Office. It has six different views of Triumph, one of which was taken during the Fourth of

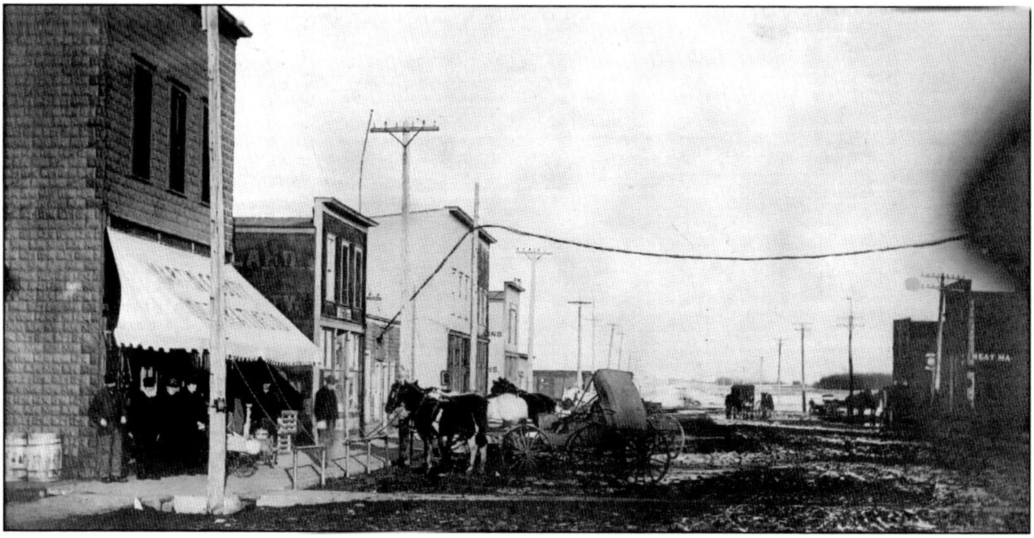

Here is Triumph's Main Street about 1908. Theodore Lundberg, a prominent Galena Township farmer who emigrated from Lumholt, Sweden, wanted to name the new town Lumholt. (Note that Lumholt is probably a misspelling and likely refers to Lammhult, Sweden.) John Steen wanted it named after the Triumph Creamery Company, of which he was a shareholder. John Steen had the honor of naming the new town. The neighboring towns of Triumph and Monterey became Trimont in 1959.

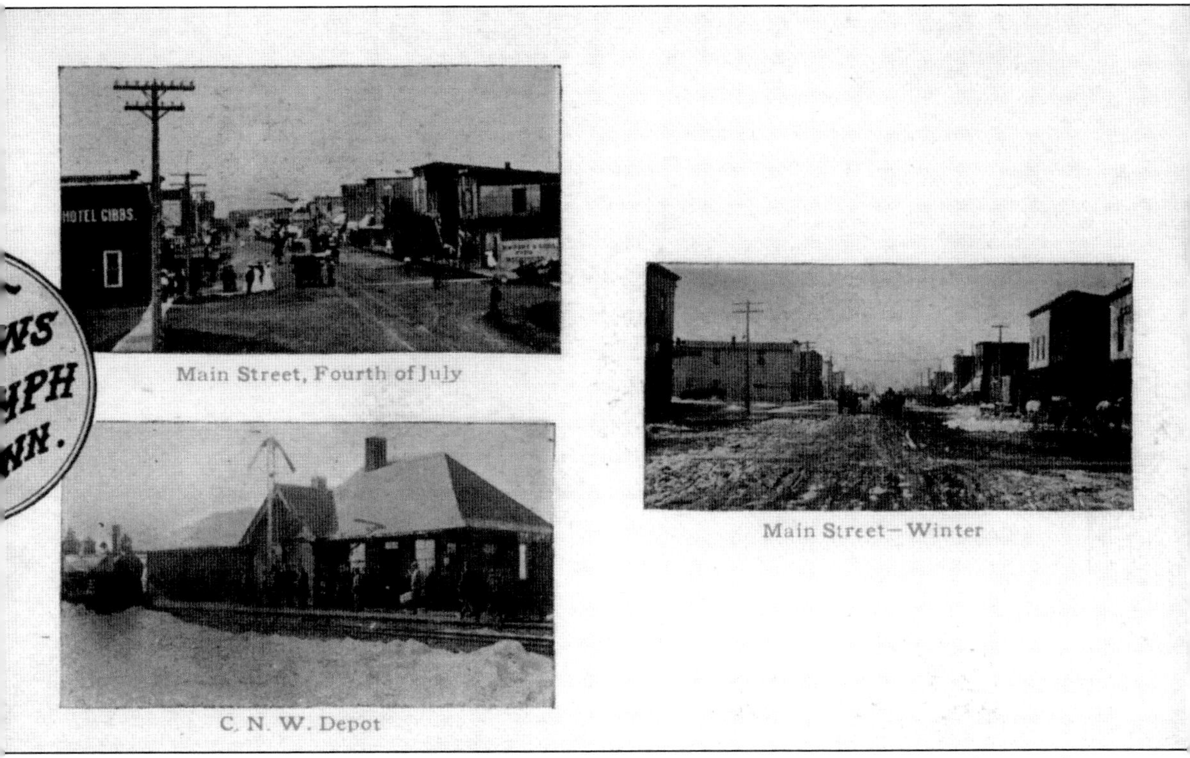

July celebration. The depot, built in 1899, and the residence of the banker F. S. Schwalen are also shown. The Triumph State Bank opened in 1901, and Schwalen was the cashier.

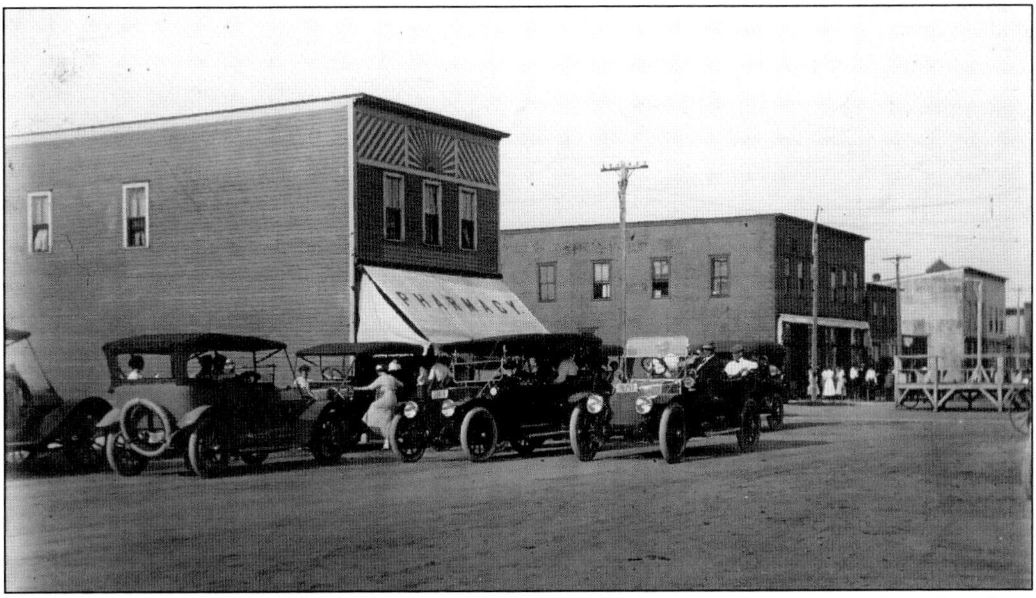

This postcard was postmarked in 1919, and the picture does not date too much earlier than that, judging by the cars. The building with the starburst front was A. D. Catlin's Drug Store, which was constructed in 1904. Catlin moved his business to Sherburn in 1908, and the building became the Stockdill Drug Store. According to Walter Carlson, the structure burned in 1932.

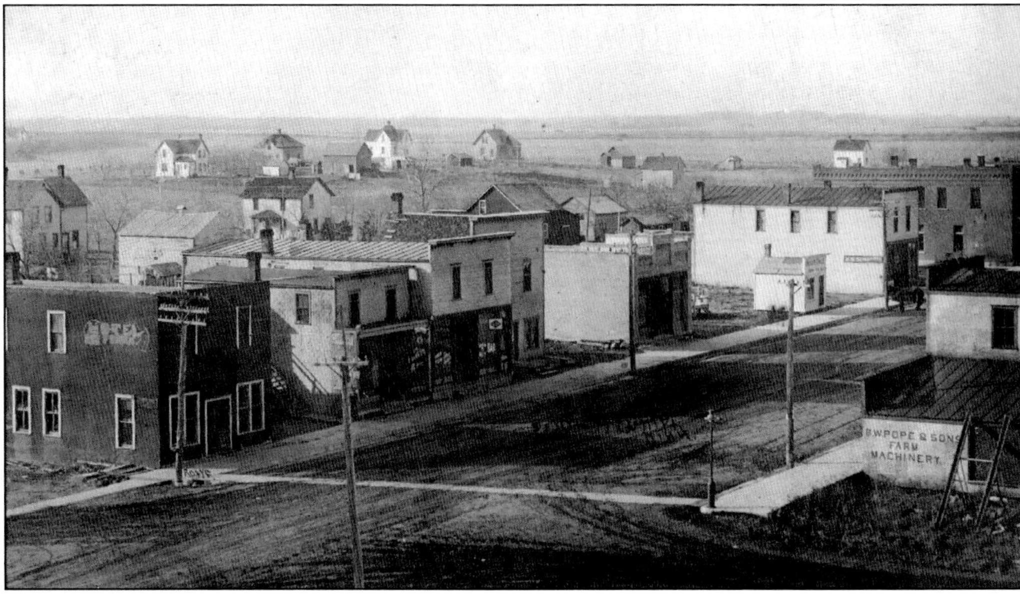

Shown here is Triumph's Main Street about 1908. B. W. Pope Implement (seen at the first building on right) began business in 1900. In 1901, the business expanded and took over the livery barn and also added a full line of bicycles. The business was booming, and Pope's sons joined him in 1901. The next year, they built an implement shed and decided to sell the livery to concentrate on the implement dealership. They sold out to John Groth in 1908. The fourth building on the left (set back from the rest) was Wally Wellcome's restaurant, built in 1899. Walter Carlson claims this was the first building in Triumph; however, the Trimont Centennial book claims the C. J. Anderson building was the first. The second and third buildings were saloons.

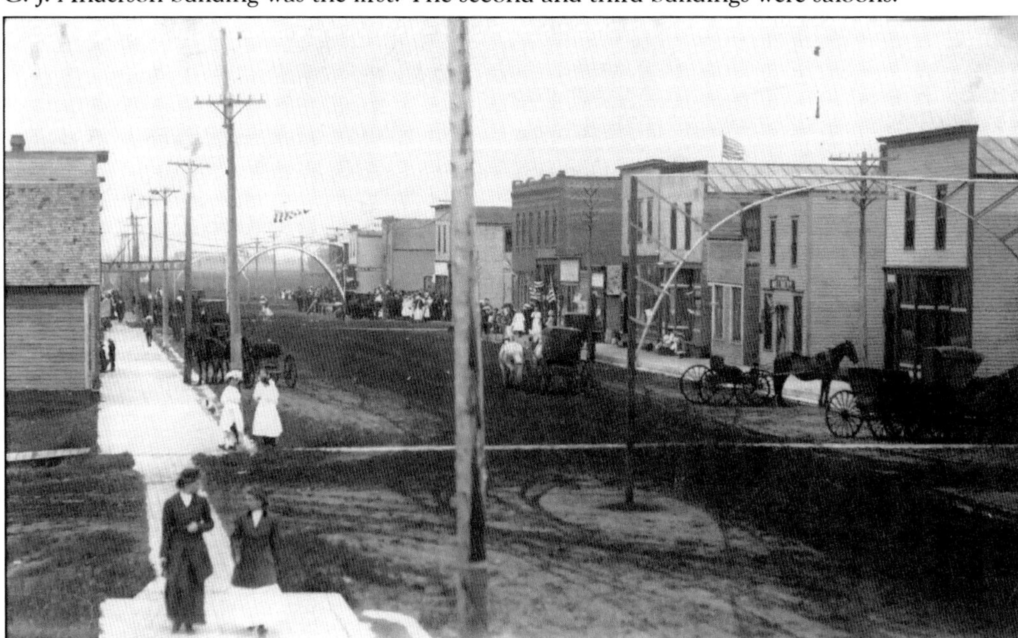

This is the opposite side of the street from what is seen in the above photograph, showing the 1907 Fourth of July celebration about to begin.

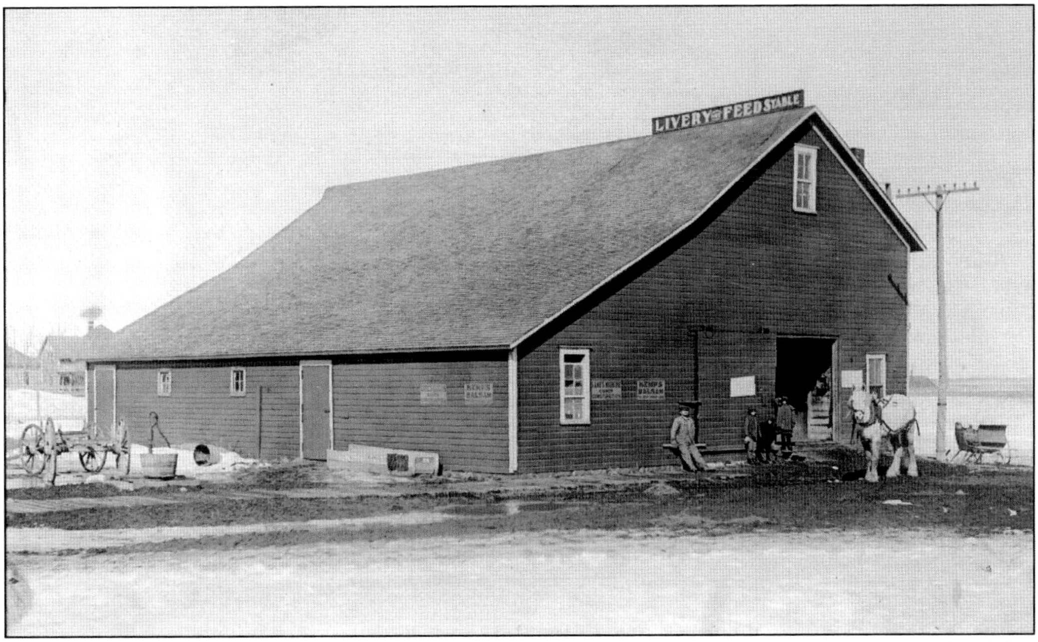

The Triumph Livery Barn was built in 1900 by F. E. Glines. In 1901, Pope took control of this livery and feed stable. B. W. Pope and Son also had a farm implement and machine business with a livery in connection. This is believed to be that livery.

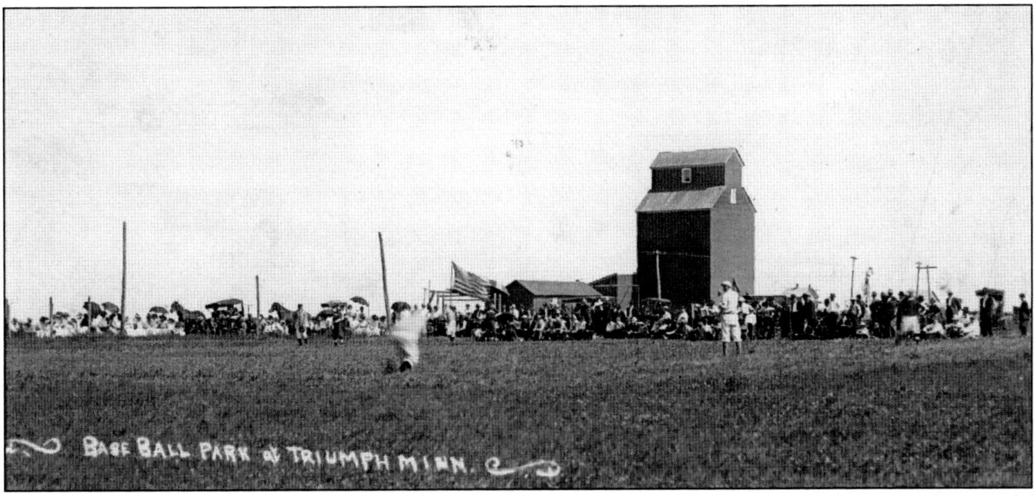

A baseball game is being played in this photograph at the Triumph Baseball Park. This could possibly be the game between Triumph and Sherburn in July or August 1909.

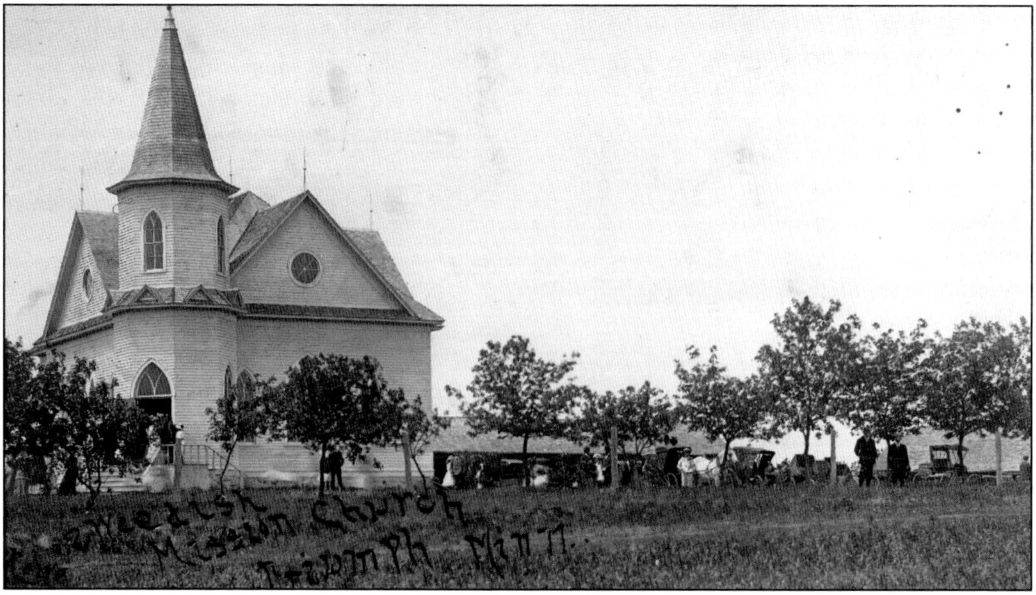

This is the first Swedish Mission Church in rural Triumph. Throughout the 1890s, this congregation used the rural Methodist church for its services until this church was built in 1901. Shortly thereafter, the church steeple was struck by lightning and caught fire. In order to save the church, the parishioners decided to chop the supports and topple the bell tower. The photograph above dates from about 1908 and shows the rebuilt steeple. In 1924, the Trinity Lutheran congregation purchased this vacated church and moved it into town.

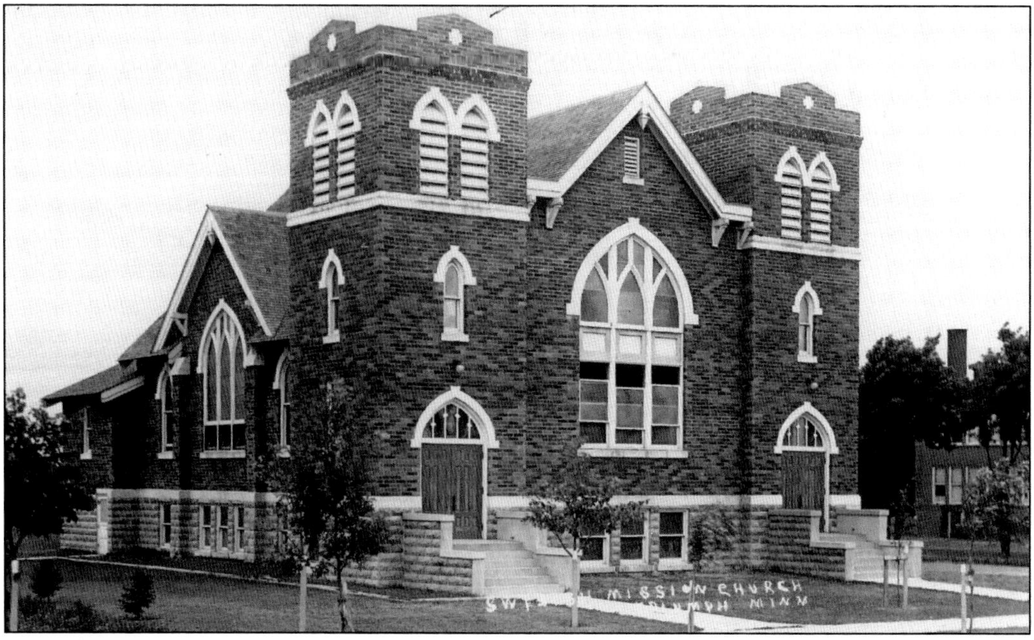

According to a 1988 Martin County history book, the Swedish Evangelical Mission Covenant Church was founded in 1885. The congregation decided to move into town and built this church in 1921. The edifice was razed and replaced by the current church in 1975. The congregation built a parsonage in 1927.

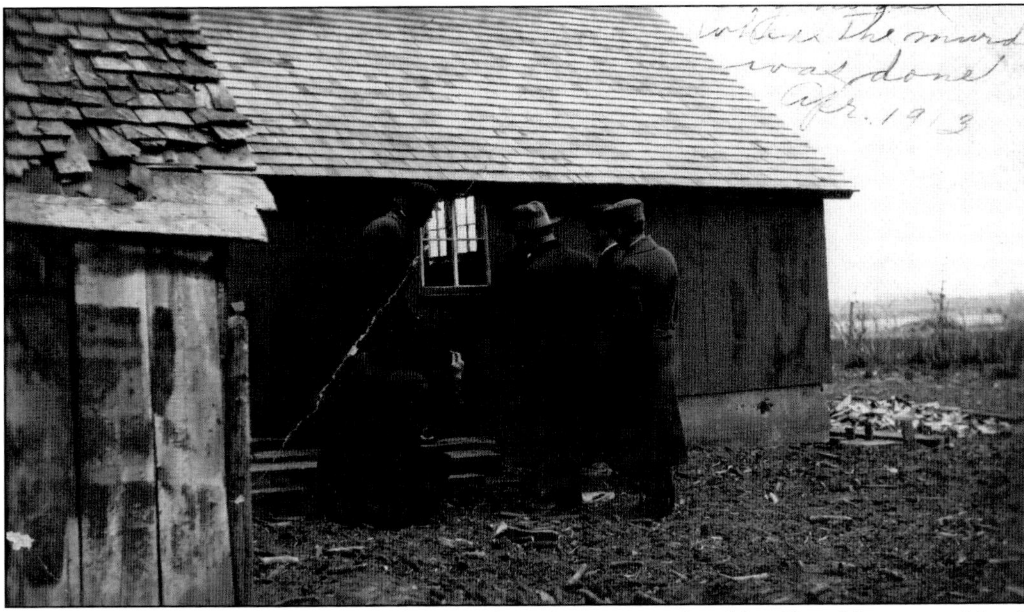

This postcard is of John Steen's hog house, where he was murdered by Chris Virgins on May 8, 1913. Apparently Virgins tried unsuccessfully to murder Steen at least twice before this. He once shot at Steen but only hit his mailbox. Another time, he tried poison beef that was hung in the Steen grove to cure, and he did manage to kill the Steen family dog. The third time, he took aim and shot Steen through the window where the men are standing above. Steen was so well known in Martin County that the trial was moved to Blue Earth.

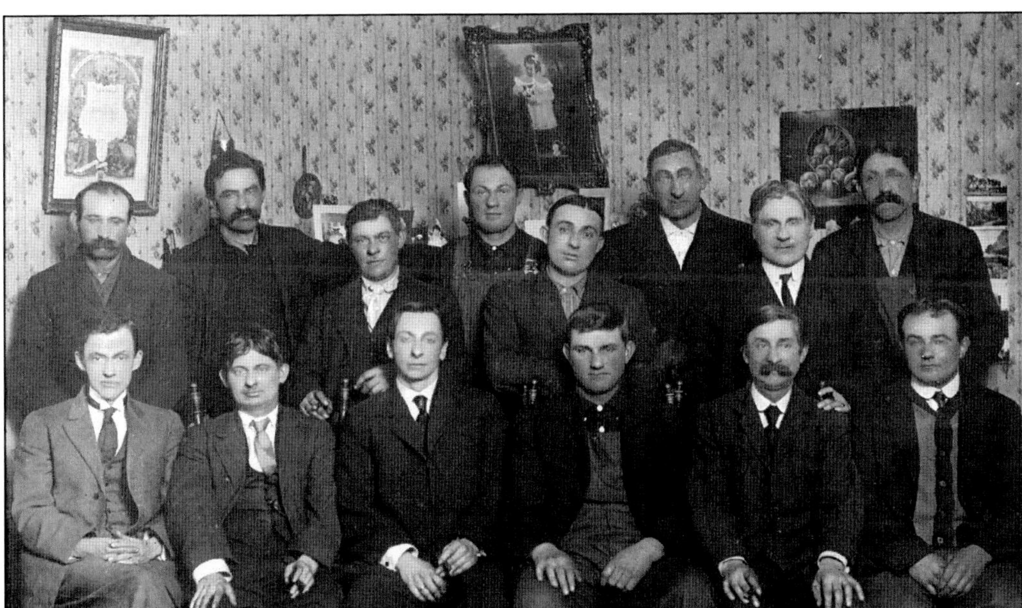

Here are the Modern Woodman of America lodge members of Triumph. Steen is in the back row, second from left. After Steen's death, the lodge was draped in black for 30 days.

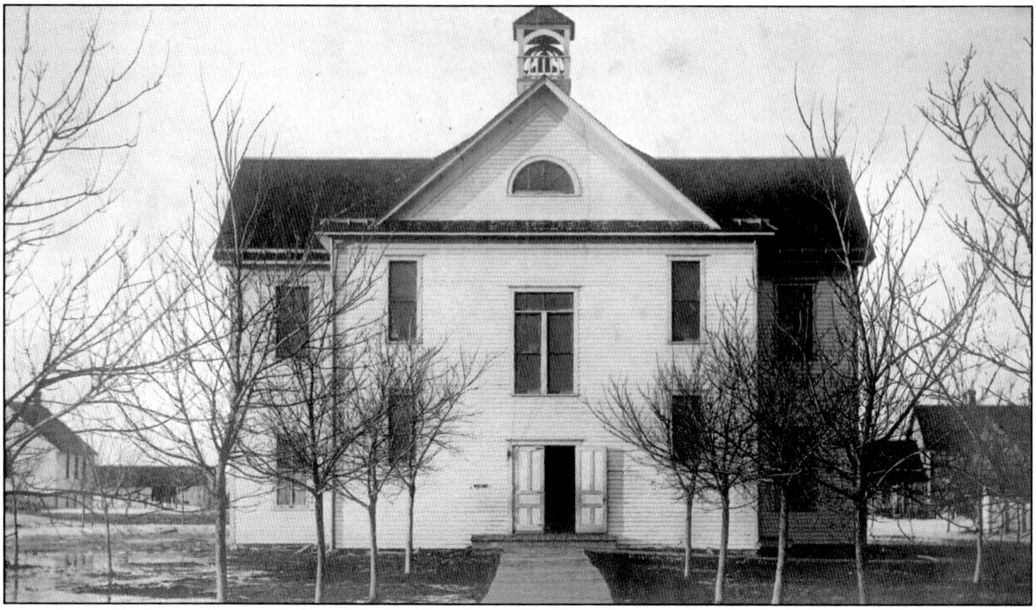

Monterey began in 1899 when the Minneapolis and St. Louis Railroad set up a station. The name Allen was suggested for the town, but Monterey was decided on. The Monterey Post Office was established on December 28, 1899. Monterey had two banks, and both of them had the luck of being robbed. The Peoples State Bank had its safe blown up on April 27, 1908, and the Farmers State Bank was held up by armed robber James Charleson in December 1939. It was believed to be his first robbery. This school was built in 1901 and was destroyed by fire on October 31, 1909. The cause was believed to be lightning.

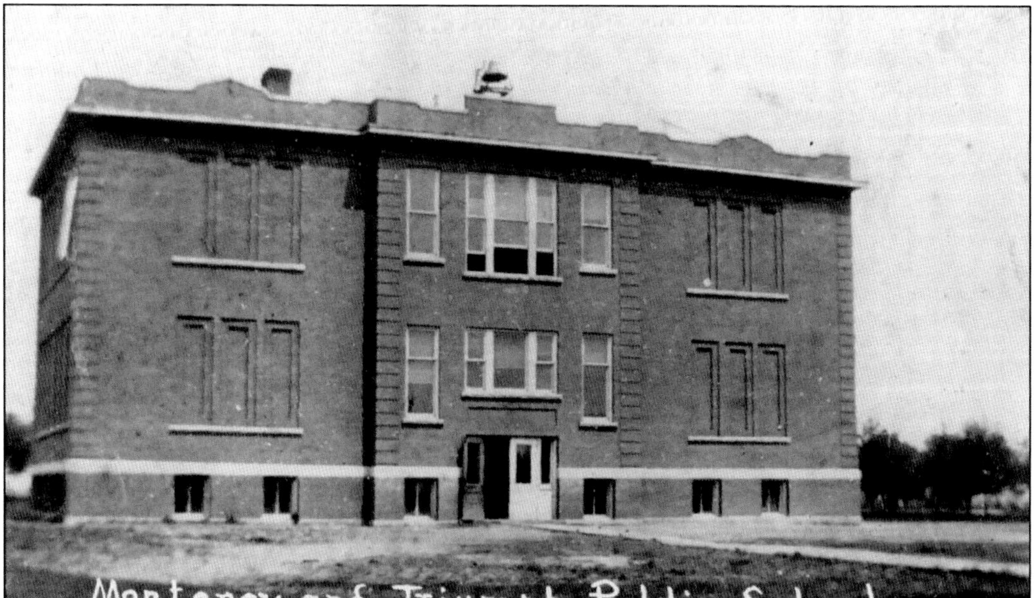

The Tri-Mont School District No. 118 was organized on January 8, 1901. In 1910, this new brick structure was built, but it was still not a high school. However, by 1916, the 10th grade was added, and 1924 saw the first graduating class.

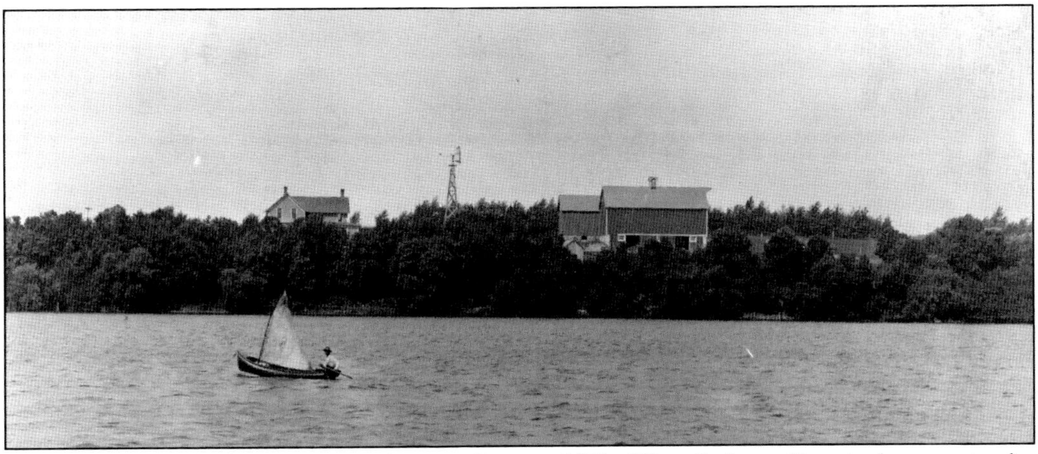

Here is Cedar Lake by Monterey, showing Bert and Ella Wetzel's farm. Bert is the man in the boat. This was believed to be located at the John Forstrom residence at 640 190th Street in section 36 of Cedar Township.

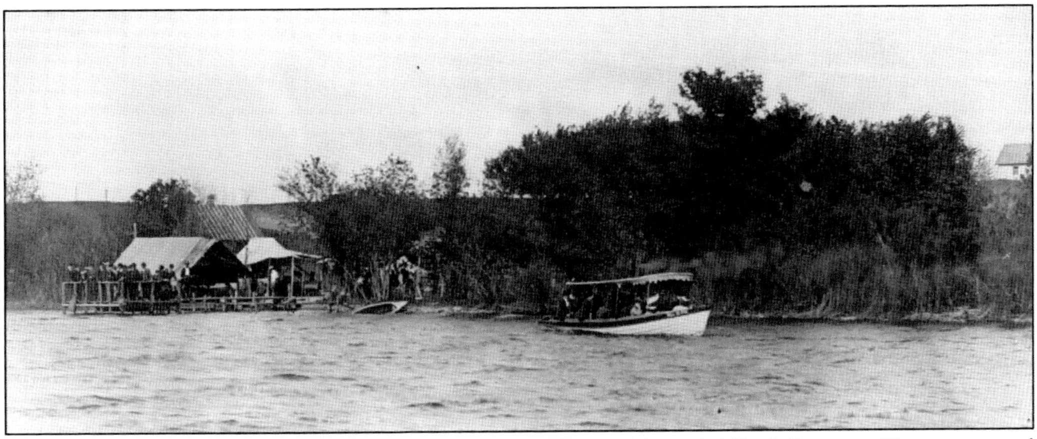

Cedar Lake, near Monterey, had a summer resort. This is Morey Miller's Summer Resort around 1910. Miller and his wife opened it in 1905.

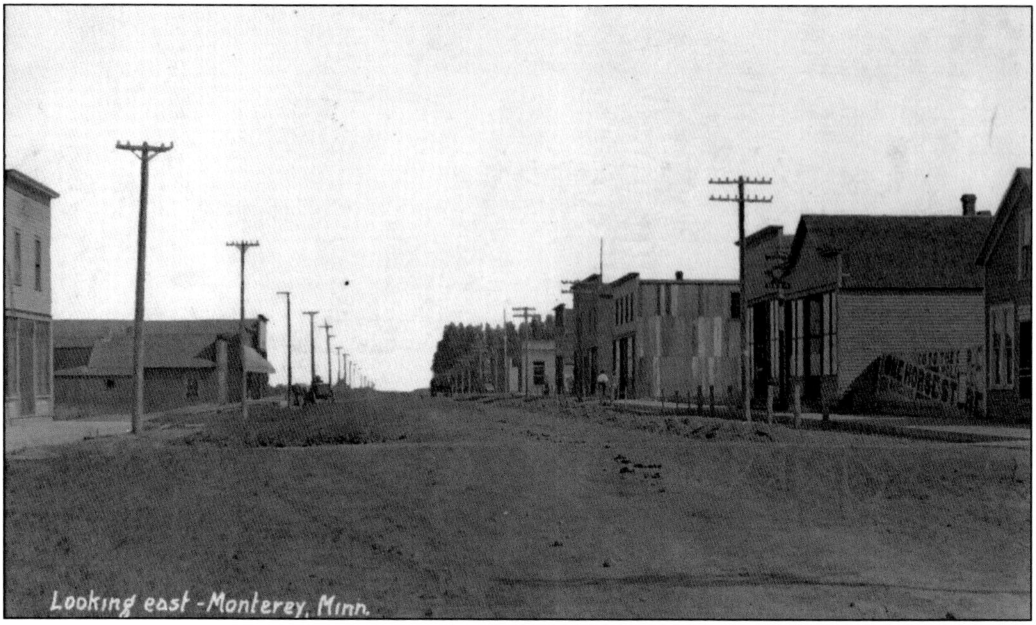

Here is the Main Street of Monterey looking east about 1909. The very first building (partially cut off) on the right is the post office. The building second from the right is a saloon. The very last building is the Peoples State Bank.

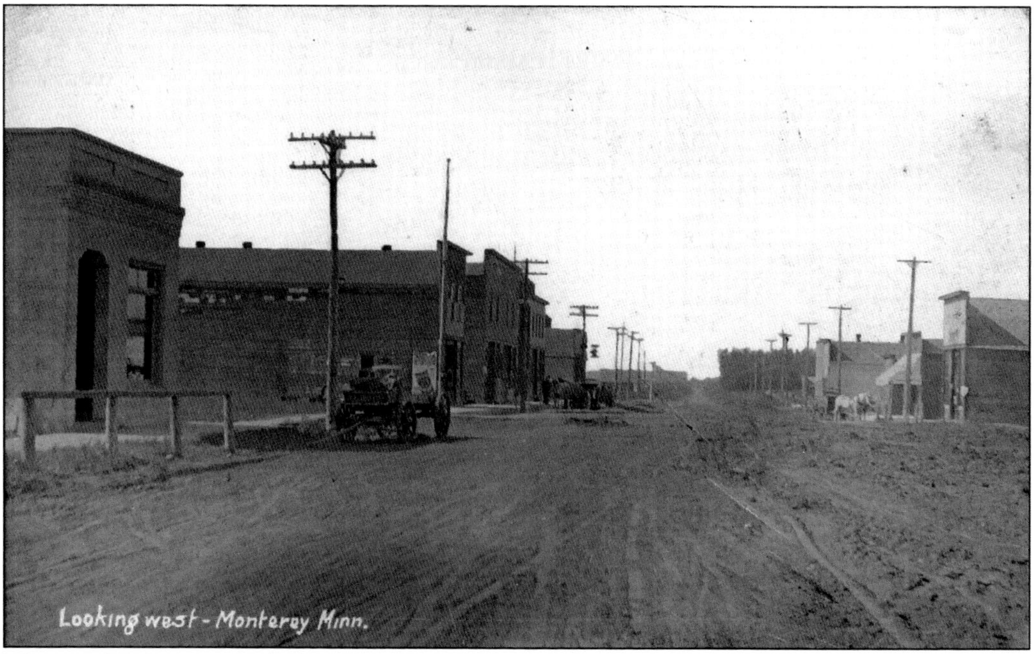

Monterey's Main Street looking west about 1909 is shown here. The first building on the left was constructed in 1904. This housed the Peoples State Bank, which originally was called the Peoples Bank of Monterey before 1903. In March 1908, robbers took $1,485 after blowing up the safe. It has not been recorded when this bank first started or closed.

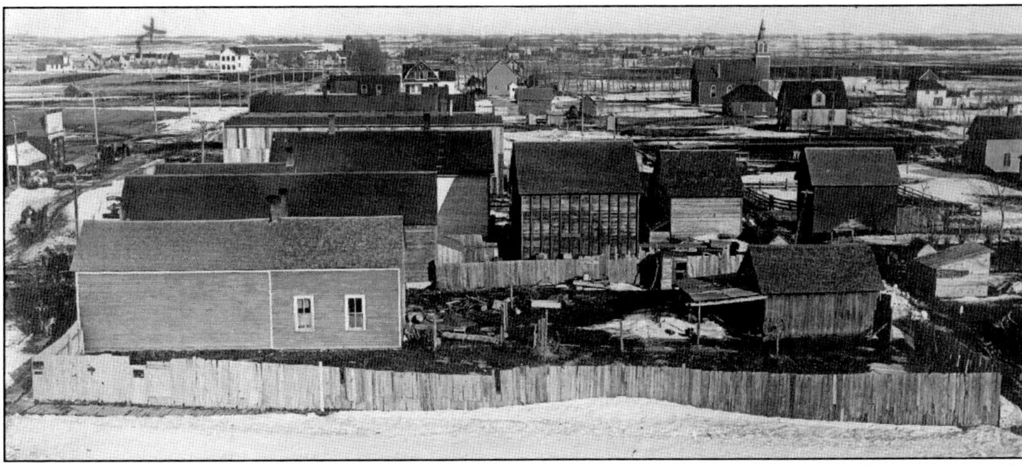

This view of Monterey was taken about 1909, and Triumph can be seen in the distance. On the far right is the Catholic church, which is now the Trimont Historical Society. The schoolhouse can be seen toward the left, and almost in the middle is Dr. Joseph Butz's residence and office. Butz came to Monterey in 1903 and built this home. It was also used as a hospital in 1906.

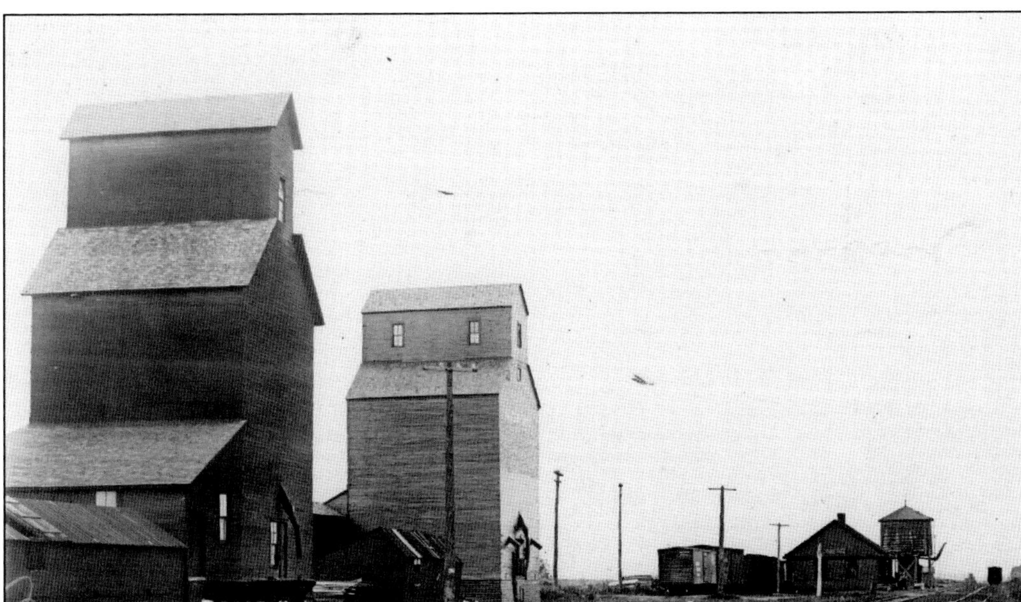

This postcard is hand dated March 16, 1916, which was almost 17 years after the first train came into Monterey on November 1, 1899. These two elevators were acquired by the Monterey Farmers Elevator Company (which began in 1905) by 1915. In 1918, they reorganized and became the Farmers Cooperative Elevator Company. A serious misfortune struck in 1934 when the elevator on the left was destroyed by fire. Gilbert Satter managed this from 1910 to 1930; Walter Benson was manager from 1930 to 1945 and Otto Isler from 1945 for many years later.

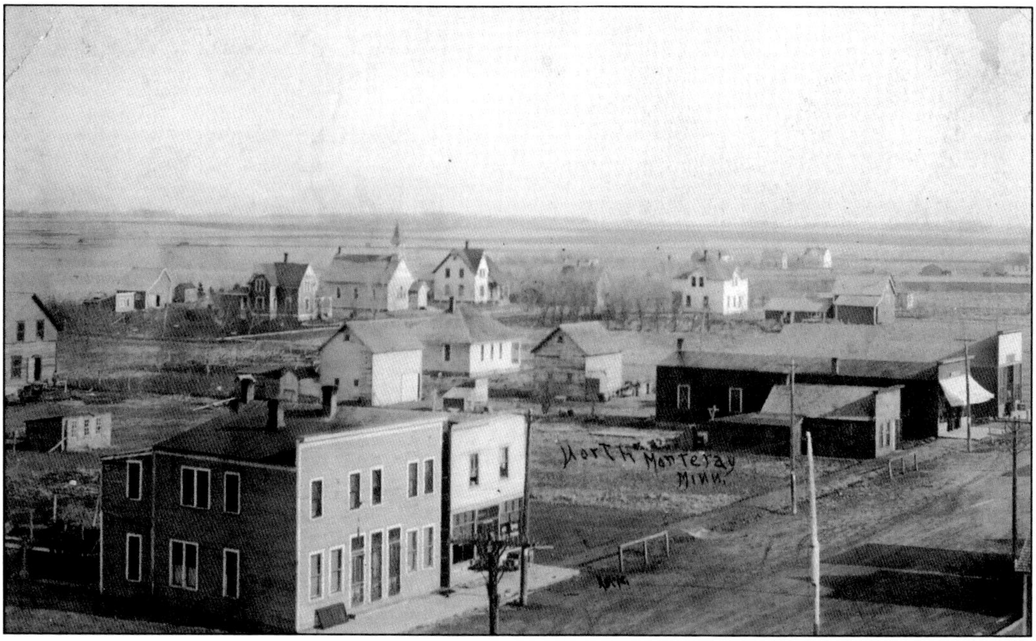

This is a bird's-eye view of Monterey about 1909 looking east. The Baptist church is in the background.

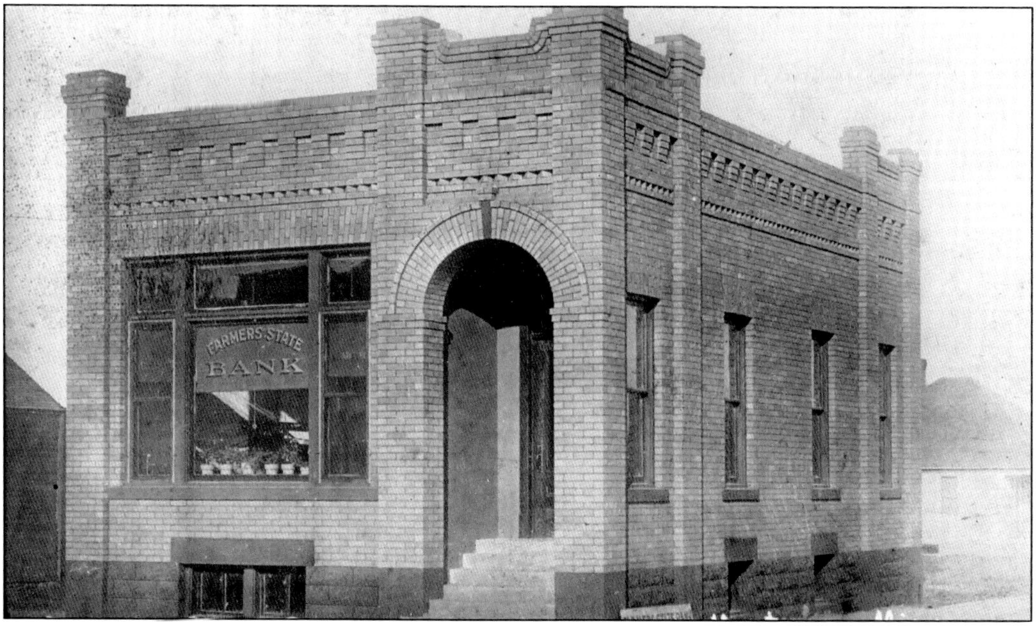

The Farmers State Bank of Monterey was started in June 1913. It was held up by armed robber James Charleson in December 1939. Charleson had already been incarcerated in 1940 on a murder charge when he was charged with this robbery. The silver dollars that were found on him were thought to be the very same ones he stole from the bank. This building later became the Signature Music Studio in 1994, with Joel and Kristin Rabbe as proprietors. This is postmarked August 4, 1915.

St. Joseph's Catholic Church was built in the summer of 1905. The first mass in this new building was on Christmas Day in 1905. This parish did not have weekly mass until 1912; before this date it was monthly, and later it was changed to twice a month. The closing mass was held on March 19, 1995.

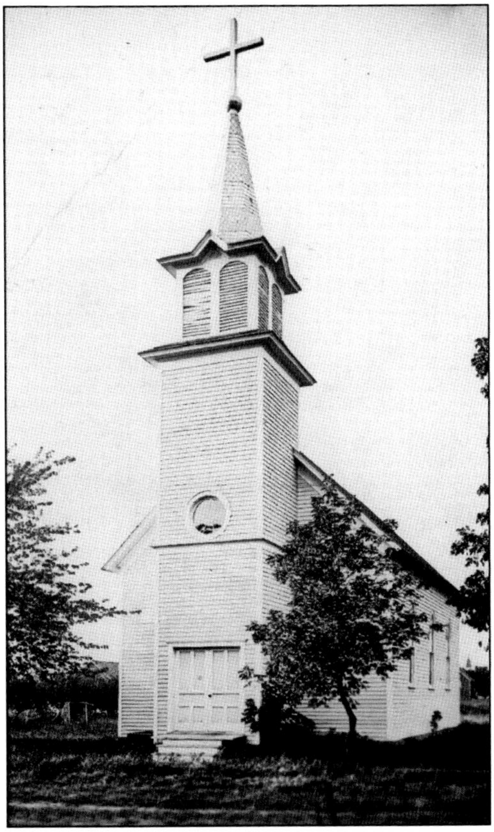

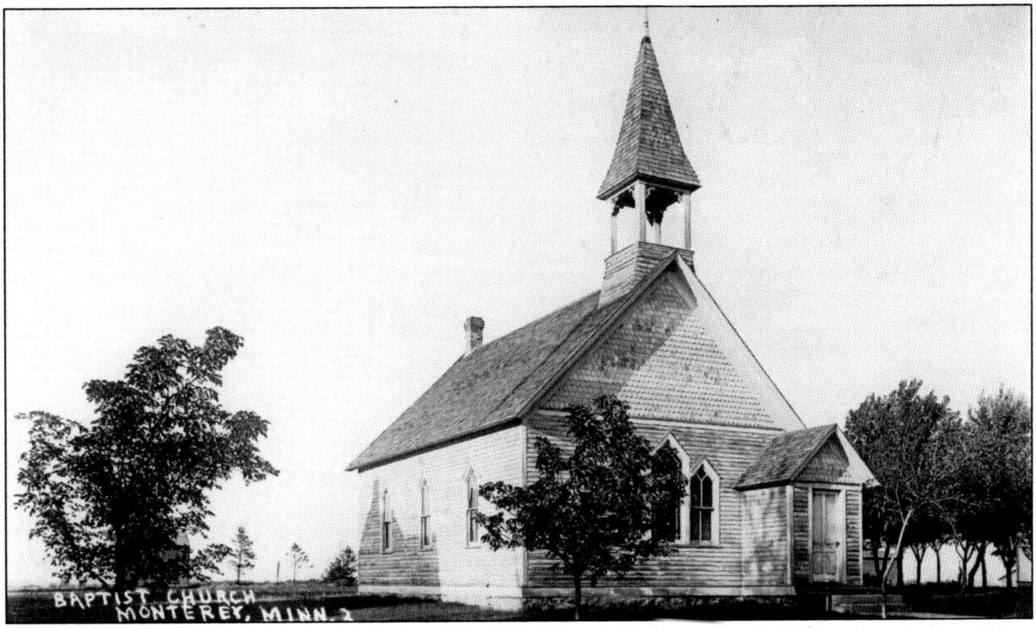

The Baptist church in Monterey was built in 1902. It is not known when the church closed, but it was probably before 1924. By the looks of the paint, the church was near the end when this postcard was taken, probably in the 1920s.

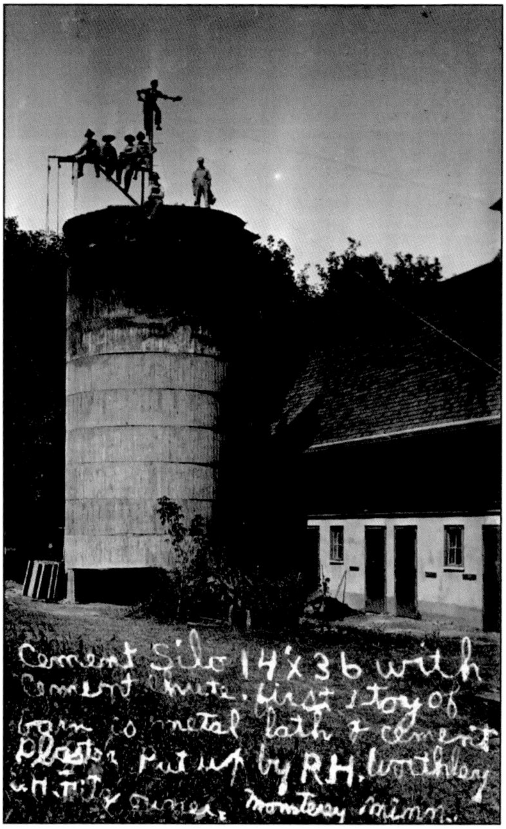

The Worthley Brothers began their cement business in 1900 and built many silos in the area. Notice the men on top.

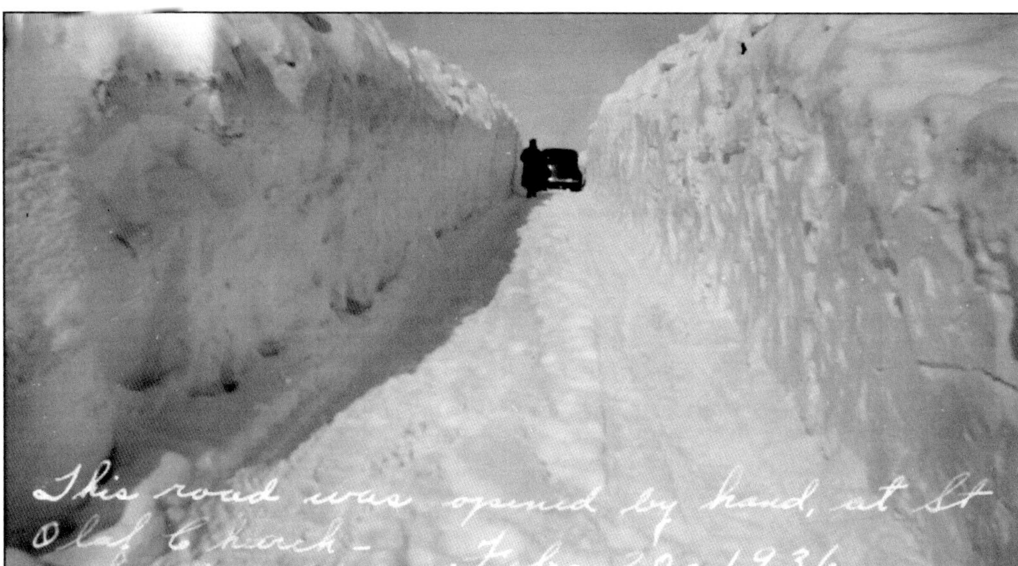

This book would not be complete without showing how much snow Minnesota can get. This shows the famous winter of 1936 and all of its snow. That winter was also incredibly cold, with 36 consecutive days of below-zero temperatures. This road near the St. Olaf Church was opened entirely by hand.

Nine

TRUMAN

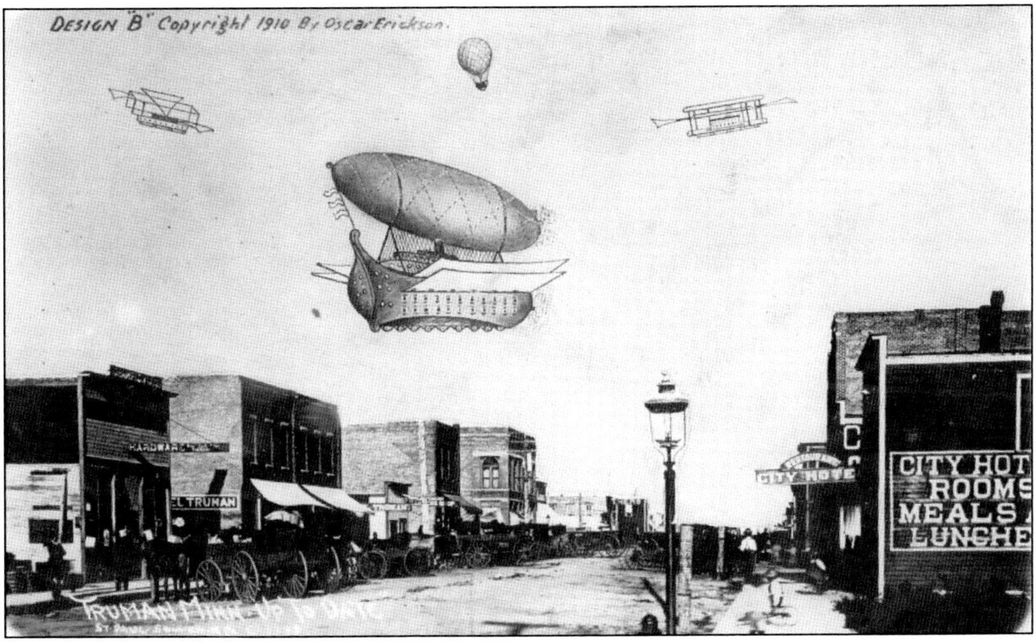

One theory of how Truman got its name was stated by Truman Loveth. He wrote a letter to the *Truman Tribune* in 1949 to lay claim of the honor. He said his aunt Mrs. Hiram Clemons was a cook working with the crew surveying the railroad and town site. One night during the evening meal, they were discussing a name for the new town. They asked Clemons what she thought. She suggested naming it Truman after her nephew and it was chosen. This is how Truman looked in 1910.

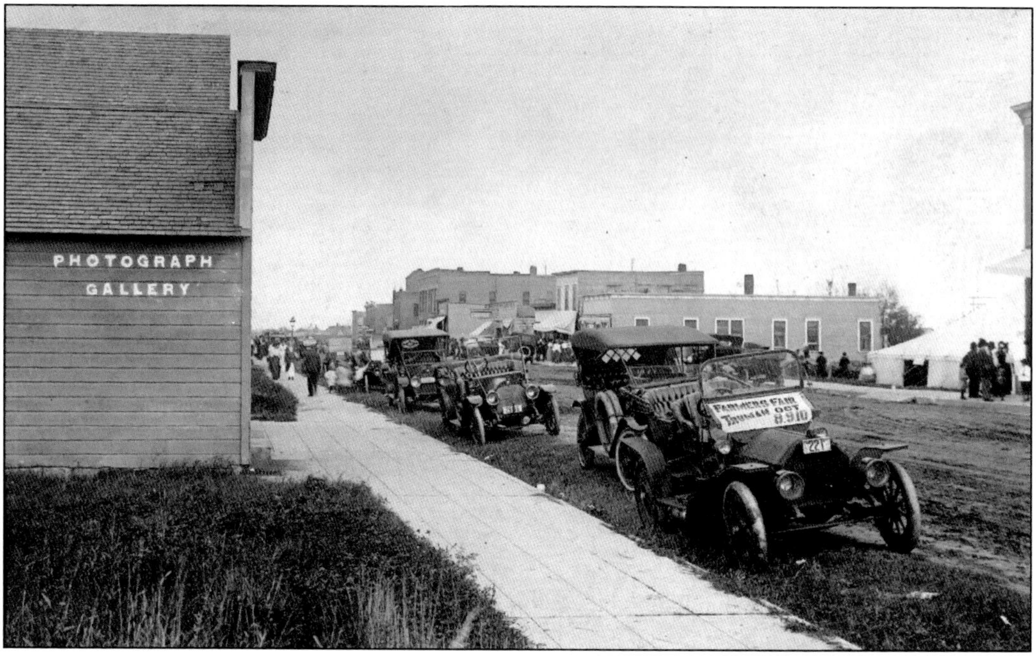

This picture postcard was taken and sent out by photographer C. D. Caulkins. On the back, he has his advertising slogan, which was, "On the best pictures, in the best homes, you will find my name." This is Main Street during the farmers' fair in October 1909. Caulkins Photograph Gallery is on the left.

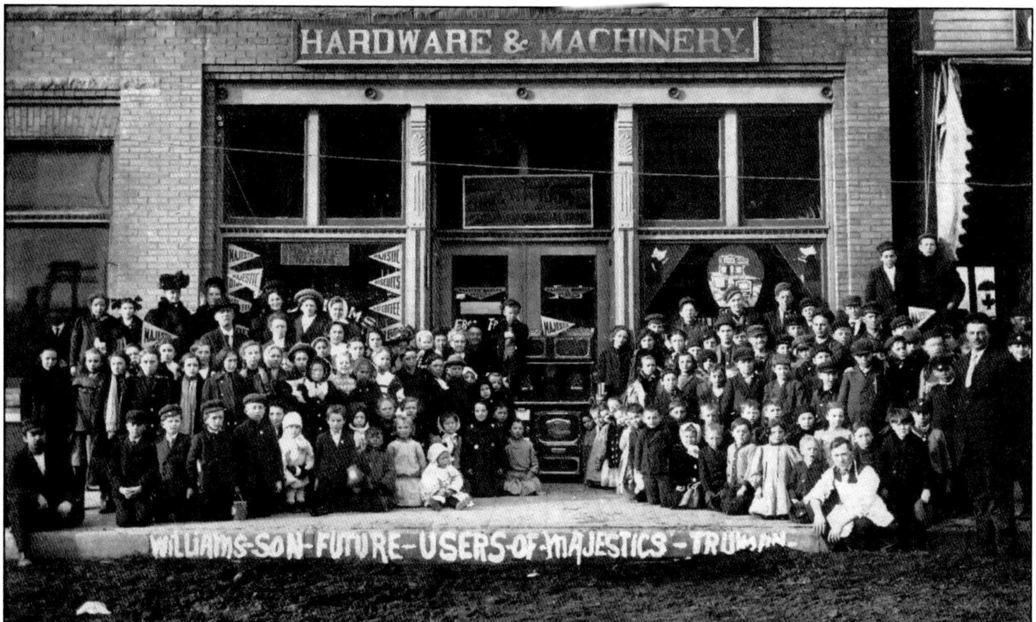

This was taken during the Harvest Twine Day celebration about 1908 and shows the Majestic Stove demonstration. The people are in front of the Williams and Son Hardware Store, with "future users" of the Majestic Stove out front. This is located at about 142 West Ciro Street.

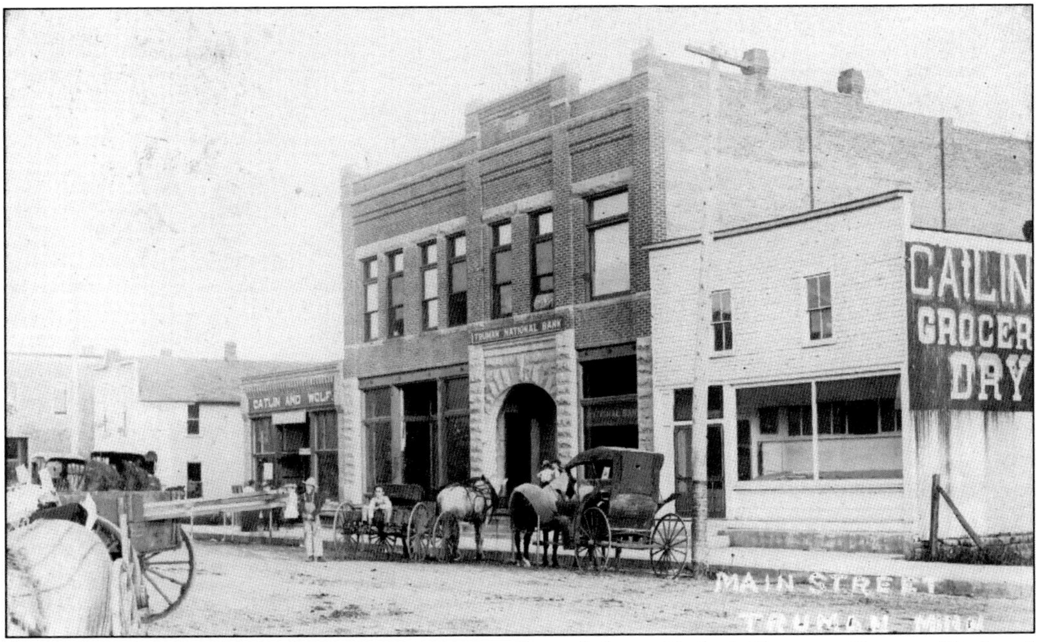

This photograph was taken about 1909. From right to left are Catlin's Grocery, Truman National Bank, and Catlin and Wolf's. Catlin's Grocery and the bank building later became Olson's Furniture Store. The bank building was erected in 1902, but all three of these structures were razed in September 2007.

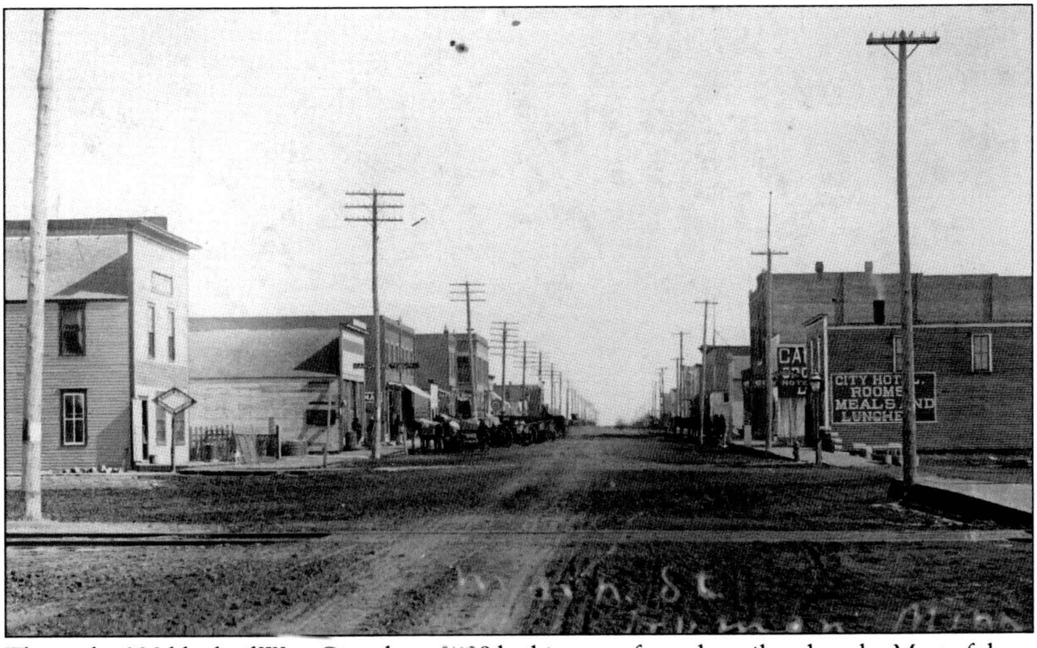

This is the 200 block of West Ciro about 1908 looking east from the railroad tracks. Most of these buildings are gone. The first building on the left is the F. C. Gleason and Company business. Second from the left is Ebert's Hardware. On the right are the City Hotel and Restaurant, Catlin's Grocery, and the Truman National Bank.

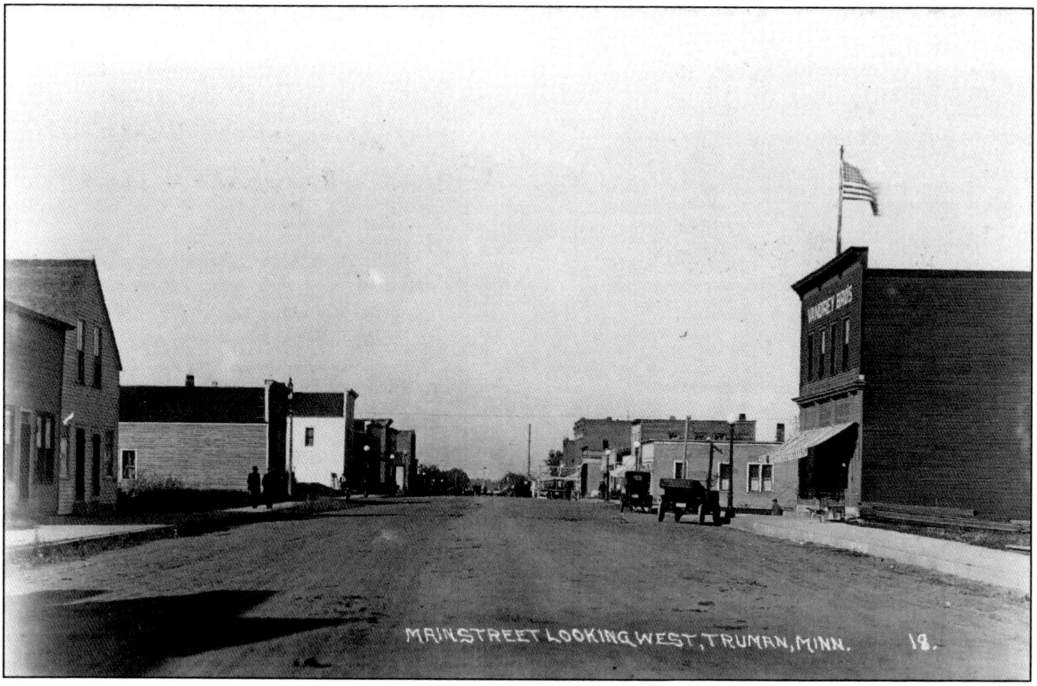

The building proudly displaying the American flag is the Vandrey Brothers General Merchandise Store, located at 114 East Ciro Street. Truman was surveyed in 1899, and before anybody knew it a town sprang up. By June, Vandrey's, three other businesses, and several homes had already been built. The next year in 1900 Truman had a state bank, telephone exchange, and a newspaper. It even had a waterworks system and gas street lighting by 1903. This photograph was taken about 1919.

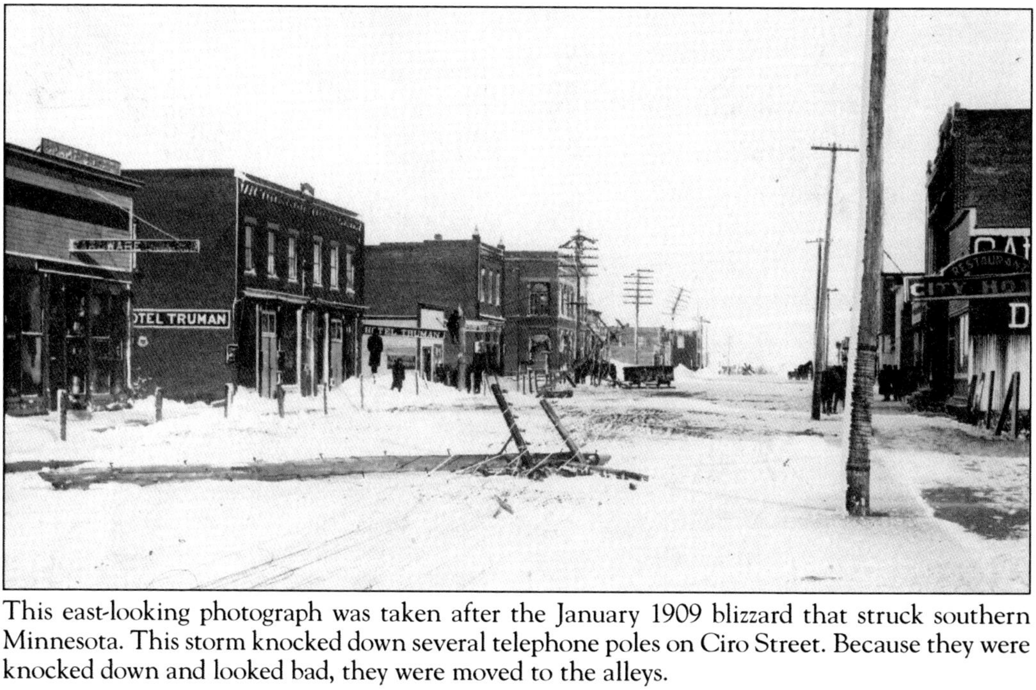

This east-looking photograph was taken after the January 1909 blizzard that struck southern Minnesota. This storm knocked down several telephone poles on Ciro Street. Because they were knocked down and looked bad, they were moved to the alleys.

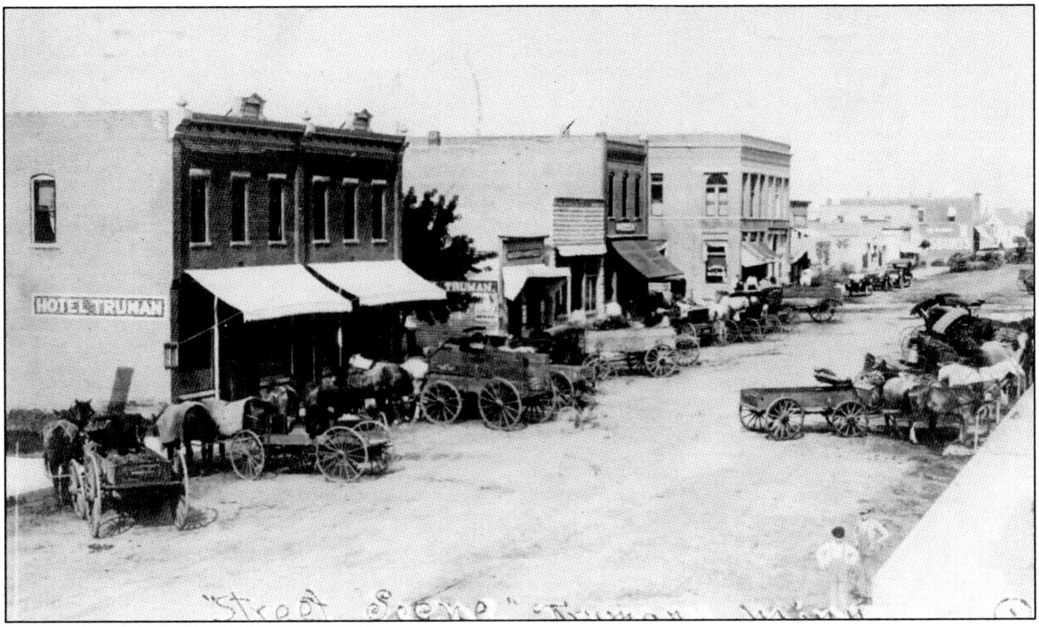

Here is the Ciro Street of Truman about September 23, 1914. The buildings are Hotel Truman, Weinkauf's Harness Shop, unidentified, Truman National Bank, and the Truman State Bank.

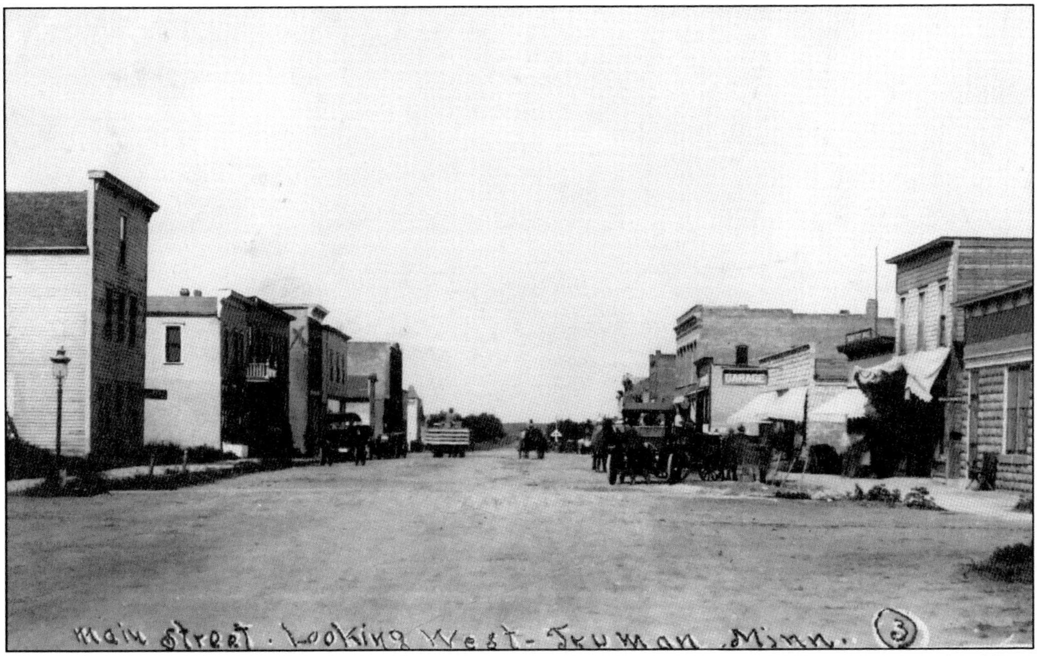

This is Ciro Street looking west about 1910. This is the 100 block of West Ciro. The first building on the left is F. H. Whitney's residence and printing office, where he published the *Truman Tribune*. Whitney first published the *Granada Journal* in Granada prior to 1905. He purchased the business in Truman in 1906 and ran it for several years. It stood at 105 West Ciro and was razed in 2008. The postcard photograph was taken in August 1909.

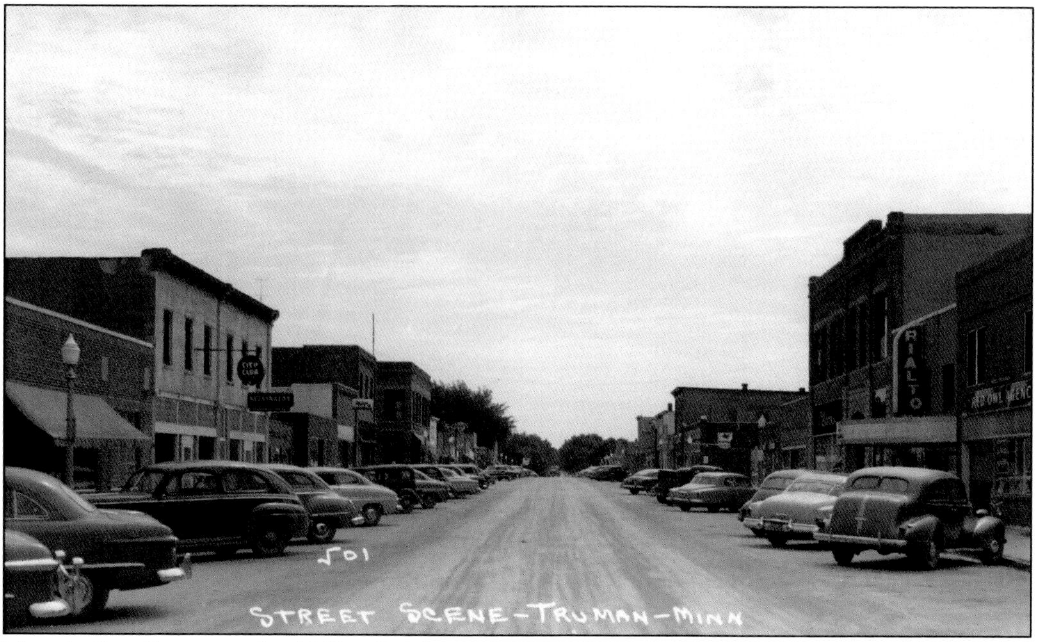

Here is Ciro Street in the 1940s. On the right are Mogenson Red Owl Store, Rialto Theatre, Olson's Furniture Store, Chat-n-Chew Restaurant, and a Mobil Oil station. On the left are unidentified, Lorig's Pool Hall, and Peterson Electric Company.

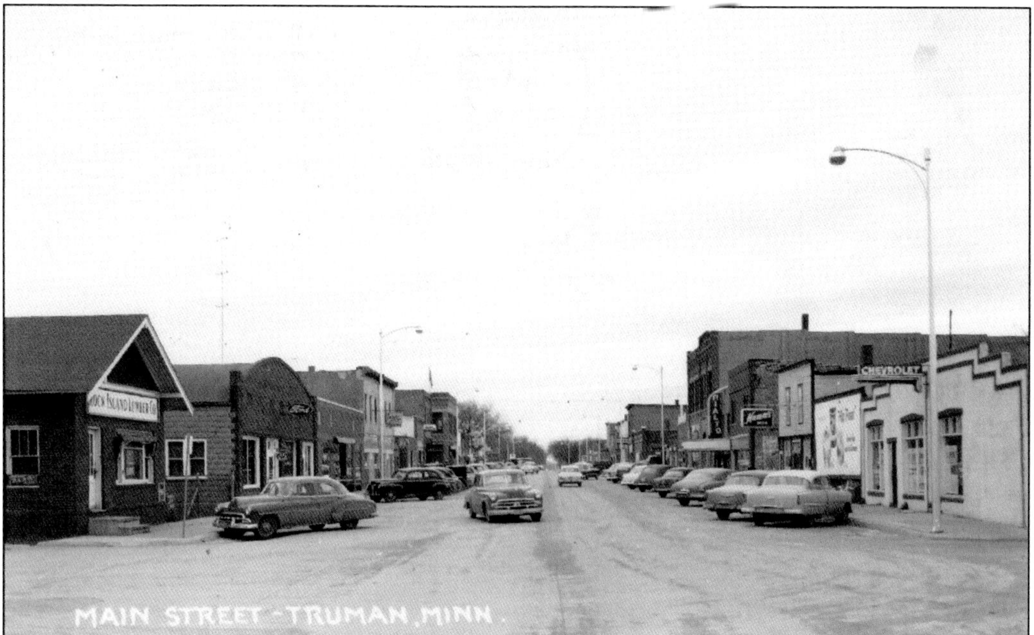

This dates from about 1957 and shows Ciro Street looking east. On the left side are the Rock Island Lumber Company and Hinton Motors Ford Garage. On the right side are the Chevrolet garage, a bar, the Red Owl Store, and the Rialto Theatre.

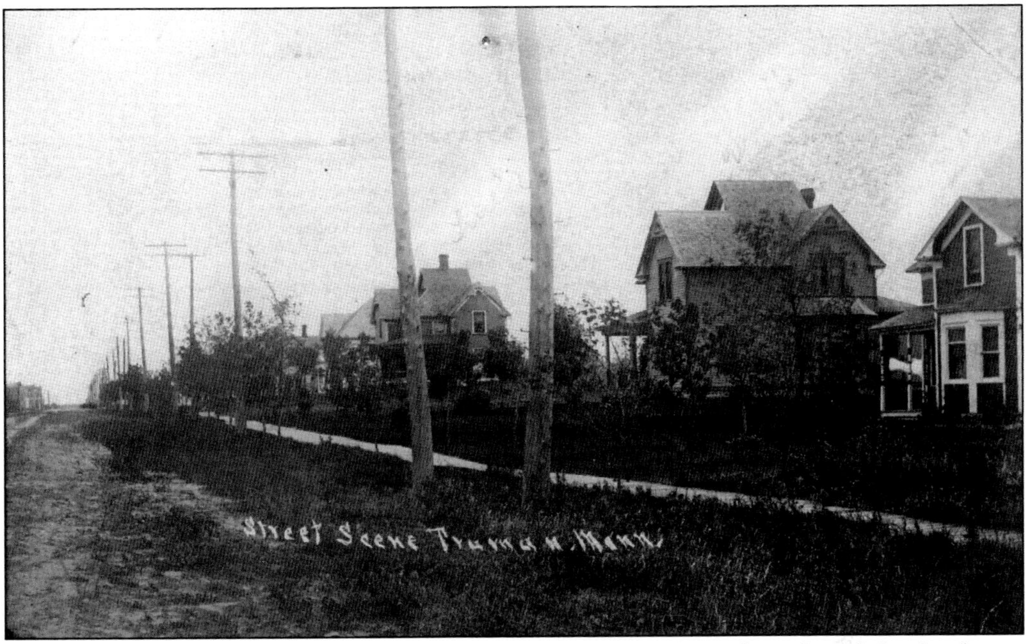

This photograph looks west into Truman about 1908. Dennis Ricard purchased the first house on the right in 2008 from Jerry Atkinson. The Truman Fire Department carried out a controlled burn there for training. Ricard purchased the former home of Marie Wood and moved it onto the site in 2008. The home had been located in Center Creek Township not too far from the Center Creek Cemetery. Continuing from the right is the Jerry Miller residence and Marvin and Mary Hoschied's home, all on East Ciro Street.

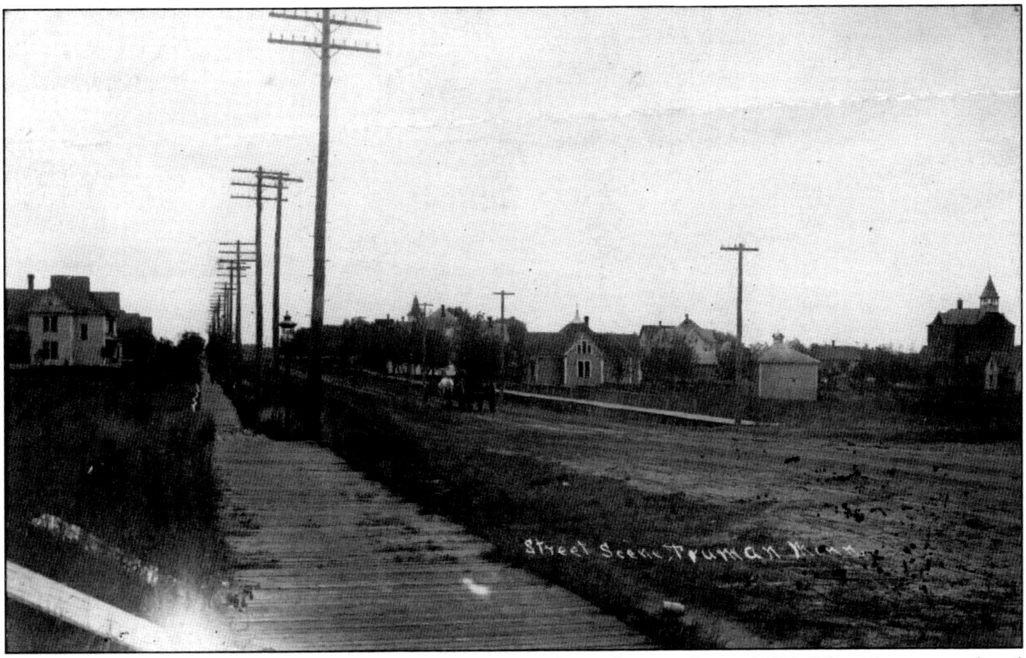

This photograph is looking east into Truman's residential area about 1907. The Truman school is on the far right. On the far left is the Zaharia Funeral Home at 302 East Ciro.

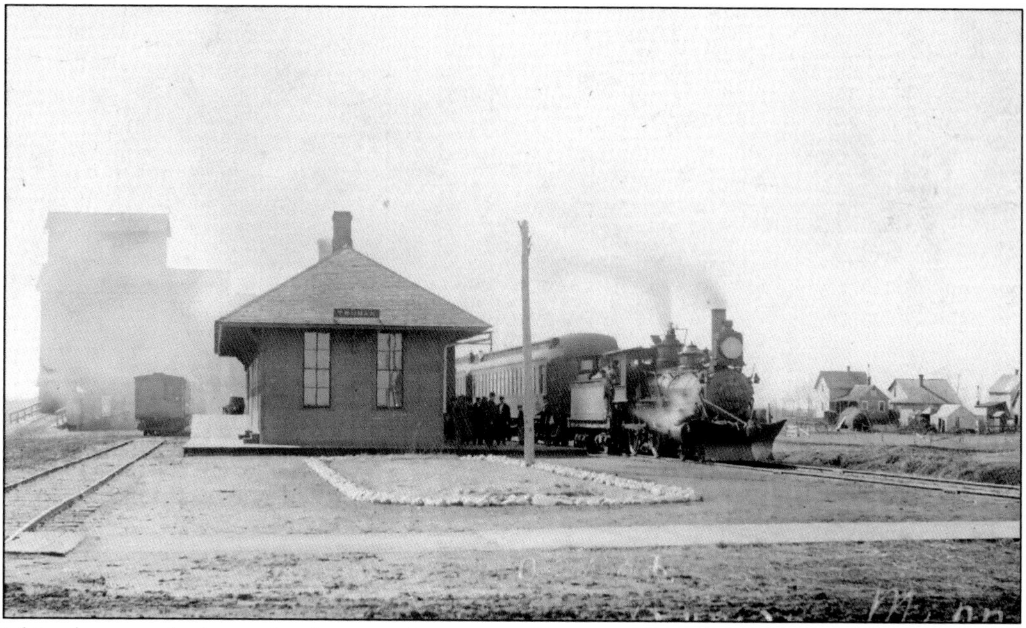

This photograph shows the depot and a train in Truman about April 1908. Notice the houses on the right. Even then the lawn was landscaped. The depot building was moved to a farm near Fairmont in 1977.

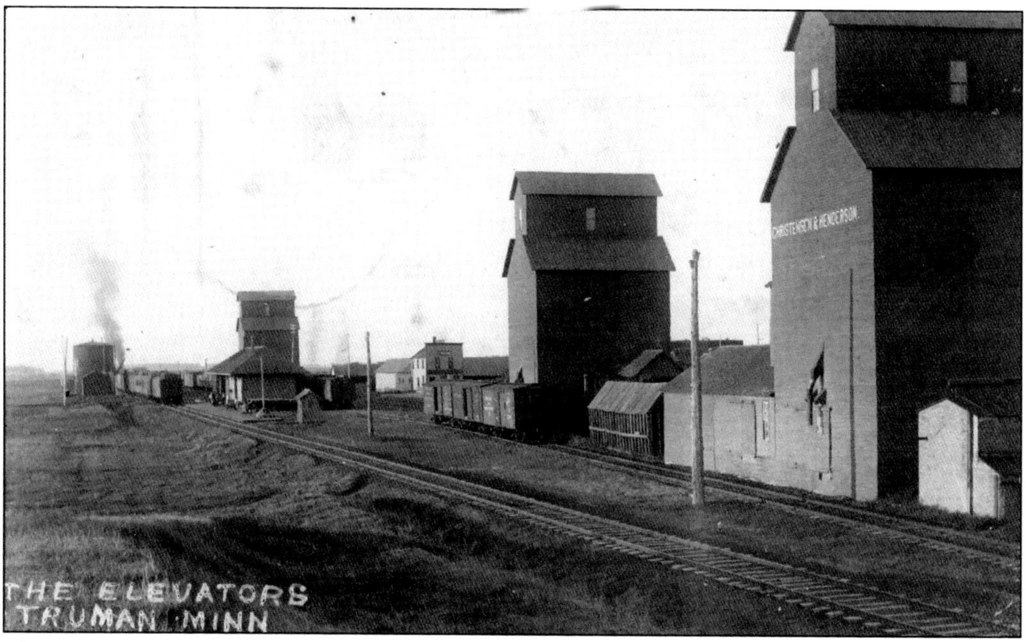

This is another view of the elevators about October 1908. The first one on the right is Christensen and Henderson's elevator. It is currently the Truman location of Watonwan Farm Services. All these elevators now are gone.

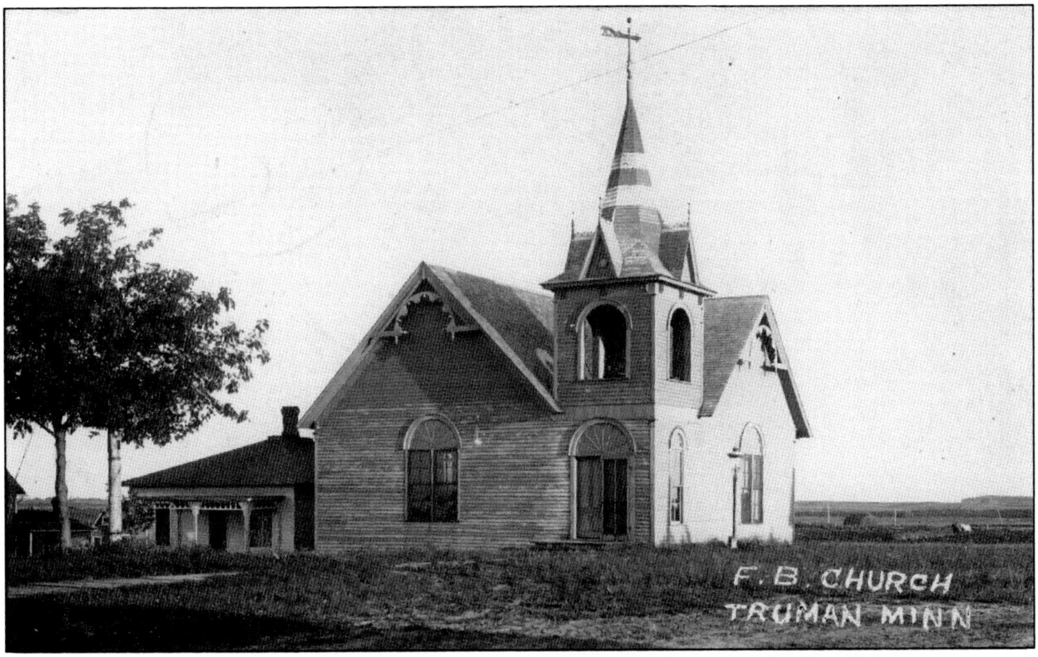

The Free Baptist Church of Westford was organized on November 26, 1884. In 1894, it reorganized as the Westford Free Baptist Church. By 1899, it reorganized again, became the Free Baptist Church of Truman, and built this structure in 1900. This photograph was taken about 1910.

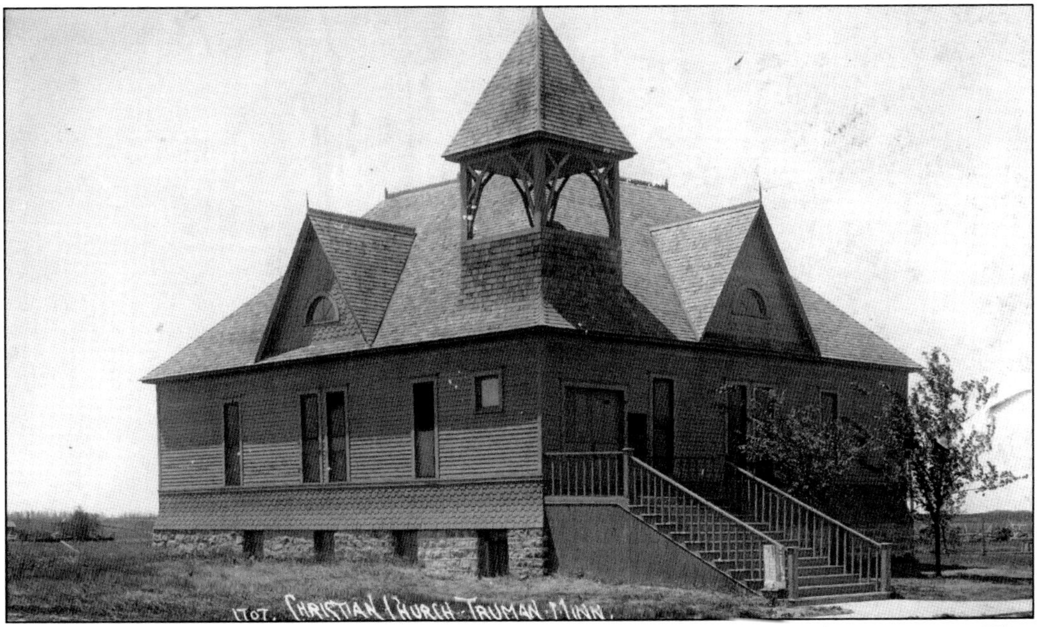

The Church of Christ was founded in October 1901 as a nondenominational congregation. This church was built in 1905 on a lot donated by Harry Fuller. It was dedicated on November 26 of that year. This postcard is dated April 9, 1911.

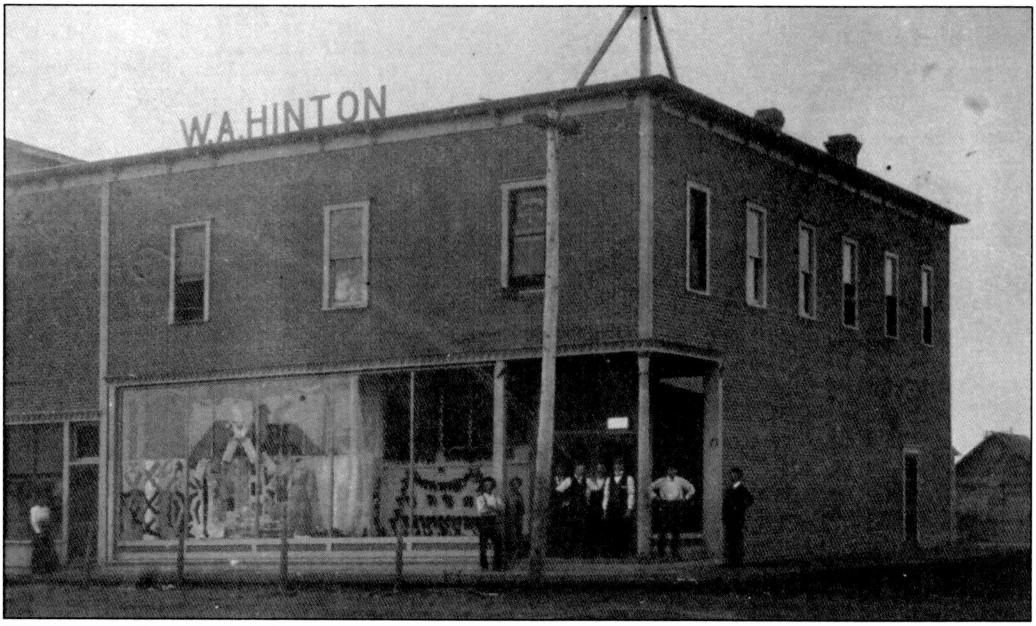

This is an advertising cabinet card from the W. A. Hinton General Merchandise Store, which was one of Truman's first businesses. It was built in 1899 with lumber hauled from Winnebago City. This was a very up-to-date store when it was built. It had an elevator, brass tacks in the counter to measure fabric, and the money was carried on a cable overhead to the cashier's office. This building was destroyed by fire in 1933.

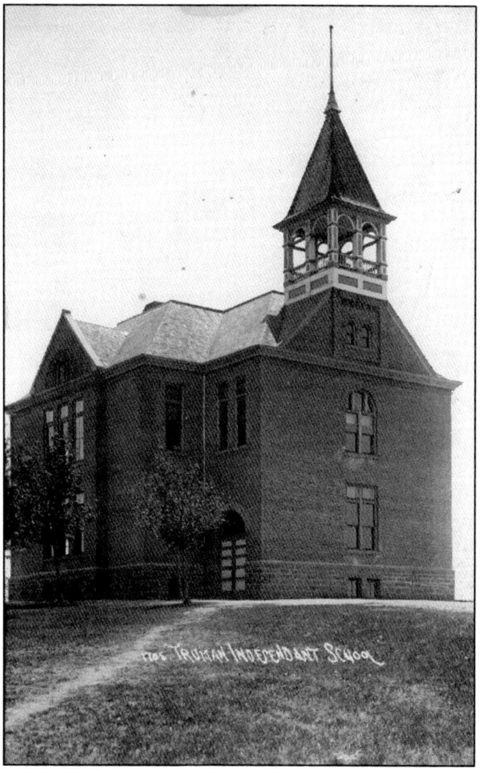

Here is a view of the schoolhouse. The Truman School was first started in 1879 just north of what became Truman. It was organized on January 5, 1881, and soon after, a new school building was constructed. The one pictured here was built in 1901. By 1912, it became a high school and an addition was built. The first graduating class was in 1913, with Ed Olson being the only senior.

Ten

WELCOME AND WILBERT

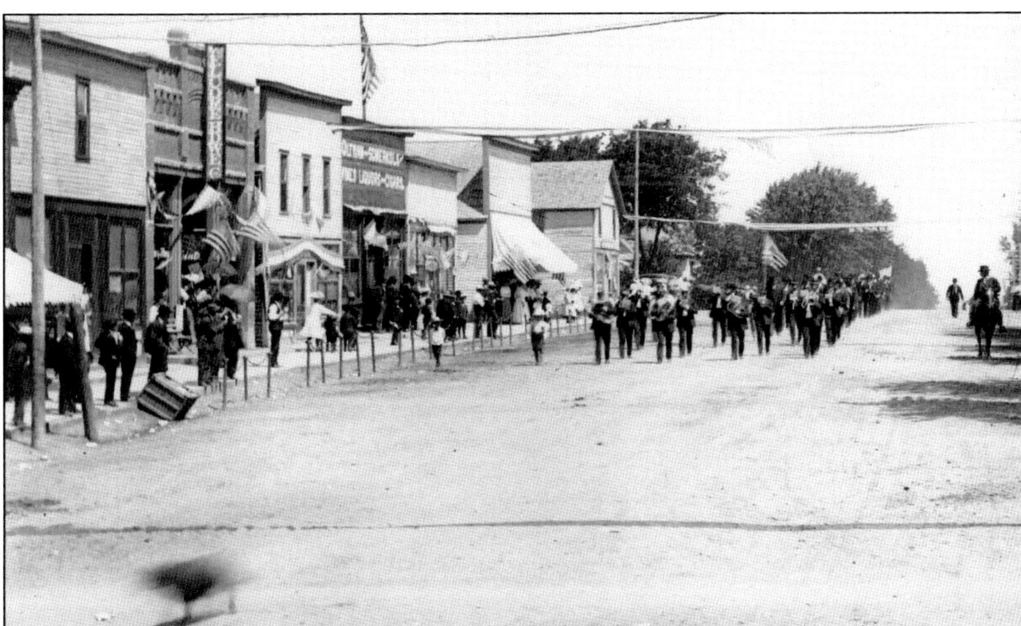

The *Martin County Sentinel* reported in May 1879 that there would be a new town near Judge Campbell's property called Campbell's Landing, but the name was not used for long. The name Lillie Creek was favored, and this stuck until shortly after the post office was established. The name of Welcome came into being on September 19, 1881. The first depot was built in 1880, but a better one was built in 1888 that had room for freight and people.

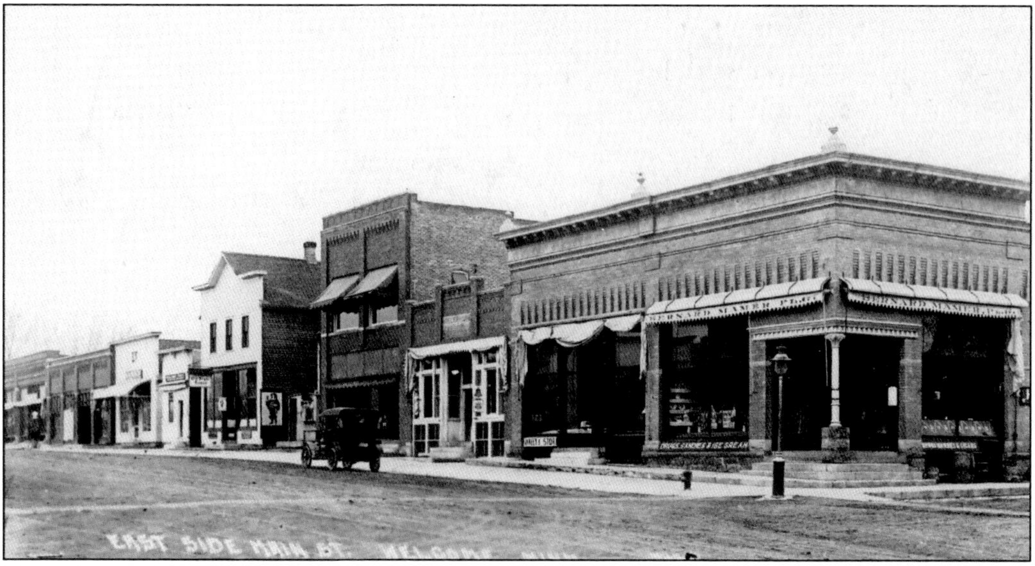

This photograph of Main Street was taken between 1910 and 1915. On the right is Bernard Mamer's Drug Store, which was built in 1898 by Dr. F. W. Weeks. It first housed Payne's Hardware and Nissen's Saloon. The next store in the same building is the H. J. Oltman and Son Variety Store. Down the street are the telephone office (constructed in 1914), the George F. Wagner Bowling Alley, and a saloon in the fourth building (which housed a harness shop in the 1940s). The short building is the Welcome Times. The last wooden building was at one time the Stockdill Funeral Home and later became a barbershop. The next building is Rosenberg's Implement Shop.

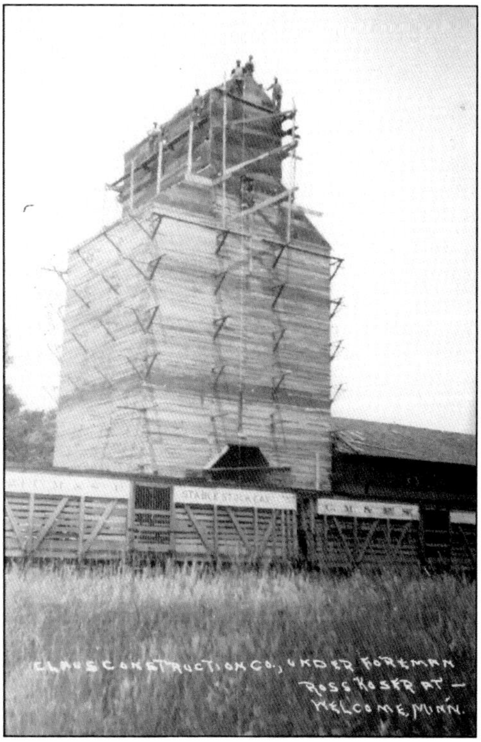

This is one of the elevators being built by the Claus Construction Company in July 1914. It cost $4,000 to build and even had a "solid foundation of concrete." Notice the men near the roof.

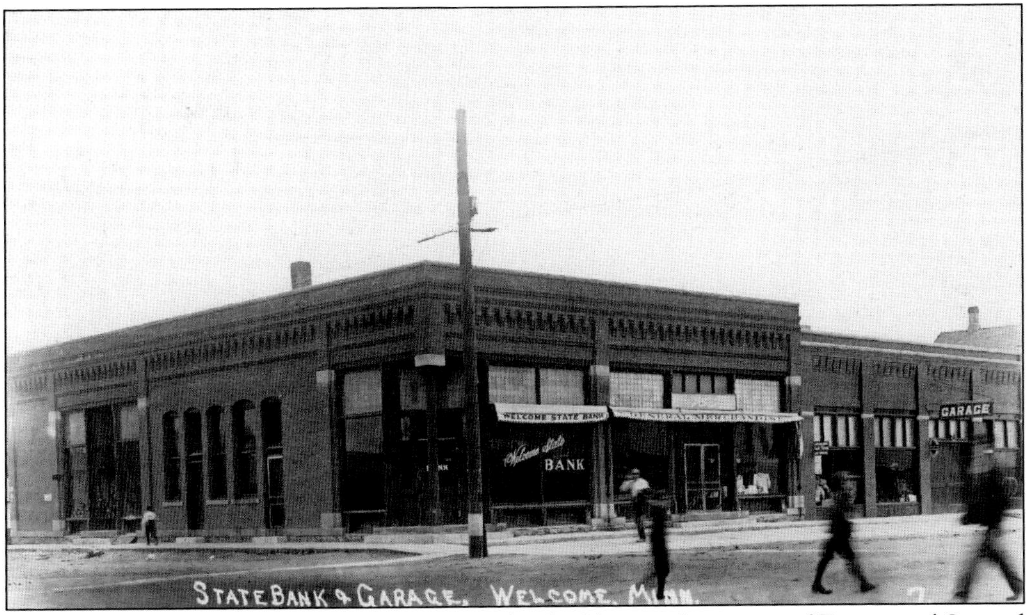

The Welcome State Bank was first located in this building at the corner of Dugan and Second Streets. It was organized in 1913, and this postcard was postmarked just three years later in 1916. Also in the same building, according to the awning, is a general merchandise store. At one time, this was also the location of the Welcome Cooperative Company. The garage on the far right may be Carl Bagley's, which he built in 1914. The storefront to the left (behind the bank) is a grocery store.

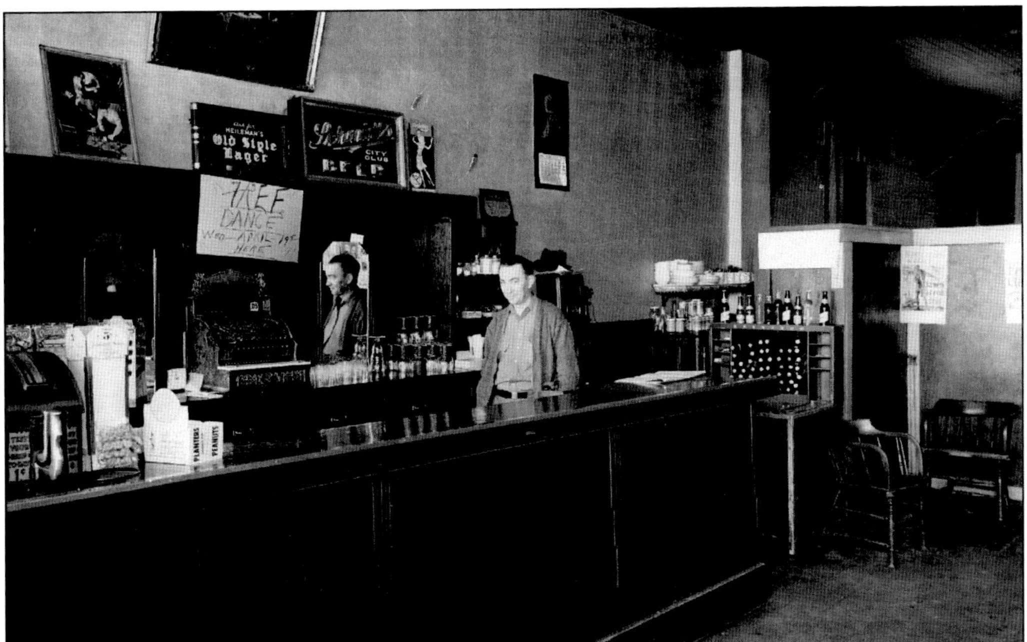

Seen behind the bar in 1939 is Lutz Hansen in the Lutz Café/Hansen Pool Hall. It was on Main Street, and just a few years later it became Rubye's Tavern. It was built in 1898 for H. A. Miller's general merchandise store. Afterward it became a saloon for William Kropp.

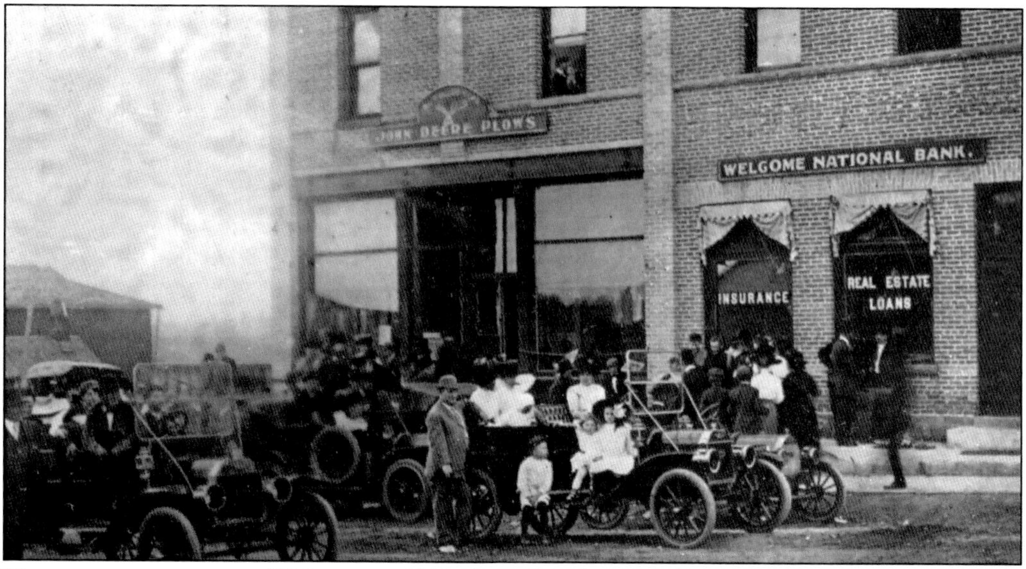

There were many cars in Welcome in 1912 when this photograph was taken. The building in the back was constructed by A. L. Ward in 1898 to house his business, the Ward Machine Company. He was a proud dealer of John Deere implements. The Ward Machine Company closed the same year this photograph was taken. Also in the same building is the Welcome National Bank. When it first started in 1897, it was a state bank. It changed to a national bank in 1902 and closed in 1929. After it closed, the Welcome State Bank moved onto the premises in 1930.

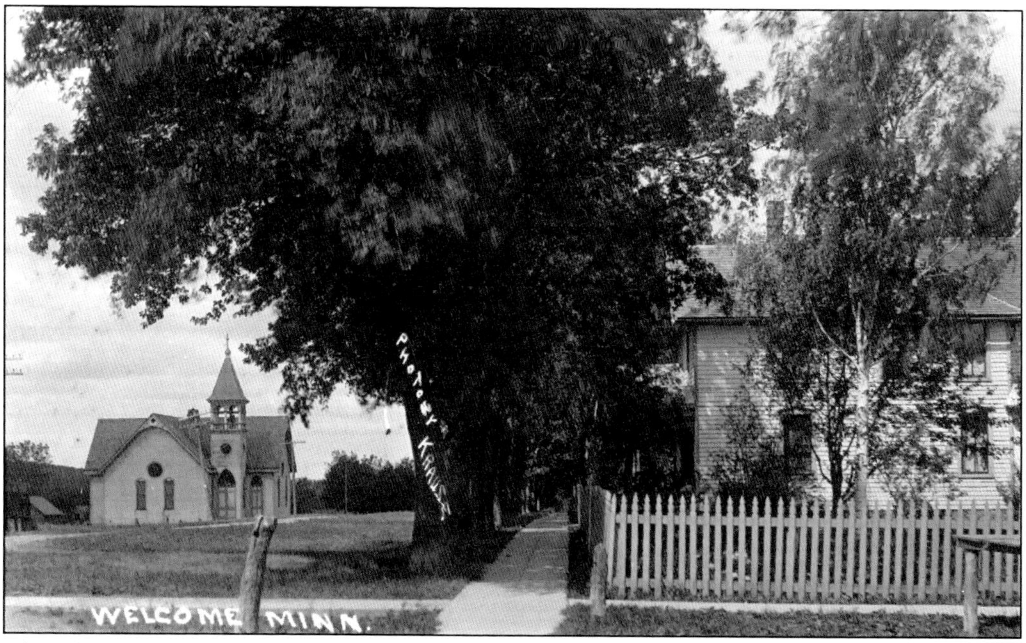

This photograph dates from about 1912. The United Methodist Church was started around 1891, with the congregation holding services in the Rolling Green schoolhouse. This church edifice was built in 1893 at a cost of $2,200 and closed on June 28, 1987. It now houses the Welcome Museum.

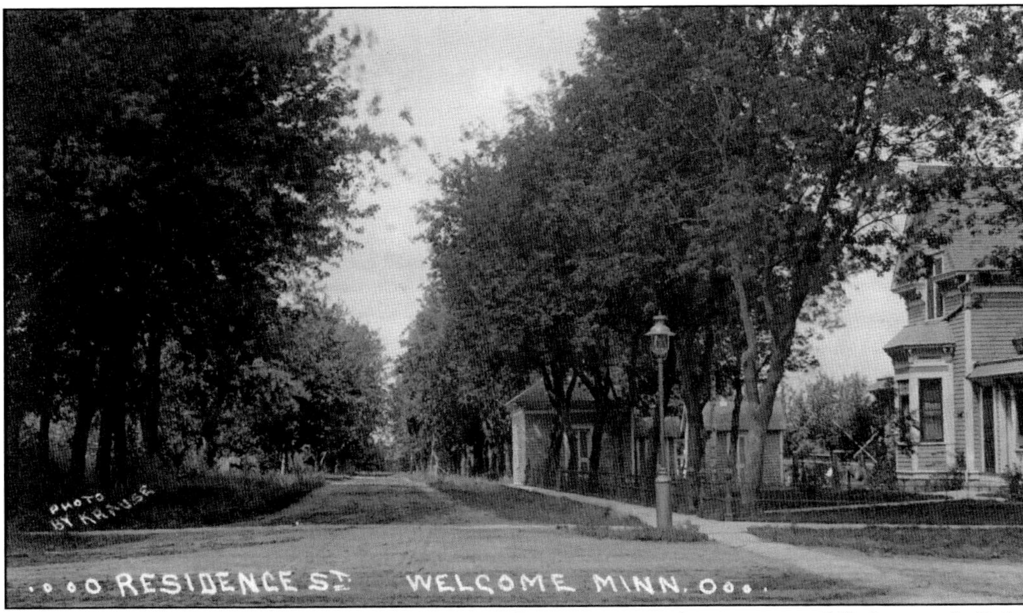

When this postcard was sent in October 1911, the writer stated it was a wet fall. It rained all day and night, and he just finished helping a neighbor get his horse out of a pond in the road. The home on the right is believed to once have been occupied by Pauline Welcome. It was built in 1895 by Henry Wackwitz.

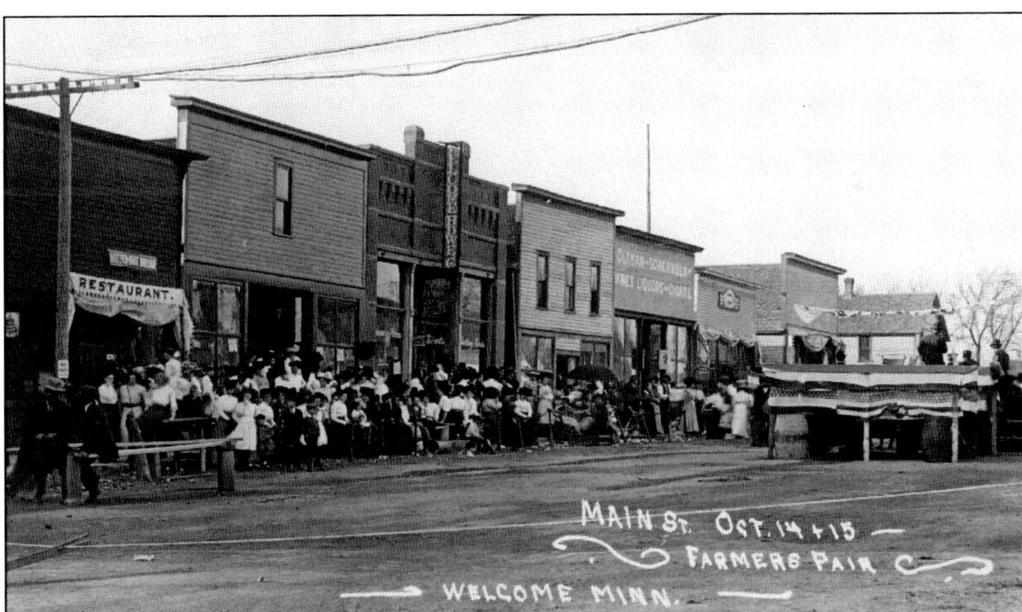

This is a farmers' fair from October 14 and 15, 1910. Ed Hanley's Barbershop and Van Amber's restaurant are in the first building. Starting from the second from left is a pool hall, Marten's and Klien Hardware (Welcome Hardware), a harness shop (later Lyle Becker's drugstore), Oltman and Schierkolk Saloon, a dry goods store, and Wilkinson's Store. In 1939, the saloon, the dry goods store, and Wilkinson's Store were destroyed by fire. On the far right is a hardware store that has most recently been known as Gerhardt's.

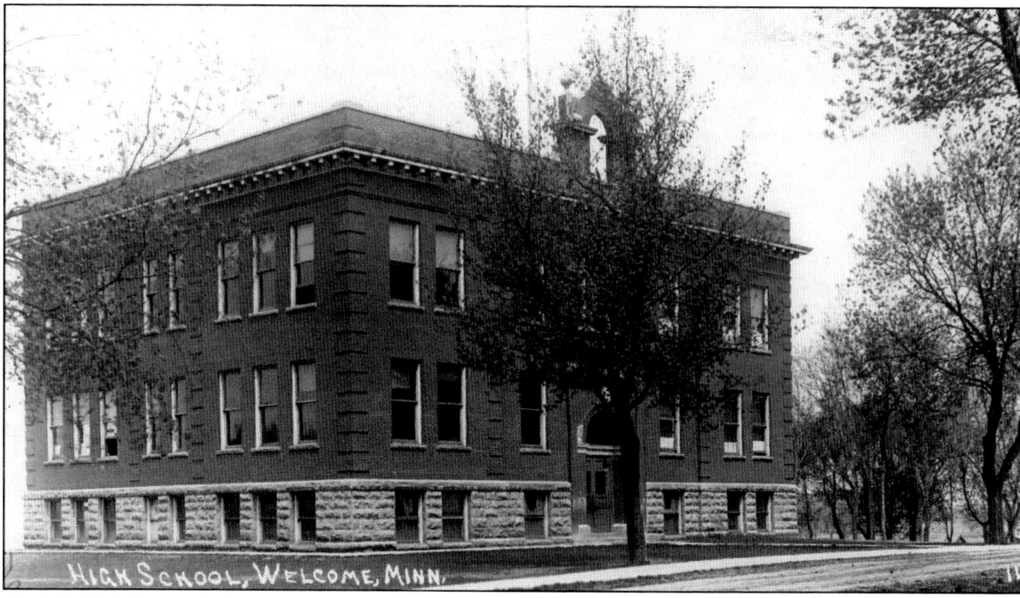

From 1867 to 1885, the children of the Welcome area went to school at various locations. A petition to have a school in Welcome was presented by Henry Kruse in 1882. The petition was granted, and in 1887, district No. 89 became official. The first building was constructed in 1885 and a second in 1895. The brick structure pictured here was built in 1907. The postcard is postmarked August 6, 1920.

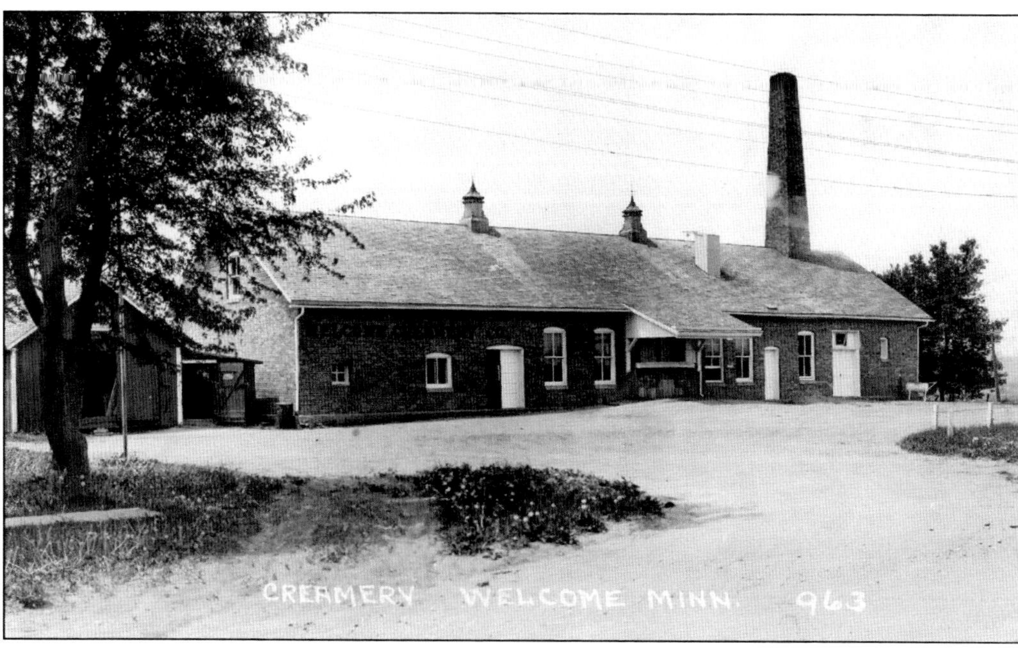

An independent creamery was started by A. R. Tuthill in Welcome in 1893. The next creamery was a cooperative, which began in 1896 and was organized by H. A. Miller. The creamery in this postcard was started in 1906, but the 1956 remodeled building is shown. This closed in 1975, "ending all creamery operations in Martin County."

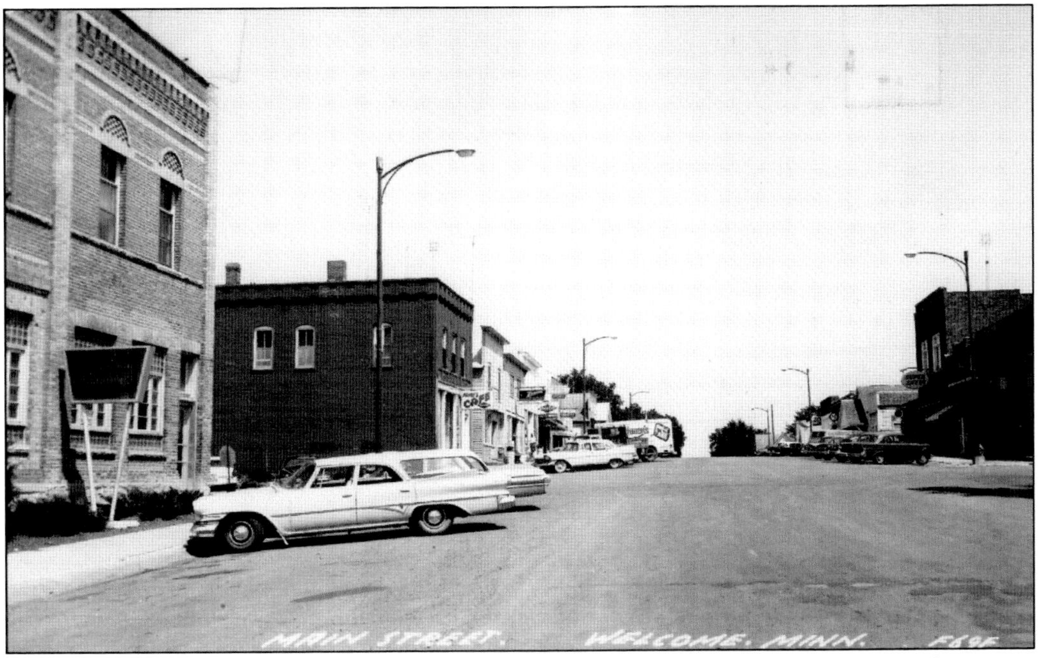

This is postmarked September 3, 1964. From left to right are the Welcome State Bank, Payne's Café, unidentified, Welcome TV Sales, a saloon/bar, Welcome Our Own Hardware Store, and Welcome Variety.

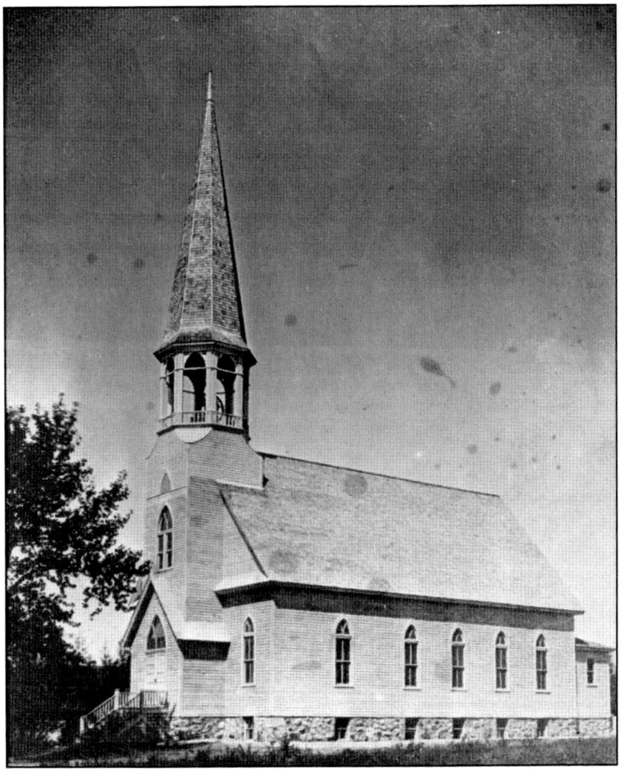

When Wilbert started, the area citizens wanted the post office to be called Tenhassen Center. The postal service declined this name because of the Tenhassen Post Office nearby. The name Wilbert was chosen after Wilbert Robinson, the first postmaster, in 1898. The German Lutheran Church of Wilbert organized and built this edifice in 1890. The day this was dedicated in September 1890, a hailstorm did considerable damage to the church, but it was quickly fixed. W. Becker was the first resident pastor in 1892, and the bell tower was added in 1895. In Wilbert, a creamery was built in 1896 and the Kellogg and Robinson store was constructed soon after. The creamery closed in the 1940s, the blacksmith went out of business in the 1930s, and the Wilbert Store shut down in about 1971.